Y0-DBZ-891

PRELIMINARY EXCAVATION REPORTS

Sardis, Idalion, and Tell el-Handaquq North

THE ANNUAL OF
THE AMERICAN SCHOOLS OF ORIENTAL RESEARCH

Volume 53

Edited by
William G. Dever

PRELIMINARY EXCAVATION REPORTS
Sardis, Idalion, and Tell el-Handaquq North

Edited by

William G. Dever

American Schools of Oriental Research

PRELIMINARY EXCAVATION REPORTS
SARDIS, IDALION, AND TELL EL-HANDAQUQ NORTH

Edited by
William G. Dever

Library of Congress Cataloging-in-Publication Data
Preliminary excavation reports—Sardis, Idalion, and Tell el-Handaquq
   North / edited by William G. Dever.
      p.   cm. — (The annual of the American Schools of Oriental
   Research ; v. 53)
      ISBN 0-7885-0315-4 (cloth : alk. paper)
      1. Sardis (Extinct city) 2. Idalion (Extinct city) 3. Ḥandaqūq, Tell
   al- (Jordan) 4. Middle East—Antiquities. 5. Excavations (Archaeol-
   ogy)—Middle East. I. Dever, William G. II. American Schools of
   Oriental Research. III. Series.
   DS101.A45   vol. 53
   [DS156]
   939′.22—dc20   96—41756
                                                       CIP

Printed in the United States of America
on acid-free paper. ⊗

Contents

The Sardis Campaigns of 1992 and 1993

Crawford H. Greenewalt, Jr.
Department of Classics
University of California
Berkeley, CA 94720

Christopher Ratté
Institute of Fine Arts
of New York University
New York, NY 10021

Marcus L. Rautman
Department of Art History and Archaeology
University of Missouri
Columbia, MO 65211

The Archaic Lydian fortification wall and nearby residential quarter of the seventh and sixth centuries B.C.E. and a Late Roman suburb of the fourth through seventh centuries C.E., all in the same locale as the city site, were again the focus of excavation and related fieldwork. One space of the Archaic residential quarter (connected to spaces excavated in 1984 through 1986) contained more than 400 ceramic, metal, and stone objects of domestic and industrial use; elsewhere, at the foot of the fortification wall, rested a hardware assemblage of more than 300 iron items. Construction details of two complete columns of the Temple of Artemis were recorded for the first time. In the tumulus cemetery at Bin Tepe, two of the three largest tumuli were further investigated: Karnıyarık Tepe ("the Tomb of Gyges") in a ground-penetrating radar survey; and the Tomb of Alyattes by limited excavation outside (which revealed remains of the crepis wall) and recording inside.

This report presents the results of excavation and related archaeological discovery and exploration in 1992 and 1993 at the city site of Sardis and in the tumulus cemetery at Bin Tepe, 8 km north of the city (not shown in fig. 1; see Hanfmann 1983: fig. 2).[1] The 1992 and 1993 seasons also included conservation, graphic recording, study of antiquities recovered in previous seasons, and site enhancement projects.[2] Since 1977 the excavation priority has been to clarify urban topography and monuments of the Archaic—i.e., Lydian and early Persian—periods of the seventh and sixth centuries B.C.E. Information in this report is derived substantially from manuscript reports written in the field by Expedition staff members; copies of those reports are filed in the Sardis Expedition Office at Harvard University.

OFF-SEASON DISCOVERIES

During the 1992–93 winter months, two notable discoveries were made by chance and recorded by the director and staff of the Archaeological Museum in Manisa: a Late Roman subterranean tomb, or *hypogaeum*, with painted decoration and an Archaic lion head in limestone.

The *hypogaeum* (T93.1) is located about 400 m west of the Pactolus stream/Sart çayı, a few meters south of the modern Ankara–Izmir highway, in a region where there were other Roman tombs, including another *hypogaeum*.[3] Like other *hypogaea* at Sardis (Greenewalt et al. 1983: 22–25; Greenewalt 1978: 61–64 and references; Greenewalt 1979: 4–8), this one is just below the modern ground surface and is a rectangular, barrel-vaulted chamber (2.80 m long, 2.29–2.34 m wide, ca. 2.15 m high). It was entered at one of the short ends through a square hold (0.59 m on a side) in the ceiling and steps made of stone slabs that project from the wall. The tomb is oriented east–west, with the entrance at the east end. The vault at the west end and the top of the west wall were broken at the time of discovery. The walls and ceiling are built of mortared rubble and brick, plastered, and painted with a decorative repertoire of motifs and colors that are standard in Late Roman *hypogaea* at Sardis and elsewhere: at

1

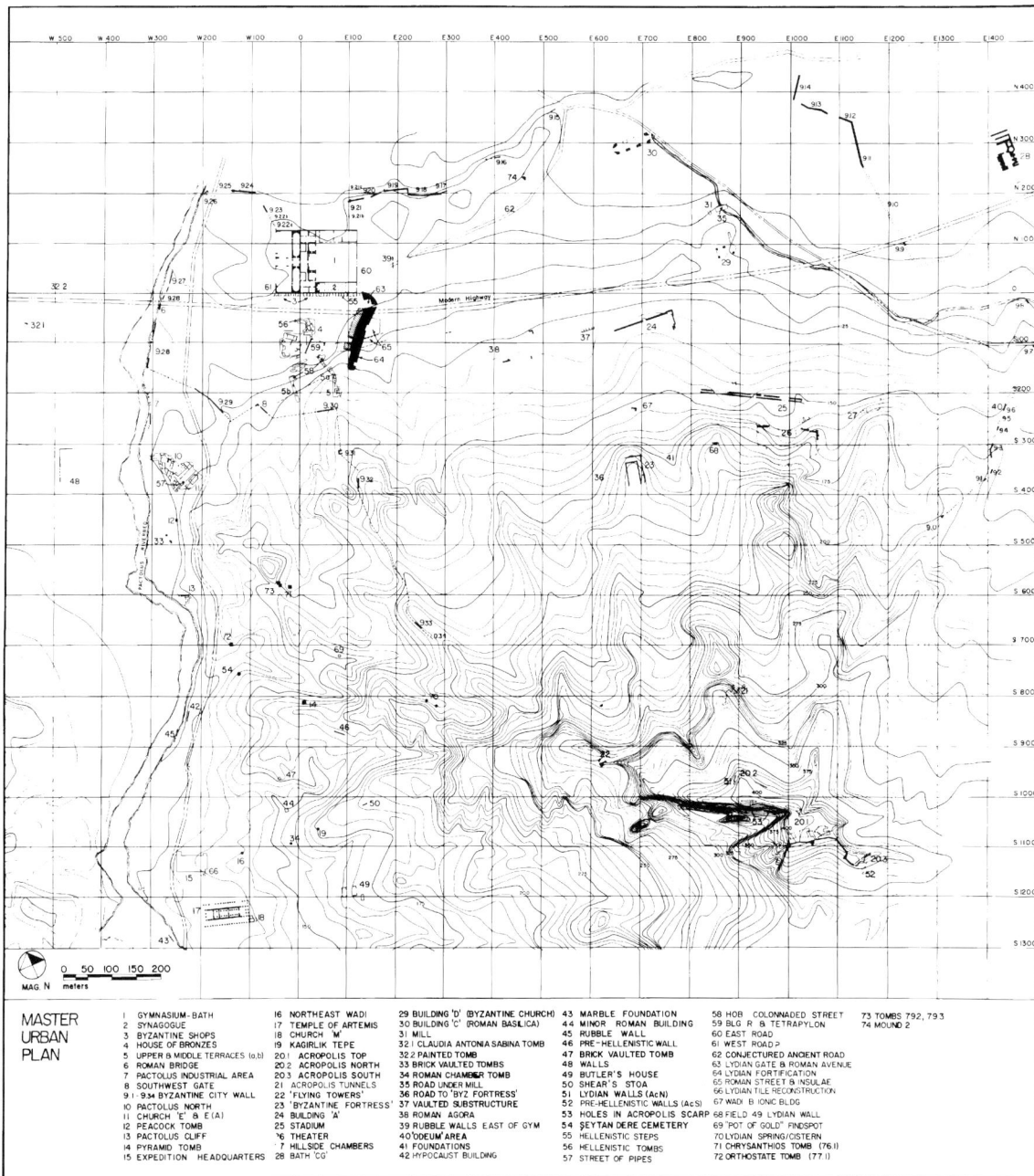

Fig. 1. Sardis, general site plan.

the base of the walls is a dado course (the decoration of which is indistinct and includes a rinceau); above, free-field motifs include baskets of fruit or flowers, garland swags, exotic birds (peacocks, pheasant?), and individual flowers (fig. 2). Dark blue, green, pink, and red are the predominant colors.

The floor is earthen. No objects or bones were recovered when the tomb was cleared by Manisa Museum authorities.

The Archaic limestone lion head was recovered on one of the artificial mounds that form a chain on the north side of the city site: "Mound 2," about 130 m

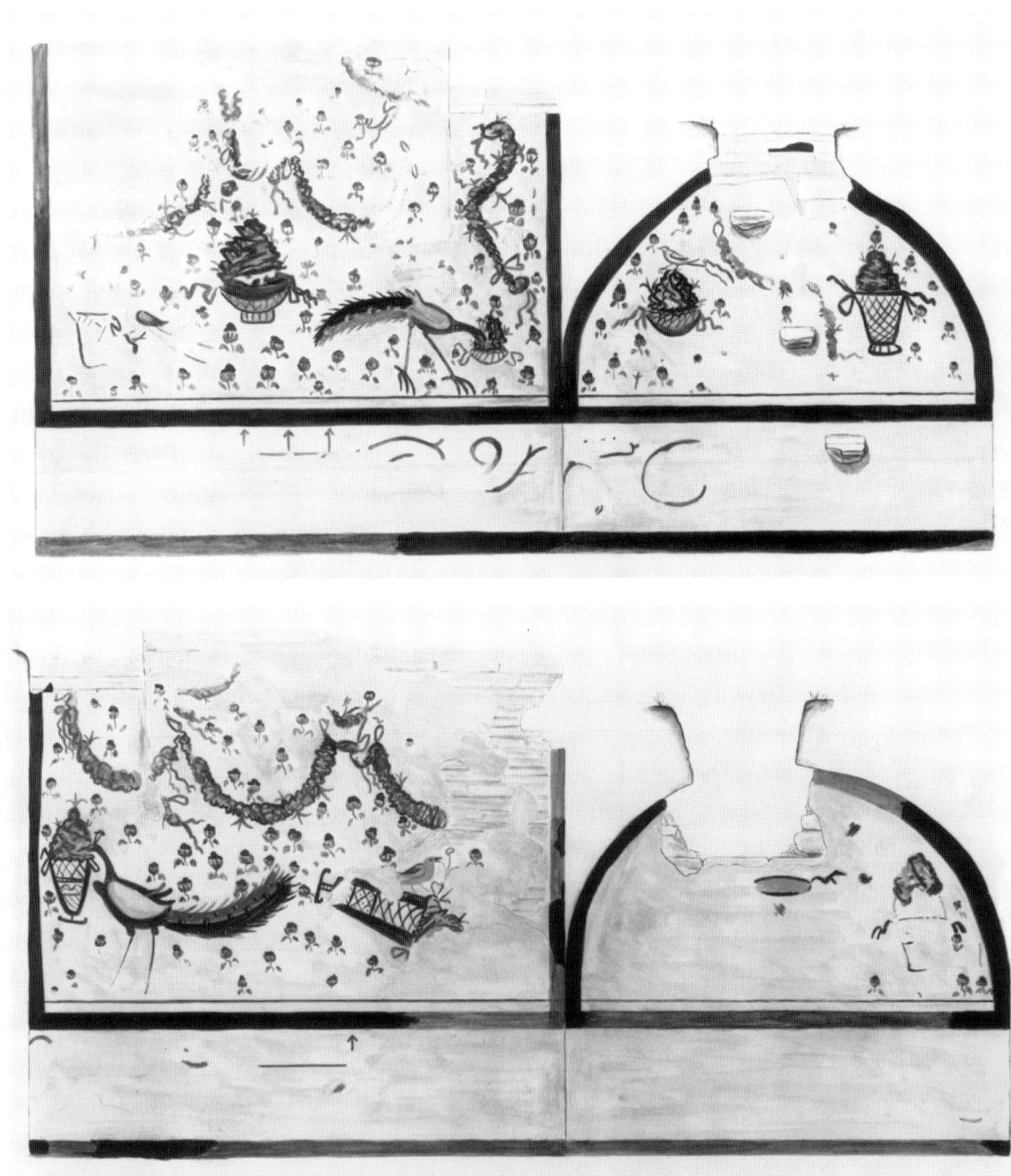

Fig. 2. Late Roman *hypogaeum* (T93.1), watercolor reproduction of painted decoration on walls and vault; by C. S. Alexander. Above, north and east sides; below, south and west sides.

west of the 1985 excavation trenches that exposed a monumental Archaic building (Greenewalt, Rautman, and Cahill 1987: 81–84). Back parts may have been cut down, and whether the head is an architectural ornament or part of a statue is unclear; the mouth cavity is closed at the back. Red paint covers the tongue. With its low brow, high cheeks, and prominent muzzle, the head resembles those on electrum coins attributed to Lydia (Manisa Museum no. 7962; height 0.285 m; fig. 3).

Fig. 3. Archaic lion head of limestone, from "Mound 2."

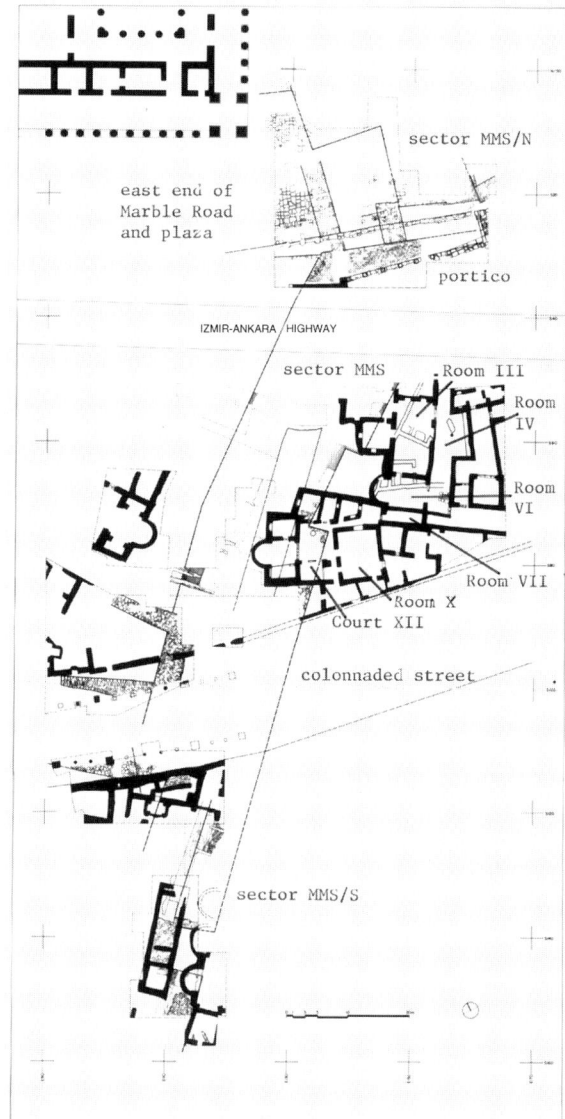

Fig. 4. Sectors MMS/N, MMS, MMS/S. Simplified plan of Late Roman features (mostly heavy black) and Archaic features (outline).

SECTORS MMS/N, MMS, MMS/S

The sector cluster is at the southwest foot of the Acropolis, ca. 300 m east of the Pactolus stream/Sart çayı, and southeast of the Roman Bath–Gymnasium and Synagogue complex (fig. 1, nos. 63–65); sector MMS/N is located north of the modern Ankara–Izmir highway, sectors MMS and MMS/S south of it. One or more sectors have been excavated every year since 1977. The principal antiquities uncovered in all three are Late Roman, fourth to seventh centuries C.E., and Archaic or Lydian, seventh and sixth centuries B.C.E. Major architectural features of both eras appear together in the plan (fig. 4). Practically nothing later than the seventh century C.E. and only slight remains from the centuries between the fifth century B.C.E. and the later Roman Imperial era have been uncovered in those sectors; occupation remains of the eighth century B.C.E. and earlier, if they exist, lie below levels reached in excavation to date.

C. H. G., Jr.

Sectors MMS/N, MMS, and MMS/S, Roman Levels

The three MMS sectors contain extensive remains of an urban quarter that flourished between the fourth and seventh centuries C.E. Work carried out over the last several years has identified colonnaded streets, shops, houses, and several buildings of uncertain function that shaped urban life in this part of Late Roman Sardis (fig. 4). Excavations in 1992 and 1993

continued to explore selected parts of the quarter and clarify its occupation history in late antiquity.

MMS/N. Previous work at Sector MMS/N exposed a broad marble-paved expanse standing at the southeast corner of the Bath–Gymnasium and Synagogue complex. Located at the east end of the Marble Road, the open, plaza-like area is bounded on the south by a monumental portico with a mosaic sidewalk similar to the colonnade in front of the

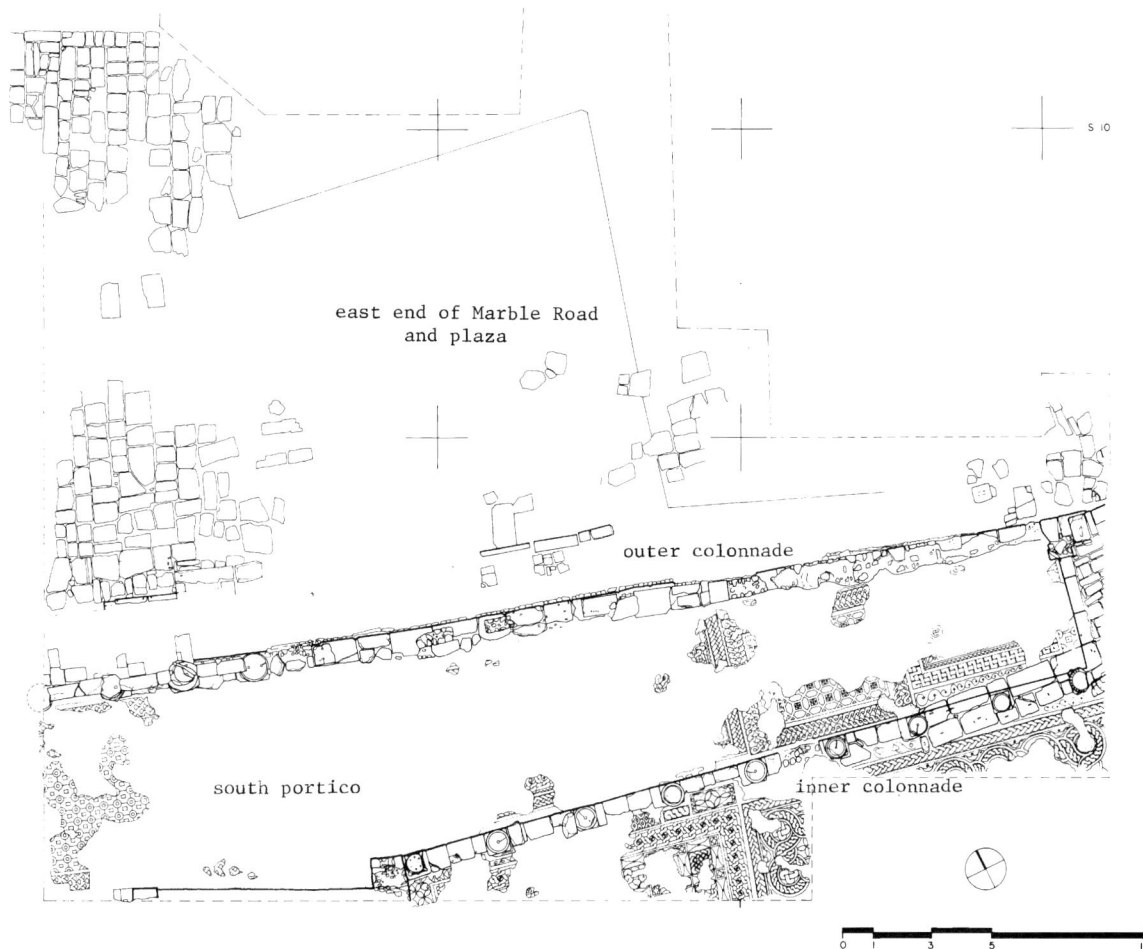

Fig. 5. Sector MMS/N, Late Roman portico, plan.

Byzantine Shops to the west (Greenewalt, Ratté, and Rautman 1994: 3–7).

Excavation in 1992 and 1993 exposed an additional 12 m of the south portico, which now measures 35 m as it stretches from the south colonnade of the Marble Road toward the northeast (fig. 5). Little survives of the main colonnade that once faced onto the plaza. The stylobate consists of an irregular line of marble blocks interrupted by brick and stone repairs, resting on deep, mortared foundations. A row of large marble columns set at 2.4 to 2.6 m intervals originally supported the portico's superstructure. Nothing remains of the entablature, which may have been made of wood, and most of the columns were apparently removed in antiquity. The mosaic floor of the portico was covered by a dense layer of fallen

brick and tile that may have belonged to an upper story. A coin of Phocas (602–610 C.E., 1992.203) recovered from the superstructure debris confirms the early seventh century date of its collapse (Greenewalt, Ratté, and Rautman 1993: 6, 39 n. 6). Both the main colonnade and mosaic floor of the portico are concluded by a row of marble blocks that extends south to join the inner colonnade. To the east lies a slightly raised, stone-paved surface that continues beyond the limit of excavation. The eastern terminus of the portico suggests the nearby presence of another major element of the urban plan, perhaps a street that continues southward toward Sector MMS.

As noted throughout its length, the main portico's upper mosaic floor is poorly preserved. The eastern part of the sidewalk presents two trapezoidal panels of poly-chrome mosaic. The eastern panel consists of a lost central zone surrounded by a modified key-meander border with patches of ivy scrolls and joined circles. The more west-erly mosaic panel presents a looped guilloche border sur-rounding a central zone with interlocked octagons made up of hexagons; the previously excavated mosaic inscrip-tion lies at the western edge of this central zone (Greene-walt et al. 1983: 13, fig. 16). Partial excavation of the bedding for this surface recovered coins and pottery dating to the early sixth century, which supports the previously suggested date of the mosaic (Greenewalt, Ratté, and Rautman 1994: 3, 5).

The inner colonnade is much better preserved; it now stands exposed to a total length of 23 m. It ex-tends from a projecting pier in the back street wall to the northeast, converging slightly toward the main colonnade; another pier or perpendicular wall may conclude the colonnade just beyond the limit of ex-cavation. The stylobate presents a row of carefully fitted white marble blocks that mark a 0.15 m rise from the outer sidewalk to the inner portico. The easternmost 5 m of the stylobate incorporates an earlier foundation of large, clamped blocks, which lies at an oblique angle to the inner colonnade. The individual blocks of the earlier foundation were cut down as needed to continue the raised step of the inner stylobate. The excavated components of the inner portico consist of nine elements: an inverted Ionic pier capital at its west end, seven freestanding Ionic bases set at intervals of 2.85 m, and at its east end a second inverted Ionic capital with finely carved egg-and-dart ornament. From the easternmost sup-port the stylobate turns to join the north colonnade. Apart from a fragmentary marble column shaft found near the middle of the colonnade, all the columns were apparently removed in antiquity.

Further traces were identified of the large polychrome mosaic panel that paved this part of the inner portico. As noted, this panel presents a three-strand guilloche frame surrounding large roundels filled with interlacing cables and enclosing Solomon knots. The roundel pattern extends to a width of four intercolumniations and concludes behind the easternmost column base. Small patches of ivy leaf scroll adjust the mosaic to the uneven south face of the stylobate. Coins found atop the mosaic floor and the inner stylobate date mostly to the fifth and sixth centuries C.E.

MMS. Sector MMS centers on the low mound immediately south of Sector MMS/N and the present highway (fig. 4). In Roman times the area was oc-cupied by a broad, irregularly shaped block that was

defined to the west and south by colonnaded streets and to the north by the open plaza at Sector MMS/N. In 1992 and 1993 excavation focused on clarifying the stratigraphy of two spaces of the main residential complex and exploring Roman features at the south-western part of the sector.

Room VII is an elongated space that stands near the middle of the main residential complex on the east side of the mound (Greenewalt, Ratté, and Raut-man 1994: 8, fig. 7; Rautman 1995). It measures 1.7 × 6.0 m in plan and has doorways at both the west and the east ends. Previous excavation cleared the latest features of the space and showed that in its later sixth century state it formed an unroofed barrier separating two independent houses. Further excava-tion of Room VII determined that in its earliest phase this space was continuous with the area to the north. When its north wall was built in the early fifth cen-tury, the newly created Room VII served as a narrow corridor joining two wings of a larger residence. At that time the room was decorated with wall paintings and had a sloping tile floor that covered a drain orig-inating in Court XII and running east. Multiple re-pairs of the floor drain suggest that it continued in use throughout the fifth century and perhaps after the eastern doorway was blocked in the sixth century.

Room X is the broad trapezoidal space that lies southwest of Room VII (Greenewalt, Rautman, and Cahill 1987: 57–59). The room is one of the larg-est interior spaces identified at the sector and no doubt it played a prominent role in household routines. A shallow sondage dug at the room's northwest corner confirmed that the room's north and west walls rest directly atop the distinctive mudbrick debris of the Archaic fortification wall ("Colossal Lydian Struc-ture"). A coin of Arcadius or Honorius (394–402 C.E., 1993.137) recovered from the foundation trench for these walls confirms their early fifth century date. In its original phase, Room X was paved with terracotta tiles set in a thick mud mortar. The floor was raised 0.10 m and resurfaced with large tiles later in the fifth century.

The southern boundary of Sector MMS is defined by the broad, colonnaded street that rises gently from west to east as it cuts through the remains of the Ar-chaic fortification wall in its earlier and later phases (below). Previous study of the street identified a central roadway flanked by a symmetrical sequence of columns and piers that supported deep porticos (Greenewalt, Ratté, and Rautman 1993: 15, fig. 10). Excavation in 1992 identified the bases of two more columns of the portico and traced westward another

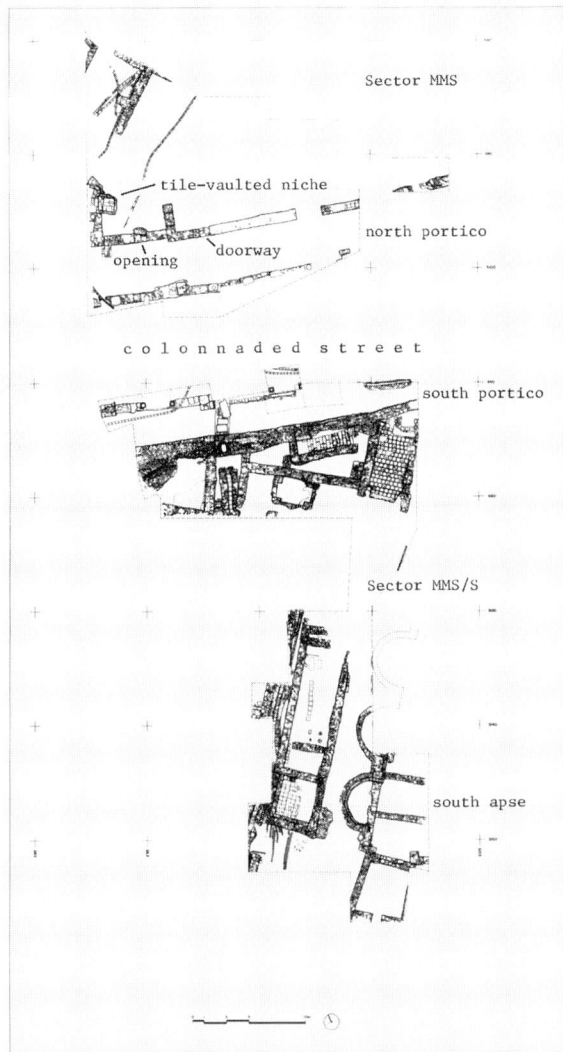

Fig. 6. Sectors MMS (west side) and MMS/S, Late Roman colonnaded street and Roman buildings to the south, plan.

Fig. 7. Sector MMS, vaulted structure.

seventh centuries (Greenewalt, Cahill, and Rautman 1987: 18–20).

The north street wall stands about 4 m from the facing colonnade. The wall was constructed of fieldstone and reused Lydian stonework with intermittent brick leveling courses. Unlike the long planar stretches found to the east, this part of the street wall was built in short, angled sections that apparently compensate for the unstable sloping composition of the mound. Opposite the most westerly exposed pier the street wall turns northward 3.1 m to define a perpendicular spur. A 0.95 m wide doorway opens off the sidewalk, perhaps to provide access to a small shop or taberna that was never completed. Another 1.1 m wide opening in the street wall's westward continuation was similarly blocked before any shop was built. Near the western limit of excavation the street wall again projects northward. A small, tile-vaulted niche was built in this west-facing wall (fig. 7). The feature measures 0.81 × 1.10 m and is enclosed by brick walls that support a shallow barrel vault to a height of about 2 m. The lower part of the niche contains a narrow ledge that stands 0.84 m above its stone-paved floor. Two or more stone steps lead up to the west. The feature was apparently built in two phases and may have housed a fountain or drain, although excavation did not identify any pipes or channels. Other poorly preserved walls were located to

7 m of the north street wall (fig. 6). Both columns originally rested on reused marble blocks built into the north stylobate; one of the displaced columns remains visible in the nearby scarp. As noted elsewhere to the east and south, the portico's packed earthen surface contains several small pits apparently used for slaking lime or mixing mortar during construction of the street in the early fifth century. The surface of the north portico rose gradually and eventually saw intermittent cooking and domestic encroachment, datable by coins and African Red Slip pottery to the sixth century. The entire street became filled with dumped debris in the later sixth and early

the north, built against and into the sloping debris of the mound.

Excavation behind and beneath these walls identified a flat working surface established atop a dump of Hellenistic and early Roman ceramic and other materials (pottery included stamped sigillate and relief wares, molds for relief ware, lamps, terracotta figurines, bone implements, fragments of Masonry Style painted wall plaster). One fragment of relief ware shows a remarkable scene of a melee with a falling man (from a horse; P93.35/10091). An early Roman sanded ware or "rough cast" bowl (P93.8/10036; fig. 8) was reconstructed from fragments. The thin wall

rises from a concave disc base to a plain vertical rim with a diameter of 0.10 m; the exterior wall is evenly covered with fine grits and a red slip (cf. Jones 1950: 190–91; Moevs 1973: 133–37). The presence within the debris of fourth- and fifth-century coins (Valens, 364–378 C.E., 1993.171; Arcadius or Honorius, 395–408 C.E., 1993.170) suggests that it was redeposited in late antiquity, perhaps at the time that the nearby colonnaded street was laid out and the quarter developed. This area became a dumping ground for Late Roman domestic refuse in the fifth and early sixth centuries. Two small rooms were built atop this fill in the sixth century. Their walls continue the orientation of the apsidal building to the north and probably lie parallel to the nearby street to the west.

Fig. 8. Roman sanded ware or "rough cast" bowl, from Roman dump, Sector MMS.

MMS/S. The large hill of Sector MMS/S rises south of the colonnaded street. Previous excavation along the northern and eastern edges of the hill identified remains of the Archaic and Hellenistic periods as well as a number of small Roman structures overlying them. Several long Roman features, including three terrace walls, were built on the lower eastern slope of the hill. Excavation in 1992 and 1993 concentrated on the lowest or easternmost terrace wall and the spaces it sheltered in Roman times (figs. 6, 9).

The terrace wall extends along the eastern edge of the MMS/S hill in a northeasterly direction. In the southern part of the excavation area the wall was founded directly atop the stonework of the east face of the Archaic fortification. Sturdily constructed of

Fig. 9. Sector MMS/S, south apsidal space, with later oven.

Fig. 10. Jug reused as a lamp, from Sector MMS/S.

mortared fieldstone, the terrace wall apparently was built to retain the rising Archaic superstructure and other dumped debris to the west. Excavation east of the terrace wall identified several surfaces and fragmentary walls that belong to an early but undated phase of activity in the Roman period.

The terrace wall was rebuilt later to include two or more broad, semicircular apses or exedrae. Both the wall and two identified apses were carefully constructed of mortared fieldstone with horizontal brick bands. The fully excavated south apse has a diameter of 3.8 m. The two apses carried brick semidomes that are preserved in their lowest courses. The arrangement of multiple apses or exedrae suggests that the area originally served a public function.

Artifacts from fills east of the apse included a glass intaglio signet/gem (with the device of a winged female figure, standing and holding ears of wheat; G93.2/10032) and a bronze weight inscribed ⟨ B i.e., two *unciae* (M93.9/10072; cf. Waldbaum 1983: 84–87 and references therein).

Excavation within and in front of the south apse identified a sequence of packed earthen surfaces contemporary with its construction and use (fig. 9). Pottery and coins (Justinian I, 546/548 C.E., C93.24)

suggest that these levels accumulated during the fifth and early sixth centuries. Sometime in the fifth century the area in front of the south apse was subdivided into three narrow spaces by two parallel walls extending eastward from the terrace wall. At least two pipes passed through the area at this time. Twenty-eight fragments of an openwork terracotta balustrade or screen (uncatalogued) were recovered from the northern part of this space. The screen consists of a network of interlocking semicircles and circles, some filled with rosettes; it may have occupied a window in the upper wall (cf. Rodziewicz 1967: 159; Frantz 1988: 47, pl. 47d, e). It is uncertain whether the space in front of the apse was roofed throughout this period.

The small trapezoidal space immediately to the south was also built about this time. Excavated in 1992, the room measures approximately 4.1 × 4.5 m, and was originally accessible by a single 0.8 m wide doorway in its south wall. A coin (Arcadius, 383–408 C.E., C92.8) recovered from the foundation trench of the east wall suggests a construction date in the early fifth century. The room apparently remained open into the sixth century.

A small, plain ware jug was recovered from the foundation trench of the room (P92.38/10000; fig. 10). The spherical body rests on a low, ring-foot base and has a maximum diameter of 0.16 m; the neck and handle are missing. The vessel apparently was reused as a lamp by knocking out four holes in its wall: one large opening was cut below the handle root; on the opposite side three smaller holes suggest a human face, irresistibly recalling a North American jack-o-lantern. The blackened interior of the vessel attests its functioning as a lamp. The findspot dates the reuse of the jug to the early fifth century.

A small bronze figural attachment was found in the upper fill of the room (M92.4/9950; fig. 11). The cast-bronze object represents a miniature herm with a maximum height of 0.06 m and width of 0.02 m. The oval head and slightly asymmetrical upper body of the figure are intact and preserve faint surface detail of hair and ears. The right leg and lower body are broken away to reveal a small interior cavity containing traces of lead and iron that indicate that the figure served as a decorative handle or finial for a pin, knife, or other domestic implement (cf. Davidson 1952: 189, 191).

In later years the use of this part of Sector MMS/S changed dramatically. In the middle or late sixth century most of the partition walls were removed. Scattered in front of the south apse were a number of architectural fragments, including a marble console block with a cross and floral ornament

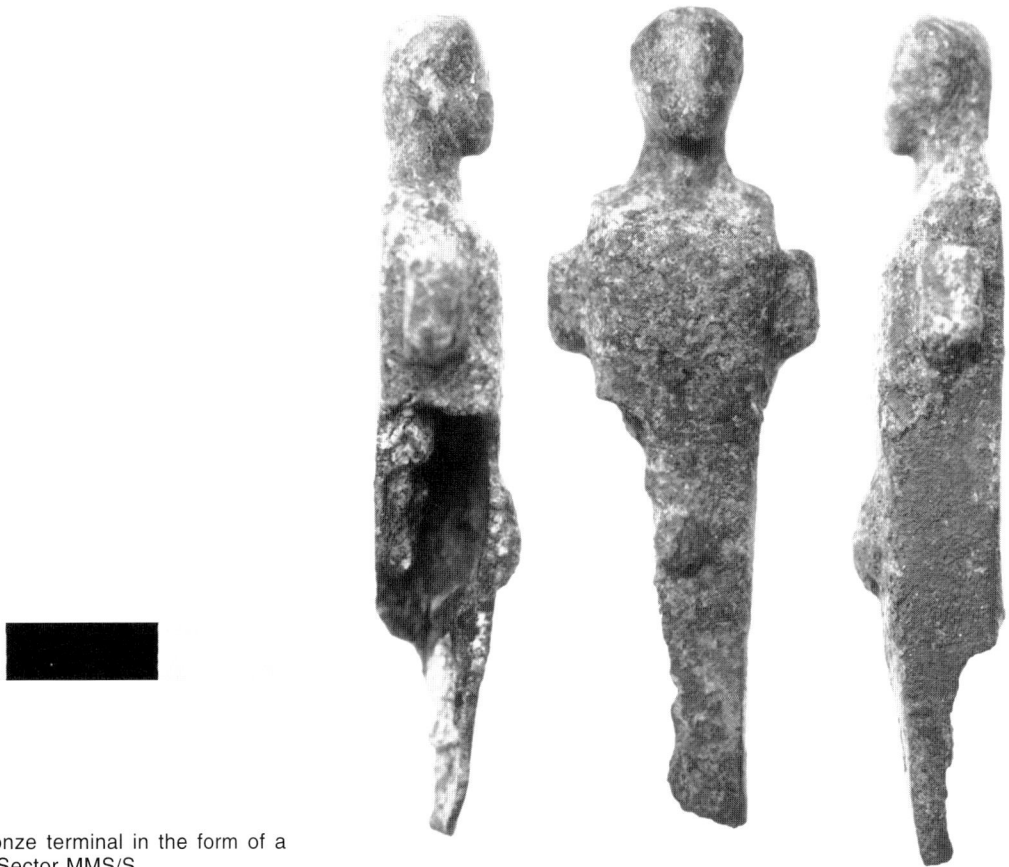

Fig. 11. Bronze terminal in the form of a herm, from Sector MMS/S.

carved in relief on its face (S93.6/10079; fig. 12). The random location of these fragments suggests that they were being assembled in the space for reuse in another building project. Shortly after, a large circular oven was installed in the south apse (fig. 9). The oven was built on a surface consisting of packed earth and small stones, and, with a diameter of 2.8 m, it occupied most of the apse. The unmortared, brick-faced platform was filled with tiles, fieldstones, and earth, and supported a tile floor at a height of 0.6 m. Above this level would have risen the tile or mudbrick dome of the oven (cf. Argoud 1980; Hirschfeld 1992: 85, 87; fig. 38). Abundant deposits of ash were found heaped on the floor in front of the apse. The superstructure of the oven had apparently been dismantled before the brick semidome of the apse collapsed onto the platform. Several fragmentary walls found at higher levels document a final phase of activity in the area.

M. L. R.

Fig. 12. Marble console block, from Sector MMS/S.

Sectors MMS/N, MMS, and MMS/S, Archaic Levels

The three MMS sectors are located on the line of an Archaic fortification wall of the late seventh and early sixth centuries B.C.E.; the wall has been traced for a distance of 170 m (fig. 4; see also Greenewalt, Ratté, and Rautman 1994: 14–15, figs. 14, 15). In MMS and MMS/S the fortification ruins still stand 8–10 m high and have helped to create artificial mounds in the modern landscape; at MMS/N, where the wall contained a gate, and between MMS and MMS/S the fortifications were cut down in later antiquity to accommodate the Roman Marble Road and colonnaded street (fig. 4; above, pp. 4–6).

The fortification wall must have surrounded part of the lower city. Its course further north may be marked by the chain of artificial mounds that extend from the northeast corner of the Roman Bath–Gymnasium complex eastward, on the north side of the city site. The line of those mounds was followed by the Late Roman fortification wall (fig. 1, nos. 9.15–9.21; Hanfmann and Waldbaum 1975: 37), which could have reproduced an older line of defense; and at the only point where one of the mounds, "Mound 2," has been excavated, it covers the ruins of a huge Lydian building that might be a fortification (Greenewalt, Rautman, and Cahill 1987: 80–84; see also above and fig. 3 for an Archaic lion head of limestone from "Mound 2").

Near the fortification wall is a contemporaneous residential quarter.

MMS/N. MMS/N is the site of a gate in the Archaic fortification wall. The gate consisted of a trapezoidal court to the west and a passage (5.57 m wide) to the east. The south side of the court and passage are formed by the north end of "Colossal Lydian Structure" (this name was previously assigned to the fortification wall in Sector MMS). The north side is formed by the structure of zig-zag, W-shaped outline that combines "Lydian Sandstone Wall" or LSS (north side of the court and extending further north) and "Lydian East Wall" or LEW (east side of the court, north side of the passage). The court was blocked in the Archaic period by a solid casement wall formed of two thick shell walls, "Lydian West Wall" or LWW (to the west) and "Wall Z" (to the east) and intermediate gravel fill (figs. 4, 13). Excavations in 1992 and 1993 aimed to clarify the appearance of gate remains, partly by removing some of the post-Archaic features that created visual obstructions and distractions, to determine the date of the court blockage, and to locate the east end of the gate passage.

Features that were partly or wholly removed included a Roman drain north of the Roman portico (10 m removed, between E. 138 and E. 148 on the "B" grid), two Roman foundations ("oblique foundations A and B," of which the upper 1 to 2 m were removed),[4] and paving, foundation, and wall remains at the southeast end of the court. The oblique foundations contained more than 75 reused limestone blocks that belong to one or more Archaic buildings; notably four segments of faceted molding, like faceted molding segments recovered in Sectors MMS/N and MMS in previous seasons (Ratté 1989: 247–48); and pottery fragments of the first or second century C.E. (Roman red-ware pitcher and bowl) that indicate an early Roman date for the foundations (which have been called Hellenistic in previous reports).

Removal of those features exposed several parts of the gate and blockage structures, including the north end of "Wall Z" (fig. 13).

The date of the gate court in its final phase depends on East Greek orientalizing pottery recovered behind gate-court walls and Middle Corinthian skyphos fragments recovered under a court surface (Greenewalt, Cahill, and Rautman 1987: 33; n. 25; Ratte 1989: 90, 237–44). The date of blockage depends on the nature of mudbrick debris and its relationship to the blockage construction. The mudbrick debris survives in relatively shallow deposits; some of it is semibaked and reddish, some of it is unbaked and gray-green. It closely resembles "Brick Fall" deposit in Sector MMS, which may be dated ca. 550 B.C.E. on the basis of ceramic evidence (Cahill in Greenewalt, Cahill and Rautman 1987: 22–24; Ramage 1986; see also below); and it covers local ceramic items—a lydion and column crater fragments recovered in 1992 (lydion inventoried P92.40/10004; see also Greenewalt, Sterud, and Belknap 1982: 21, n. 16)—similar to those covered by "Brick Fall" deposit in Sector MMS. If the mudbrick debris in Sector MMS/N is "Brick Fall," therefore, it also would have been deposited ca. 550 B.C.E. Its identification as "Brick Fall," however, may be questioned: in some places semibaked and unbaked components occur in separate strata, which could be fortuitous (semibaked and unbaked bricks are sometimes separately clustered in the "Brick Fall" of Sector MMS) or might signify separate deposits; and if semibaking is a factor of manufacture rather than of destruction, as Cahill has argued, it is not by itself a reliable

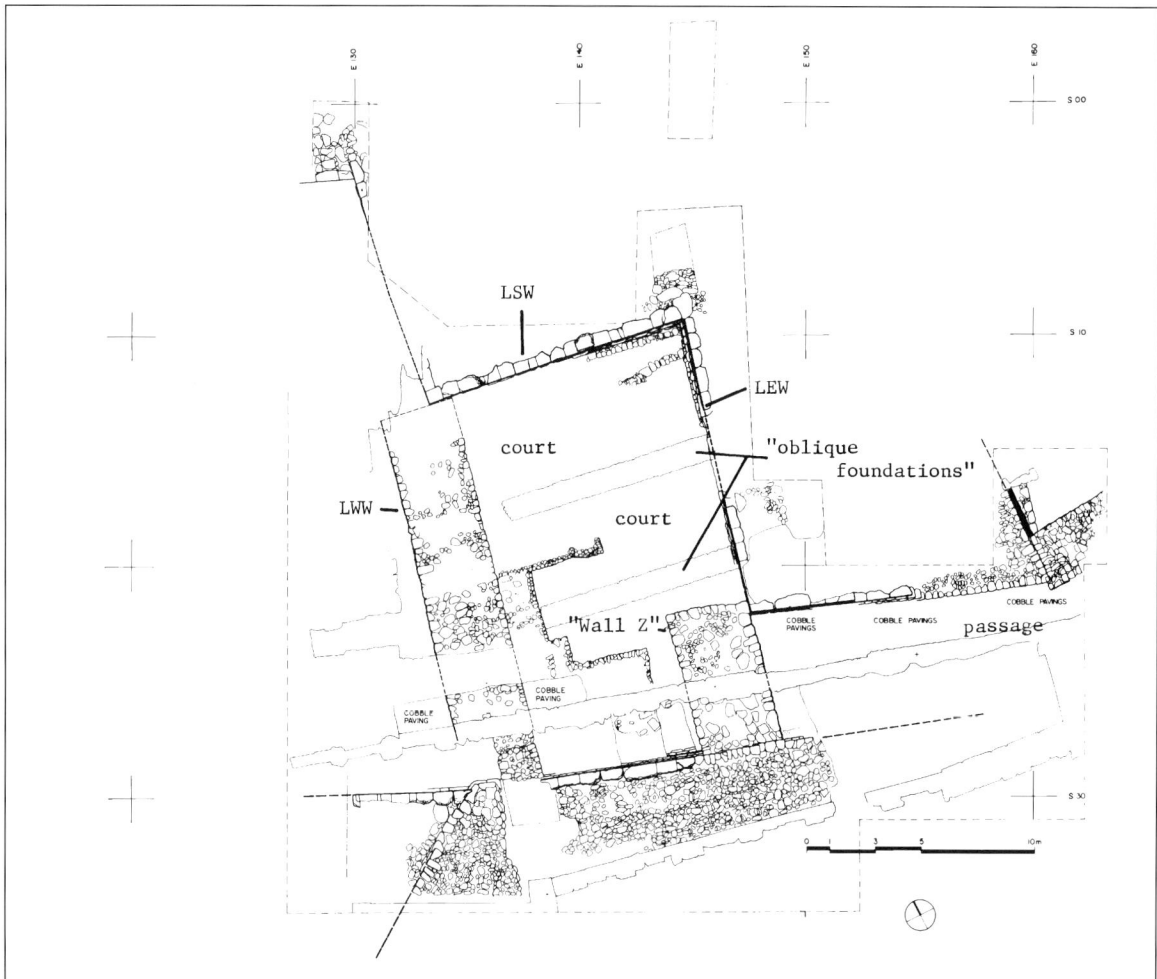

Fig. 13. Sector MMS/N, Archaic features, plan.

chronological indicator. The shallowness of the deposits in Sector MMS/N and the uncertain chronology of local ceramic styles are major factors in these uncertainties. Mudbrick debris with semibaked inclusions underlies parts of the gate-court blockage ("Wall Z," the south end of LWW, and at least some intermediate gravel fill) but apparently not others (north end of LWW); and where debris adjoined one side of the blockage (LWW, west side) it appeared to rest against rather than be cut by blockage (Greenewalt, Sterud, and Belknap 1982: 20). Whether the gate court was blocked before or after the mid-sixth century B.C.E. destruction, therefore, remains problematic.

Excavation east of the gate passage uncovered the east end of the passage on its north side, 13.2 m east

of the northwest corner: an acute salient corner, with return to the north. Built against the east face of the gate and projecting slightly into the passage is a masonry adjunct, possibly the east end of a wall or tower (fig. 13). The design and chronology of these features remain to be clarified.

Several stratified gravel surfaces were exposed in the gate court and passage and east of the passage. Most of them evidently belong to phases of an east–west thoroughfare. The oldest surface, east of the passage, may be dated to the eighth century B.C.E. on the basis of local Geometric-style pottery fragments recovered from fills above and below it; that surface is less compacted and less stony than the others, however, and may merely attest to occupation. One of several gravel surfaces in the court extends underneath masonry that defines the south side of the court (i.e., the north side of Colossal Lydian Structure) and so must be older than the gate building in its final, predestruction phase. Above that surface is another, on which rested the lydion and column crater fragments cited above.

MMS.   The aim of excavation (in 1993) was to uncover more of the Archaic residential quarter located east of the fortification wall and destroyed together with the wall in the middle of the sixth century B.C.E. The excavation space is under Late Roman Room IV (fig. 4) and measures roughly 5 m × 12 m (the Late Roman wall separating Room IV from Rooms III and VI and the steps at the south end of Room IV were removed in 1990 and 1993; Greenewalt, Ratté, and Rautman 1994: fig. 7; and fig. 4 above). Below Roman fills (excavated in 1990) were strata and fills of the Hellenistic Age and fourth and fifth centuries B.C.E. Three east–west walls could be assigned to those eras on the basis of context pottery (e.g., fragments of a molded relief-ware bowl, a Hellenistic lamp, and black-glaze, palmette-stamped bowls; walls omitted in the plan, fig. 14). Culturally noteworthy items included fragments of an Attic cup decorated in black and intentional red glaze, many Achaemenid-type bowl fragments, a terracotta revetment tile with conventional star motif, three glass beads, a bronze knife or dagger handle, and four bronze arrowheads, three of them trilobate, one leaf-shaped.[5] About thirteen fragments of opaque, red-glass cullet and two pieces of obsidian may have been tossed up from the lower stratum with the mid-sixth century B.C.E. terminus, when that stratum was disturbed shortly after the destruction (below).

The earliest chronologically diagnostic material above the stratum with the mid-sixth century B.C.E. destruction appears to be of the mid-fifth century B.C.E., which suggests that the locale may have been unoccupied for a century after the destruction.

Part of the occupation stratum with the mid-sixth century destruction had been excavated in 1984–1986. Those excavations had uncovered an oblong space, ca. 6 × 18 m, with spatial components of workshop, yard, kitchen, and a living space of undetermined kind (Cahill in Greenewalt, Cahill, and Rautman 1987: 26–31; in Greenewalt, Rautman, and Cahill 1987: 62–70; in Greenewalt et al. 1990: 143–55). The part of the stratum excavated in 1993 is immediately east of the part excavated in 1984–1986 (fig. 14).

Most of the stratum excavated in 1993 was undisturbed (although it may originally have been somewhat thicker and its top part subsequently shaved off). It did not contain a cover layer of "Brick Fall" destruction debris, which had covered yard, kitchen, and living space; but it did contain clots of "Brick Fall" mixed with debris from the residential buildings. The only disturbance had occurred on the northeast side, which corresponds to the east side of the workshop; the main part of it, excavated in 1986, also had been disturbed. The disturbance may have taken place soon after the destruction, since the disturbed part corresponds precisely with the workshop and its limits, which presumably would have been forgotten a decade or so after the destruction. The fragments of opaque red glass cullet and obsidian, which were recovered from an upper stratum east of the workshop (above), might be workshop contents that had been removed at the time of disturbance (for opaque red cullet recovered from the workshop in 1986, see Cahill in Greenewalt et al. 1990: 153–55; Brill and Cahill 1988).

That the occupation in the stratum ended with an intense conflagration is indicated by the burnt condition of many and varied items: most conspicuously pottery—the predominant class of artifact—many fragments of which rested in or next to concentrations of burnt material; also wood, straw, rush matting, seeds, vitrified mudbrick, and charred bones. Joins between burnt and unburnt fragments of many pottery items (e.g., marbled bowl P93.37/10093; Lebes with orientalizing decoration P93.25/10069; an Attic black-figure closed vessel P93.44/10109; figs. 15–18) indicate that some artifact destruction preceded conflagration. The survival of only a few average-sized stones and the gravel bedding from the east wall of the workshop indicates that the wall had been deliberately destroyed; but its destruction may have occurred after the conflagration, when the workshop fill was disturbed.

Apart from the east side of the workshop, the space excavated in 1993 represents more open yard. Walls appear at the north and south ends: at the north end was found the south terminus of a wall projecting from the north scarp; at the south end there was an extension of the south kitchen wall, which extends into the east trench scarp (and shows two phases of construction). A drain extends from the middle of the space into the north trench scarp. Its cover slabs of stone are supplemented by smaller stones (including a worn upper grindstone) to seal

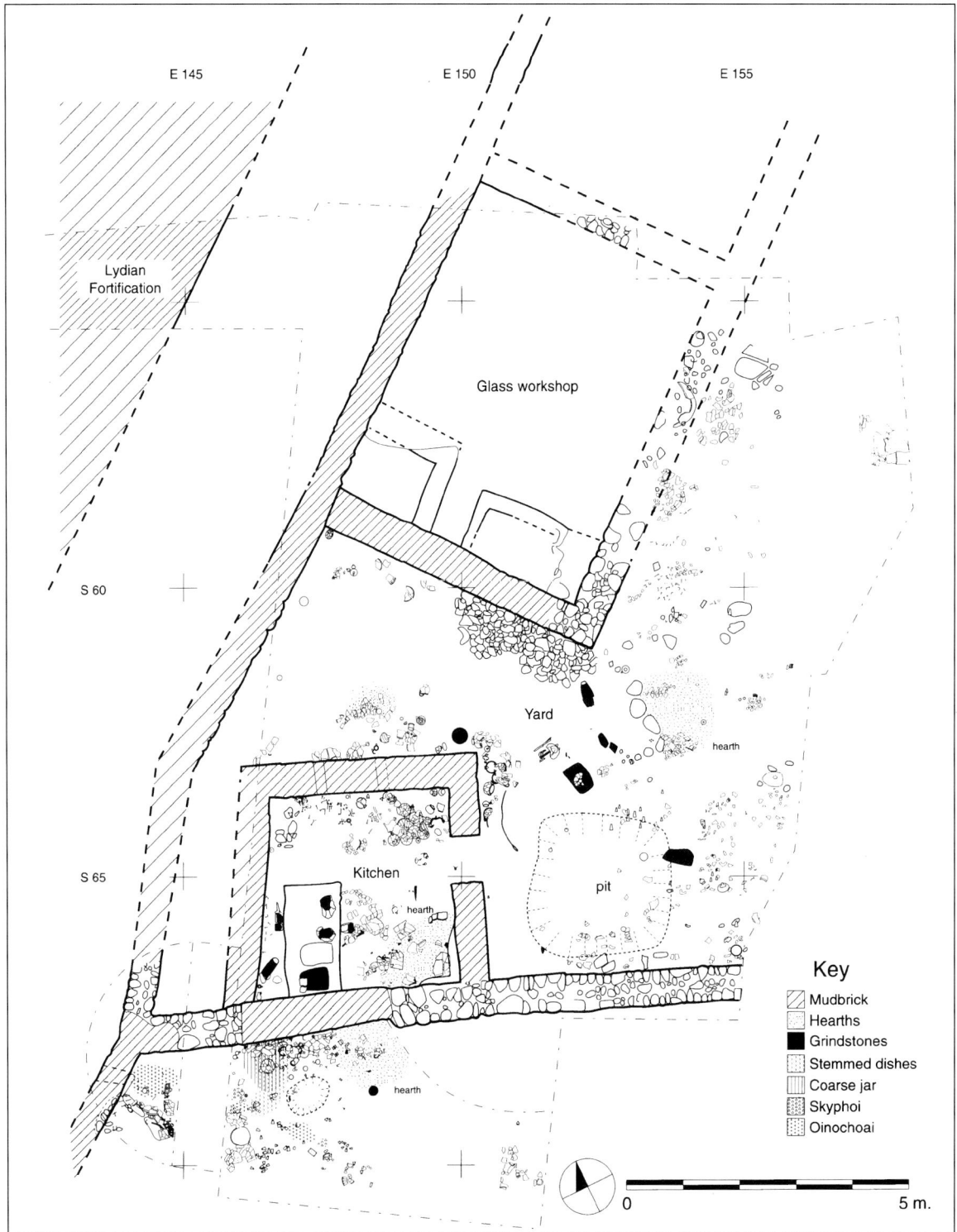

Fig. 14. Sector MMS, Archaic residential quarter, plan.

Fig. 15. Skyphos and bowl with marbled decoration; a. interior; b. exterior, from Archaic residential quarter, Sector MMS.

Fig. 16. Lebes with orientalizing decoration, from Archaic residential quarter, Sector MMS; reconstruction by I. Tokumaru, with infilling by M. J. DiLisio, 1994.

the chinks; fig. 14). The sides and bottom of the drain are made of small stone slabs (like the drain under one wall of the living space south of the kitchen; Cahill in Greenewalt, Rautman, and Cahill 1987: 64). During the final use of the space, the drain evidently no longer functioned. Remains of two walls from an earlier occupation phase appear in the northeast corner of the space: these were the stone foundations of a wall that had been cut by the drain (fig. 14); and a mudbrick wall, further northeast (not shown in fig. 14).

The floor of the yard is a hard, clayey surface at the north and south, a mixture of sand and gravel—perhaps associated with the drain—in the middle. The floor surface is relatively level in the north half of the space but uneven in the south half, where it dips down gradually to an oblong pit, the steep west side of which had been excavated in 1986. A hearth rested on sand and gravel in the middle of the trench

(fig. 14). Carbonized wood remains at the north side of the pit were consistent with similar evidence previously recovered and suggested that the pit had been covered by planks supported on wooden posts (Cahill in Greenewalt et al. 1990: 150). Other carbonized wood remains, together with iron brackets and nails in the pit, might—in view of loomweights also recovered there (below)—have belonged to a loom. Carbonized wood and pottery scatters near the extension of the kitchen south wall might be remains of shelves or a table that supported pottery. Traces of matting were detected over much of the south side of the space, including the periphery of the hearth. Much burnt straw, recovered in the southwest part of the space and resting at an incline, downward to the northeast, might be roof thatch from the kitchen or simply straw heaps.

A variety of artifacts and food remains were recovered throughout the stratum. They included pottery (large to miniature vessels, luxury and plain, imported and local wares, ordinary and unusual shapes; containers for food, drink, and cosmetic substances), lamps (more than ten, including L93.2/10031; L93.4/10100; L93.5/10110), terracotta loomweights and spindle whorls, stone and glass, bone and ivory, metal (iron and bronze), wood, basketry, grain, and bones.

A total of 214 kg of pottery was recovered, representing over 200 items. Almost all the pieces were recovered in fragments, many fragments of

Fig. 17. Orientalizing decoration of Lebes in fig. 16, C. S. Alexander.

individual items widely scattered. Most are incomplete, some by as much as 75% or more, which probably reflects widespread scattering—beyond excavation limits—at the time of destruction rather than incomplete condition before destruction. Breakage of pottery before burning is noted above.

The pottery includes a standard repertoire of Lydian shapes and decorative conventions. Shapes are primarily those associated with the preparation and serving of food and drink, and with the storage of cosmetic unguents and salves. The following shapes are represented:

Pithos (2; one upside-down over workshop east wall foundation);

Amphora (2; of "Myrina"-type shape and decoration and consisting of many fragments drilled for repair (one almost complete, P94.41/10202);

Hydria (6, including 5 of wavy-line type);

Oinochoe (15, including 4 with pendent decoration);

Mixing bowls (about 6, including column crater, skyphos crater, lebes [the last described below]);

Plain bowls (22; of the same kind as the "coarse bowls," often with lopsided rims, recovered from kitchen and yard; see Cahill in Greenewalt et al. 1990: 149, 151;

Fig. 18. Pottery made in Greece, from Archaic residential quarter, Sector MMS. Upper right, Attic closed vessel with narrative scene and animal frieze. Lower right, Attic Little Master cup. Lower left, Corinthian cup. Upper left, Lakonian cup.

Stemmed dishes (22);

Skyphos (42);

One-handled cooking pot (9, including 1 *chytra* holding grain and recovered near the hearth);

Cooking stands (5);

Bread trays (6);

Lekythos ("Lydian/Samian" type; at least 3; including an unusually small one [below]);

Lydion (about 17, including P93.53/10121; P93.54/10122; P93.55/10123);

Askos (1; miniature [below]).

Standard decorative conventions include gray ware; streaky glaze with and without simple linear decoration and dots in white; bichrome; marbling (the last on small fragments, with the exception of a skyphos, P93.48/10114).

Unusual vessels include the miniature askos (with simple linear decoration over light slip, burnt; P93.43/10105); an unusually small lekythos of "Lydian/Samian" type (with streaky-glaze decoration; P93.52/10120); two "bobbins" (with simple linear decoration and dots over light slip, burnt; both recovered near the hearth; P93.23/10063; P93.39/10095); a jug with spout in the form of a phallus (with testicles in relief, painted pubic hair; P93.38/10094; fig. 19).[6]

Luxury-ware items include a skyphos, ca. one-third complete, with marbling inside and out (P93.48/10114); a bowl, nearly one-fourth com-

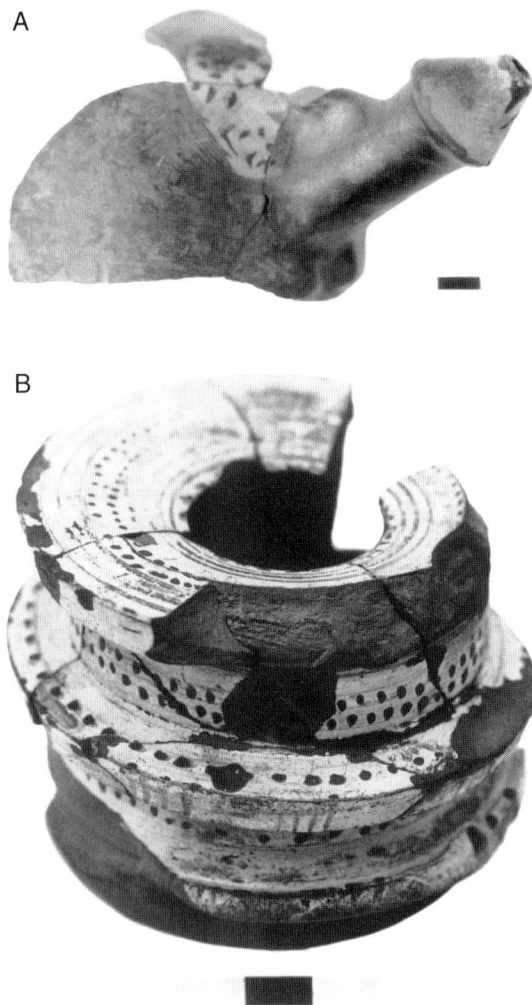

Fig. 19. A, Jug with phallus spout, and B, "bobbins" from Archaic residential quarter, Sector MMS.

plete, with curled or scaled marbling inside, outside cream slip over which a simple band of pattern below rim (P93.37/10093; both fig. 15); several vessels with orientalizing decoration, including stemmed dishes (P93.26/10070; P93.41/10103; P93.42/10104; P93.47/10113), the Myrina amphora mentioned above, and a lid (P93.46/10112). The finest orientalizing vessel is a lebes with painted decoration featuring two water serpents or *ketoi* (figs. 16, 17).

P93.25/10069. Broken twice in antiquity: repaired after the first break (drill holes for clamps between the *ketoi*); after the second, fragments became scattered and some were darkened by burning. Four symmetrically spaced lugs on top of rim (one lug is a floater in the restoration, another

Fig. 20. Attic Little Master Band Cup, from Archaic residential quarter, Sector MMS.

is restored from a rim scar). Flat disk foot. Inside and on lugs, dark glaze. Outside, cream slip over which decoration in dark glaze (no added red or white was discerned). On rim, contiguous double circles, seven circles per space between lugs. On shoulder, two confronted *ketoi* with fish (seven; one large, the rest small) between; at "back," confronted ducks on either side of floral ornament (of symmetrically organized volutes and palmettes). The floral ornament is framed by two pairs of vertical lines. In the field, filling ornament, which includes large, half-rosettes with round-tipped, solid petals, circle, and dot and cross motifs. At mid-belly, two pairs of narrow and broad bands frame pseudomaeander S-pattern. Just below mid-belly, lotus flower and bud chain. Flowers inside petals contain groups of plain or outlined dot-in-square-filled lozenges and triangles. Below lotus chain, alternating broad and narrow bands (three broad, four narrow). Framing the flat disk foot, narrow band and roundel of glaze that also covers foot. Height without lugs, 0.267 m, exterior mouth diameter 0.26 m. Estimated capacity about 21 litres (Greenewalt 1994).[7]

Several imported pottery items, all less than 25 percent complete, support or are consistent with a mid-sixth century B.C.E. destruction date: three Attic black-figure items (Little Master Cups P93.36/10092; P93.49/10117, the former a Band Cup (fig. 20), the latter probably the same, with a lion or other carnivore in the tondo), a closed vessel decorated with a narrative scene, perhaps Achilles' ambush of Troilos, and an animal frieze, in a style resembling those of the Camtar Painter, the Painter of London B 76, and Tyrrhenian amphorae according to A. B. Brownlee (personal communication; P93.44/10109); and Corinthian and Lakonian black-figure cups (the former a rim fragment, P93.45/10111; the latter a tondo fragment, P93.56/10124; figs. 18, 20). Much older is a small fragment of a Protocorinthian aryballos (P93.57/10125).

The excavator recovered 89 clay loomweights from the pit (together with remains of a loom?; above) and the southeast part of the space (underneath grain; below). One loomweight is round (with a weight of 0.341 kg); the rest are either squarish (5, with an average weight of 0.107 kg) or pyramidal (83). Of the pyramidal kind there are four sizes: large (19; with an average weight of 0.287 kg); medium (21, with an average weight of 0.113 kg); a small, fat variety (9, with an average weight of 0.074 kg), and a small thin variety (34, with an average weight of 0.037 kg). The pit contained most of the large and some of the medium loomweights; the southeast locale two large, some medium, and all the small ones (11 loomweights were inventoried, T93.10/10116 A–K).

More than 16 clay spindle whorls of various sizes were recovered; most of them near the hearth, together with the two bobbins mentioned above (seven spindle whorls were inventoried, T93.9/10115 A–G).

Stone items include a dish of granular texture with lug handles (ca. one-fifth complete, burnt), three water-rolled black stones that might have been used as touchstones (all recovered from the pit; S93.3/10058; S94.1/10129; S94.2/10130), and several pieces of rock crystal. The last included one piece that resembles a natural crystal but is partly cut, and fragments of one or two "ear plugs" like those recovered in the Artemision at Ephesos, one of them drilled (J93.1/10077); the rock crystal pieces were recovered in the southern part of the space (i.e., not near the workshop).[8]

Bone and ivory items include two semicylindrical bone lugs, articulated with lathe-turned flutes and astragal moldings (BI93.3/10068) and with wide and narrow astragal moldings (BI93.7/10076); and a very small ivory rim fragment.

Metal items were predominantly iron: 21 "brackets" (like examples recovered in and near the kitchen; Cahill in Greenewalt et al. 1990: 146, 151; and others from Sector MMS/S; below) and 19 nails (some of both from the pit, possibly belonging to a loom [above]); fragments of two knives, one with a vitreous accretion at one end (possibly indicating use in the workshop, where much glass was recovered; M94.6/10177); a hooked chisel; two pairs of tweezers; a crank-shaped rotary handle (for a Lydian car?; M94.8/10197); a hinge; two small rings (recovered on the floor east of the hearth); fragments of one or more horse snaffle bits (M94.7/10178); and unidentified items. Bronze items included a square ornament of embossed sheet (decorated with cross and circles; without perforations; M93.10/10126), three to six "finials"; a bridle attachment (*Riemenkreuzung*; M94.1/10131); and small amorphous scraps.

Remains of rush matting rested over much of the floor surface in the southern part of the space, and over basketry (for loomweights?) in the pit. Much wheat and barley grain was recovered, some of it in a cooking pot resting near the hearth, some in the southwest corner of the space. About 0.3–0.4 m³ of bones probably belong to ovicaprids, pig, poultry, and *bos*.

Clayey earth that probably consists of disintegrated mudbrick from the fortification wall and "Brick Fall" deposit was removed from behind the west wall of Late Roman Room II and the apse of Room VI (fig. 4) in two small ditches. The ditches were dug to prevent ground salts from penetrating the walls and efflorescing on the interior painted wall surfaces of those rooms. No chronologically diagnostic artifacts were recovered.

On the west side of Sector MMS (figs. 4, 21) excavation aimed to locate the west end of the deep recess (which had contained a helmet and a skeleton; Greenewalt, Ratté, and Rautman 1993: 20–21 and references therein) and to regularize the west limits of excavation in an even line.

Below the Roman deposits (above) is a thick, earthy stratum distinguished by small, fragmentary brick inclusions, some of them semibaked. The stratum evidently belongs to an earthwork glacis of the late Archaic fortification, which has been identified elsewhere in sectors MMS and MMS/S, and which, together with the 5 m thick stone "secondary wall," replaced the fortification ruined in ca. 550 B.C.E.[9] The surface of this stratum—or what appears to be its surface—was exposed in a narrow cut (ca. 3.5 m × 7 m); it slopes down from east to west, i.e., away

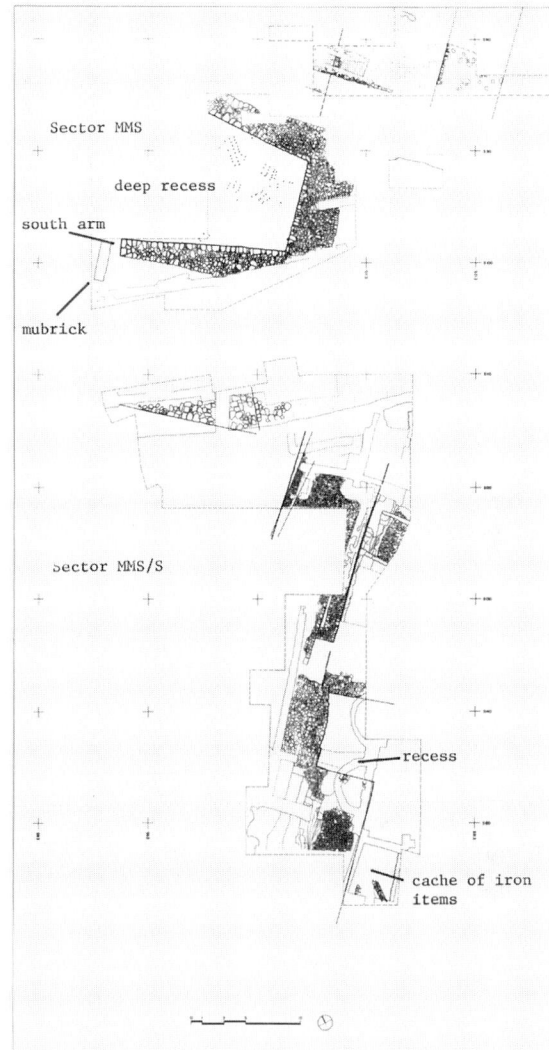

Fig. 21. Sectors MMS (west side) and MMS/S, Archaic features, plan.

from the "secondary wall" that was evidently its crowning feature, in an angle of ca. 35° (fig. 22).[10] Excavation in a few places below that stratum (e.g., at the bottom of the Late Roman vaulted structure; above) exposed "Brick Fall" destruction debris; whether that debris is original deposit or redeposit was not determined.

The west end of the south arm of the recess in the older fortification is 15 m from the back of the recess. Only the bottom course of stones survives. The south arm may have retained an earthwork glacis, as the north arm certainly did (Greenewalt, Ratté, and

Fig. 22. Sector MMS, west side. Late Archaic earthwork glacis (?), exposed under Roman dump. (The *tableau vivant* is meant to communicate the difficulty of ascent on the sloped surface.)

Rautman 1993: 15–16), which sloped down from east to west, like the later one (above). A narrow line of mudbrick (two to three bricks high, one to two bricks deep) that extends 2.5 m south of the arm foundation at a right angle to it and at ancient ground surface might belong to a curb for such a glaçis (fig. 21).

Sector MMS/S. Excavation took place below spaces of the Late Roman apsidal building and south of the recess in the east face of the Archaic fortification (figs. 4, 6, 21; for the recess, Greenewalt, Ratté, and Rautman 1994: 19–20). Strata below Roman fills contained diagnostic pottery of Hellenistic era and fourth century B.C.E. types and Archaic styles,[11] and slight architectural features (piles of large, un-

worked fieldstones). The east face of the Lydian fortification rests below the west wall of the Roman apsidal structure. The two walls have slightly different orientations; where they coincide, just south of the Archaic fortification recess, the later wall is built directly on the earlier one. The east face in this locale is aligned with the segment of east face exposed 60 m to the north (fig. 4; for the northerly segment, Greenewalt, Ratté, and Rautman 1994: 18). The MMS/S segment has a maximum preserved height of 2.7 m, is vertical, built of stone, and has been traced for a distance of 10 m (south of the recess). The masonry is quasipolygonal, except at the (south) salient corner of the recess, where it has ashlar coigns. The south side of the recess at its east end, below the south apse of the Late Roman apsidal

Fig. 23. Selection of iron items recovered at the foot of the Archaic fortification wall, Sector MMS/S.

building, is defined by the vertical face of "Brick Fall" destruction debris, which had pressed against the south wall of the recess. The south wall itself has been robbed—to the depth reached in excavation— but the "mold" of destruction debris preserves its form and location, which is also aligned with stone masonry of the southwest corner of the recess, just west of the Late Roman apse (figs. 6, 21; Greenewalt, Ratté, and Rautman 1994: 19–20).

The Archaic occupation stratum that has an occupation surface at the foot of the fortification wall and is contemporaneous with that wall was exposed in a small 2.5 m × 4 m space, 7.5–1 m south of the recess against the fortification east face (and below the south half of the trapezoidal room that belongs to the Late Roman apsidal building; figs. 6, 21).

"Brick Fall" deposit, a common feature of the occupation stratum near the fortification and particularly against its faces (e.g., in the recess located a few meters to the north; Greenewalt, Ratté, and Rautman 1994: 19–20) appeared only in the eastern and central parts of the stratum and was absent close to the fortification, where the stratum was distinguished from deposit above only by a few thin layers of carbonized material (recognized in the south scarp). The only architectural feature, apart from the fortification wall, is a narrow wall with a fieldstone socle and mudbrick or pisé above (the equivalent of two or three mudbrick courses *in situ*) that extends 1.5–2 m into the excavation space from the southeast corner (fig. 21). A thick deposit of "Brick Fall" covered and rested against the east side of that wall.

Only parts of the exposed stratum were excavated to occupation surface, due to time constraints at the end of the 1992 season and the complexity of the artifact deposit. Many iron artifacts rested on or slightly above the occupation surface in the west side of the trench and in "Brick Fall" deposit in the central part. More than 300 iron items were recovered (the locations of most were individually plotted) and more evidently rest in unexcavated parts. Recovered items include the following (a selection appears in fig. 23):

2	U-shaped handles
1	loop
15	rectangular strips, some straight and some bent, perforated with nails or rivets
4	ring fragments
2	"braces," i.e., rectangular or butterfly-shaped plaques in pairs or "fours," attached with nails or rivets
3	rivets
12	complete nails
259	fragmentary nails
4	C-shaped clamps
12	fragments of sheet
4	"brackets," i.e., L-shaped items of bent sheet
3	miscellaneous fragments

TEMPLE OF ARTEMIS

In connection with F. K. Yegül's graphic recording project, scaffolding was erected around the two complete columns of the Artemis Temple, nos. 6 and 7, to permit inspection of the capitals and upper shafts (for the column numbers, Butler 1925: pl. A; for Yegül's project Greenewalt 1990: 23, n. 4; for the scaffolding, n. 1 here). Several features were thereby recognized and clarified. The columns are 17.80 m high; Column 6 has a slenderness ratio of ± 1/8.9. The capital of Column 6—capital A, more sensitively carved than capital B of Column 7 (Butler 1925: 64–65)—is the only capital of the Temple that is carved together with the (fluted) upper part of the shaft in a single block.

The top drum of Column 7 is incised with guidelines that indicate design features. According to Yegül, a heavy vertical line facing east marks the central axis of the column. Just below the flutes (20 cm wide, separated by fillets 3 cm wide) a pair of very fine vertical lines marks the width of the flutes and a third vertical line between them marks the center. Seven of the 24 flutes are so marked. A small, finely-polished rectangular area, 2 cm by 3 cm, occupies the upper part of many fillets; a fine horizontal line that crosses the middle of that smooth part in 14 (of the total 24) fillets marks the bottom of the apophyge. Vertical lines (straight line or T) on the capital and six drums establish the center of the south side of the column (from Yegül's unpublished field report, with modifications).

In both capitals each round volute "eye" has a small rectangular cutting, ca. 1.0 cm × 4.5 cm: the socket for a bronze ornament (a rosette or the like; for their use elsewhere, see Stevens et al. 1927: 22–23, 82; Miller 1990: 70). All four volute cuttings of Capital B, Column 7, contain lead casings for ornament stems, and the southwest volute cutting also contains the bronze stem.

Marble repair plugs, called "dutchmen," were noticed in the shaft of Column 7 (three, in Drums 15 and 16 from the bottom) and in the bottom of the southeast volute of Capital A, Column 6 (fig. 24; for "dutchmen" in the Erechtheum at Athens, see Stevens et al. 1927: 206–14). These plugs are a common feature of the lower shafts and bases of columns at the east end of the Temple and are attested by cut-outs in fluted drums at the west end.

The later history of the Temple is documented by holes in the column shafts made to extract metal dowels (five) and to socket beams ends (four), three modern graffiti, and one dipinto. The graffiti are in modern Greek; two are dated, 1784 and 1874. The dipinto, in blue paint and Latin letters, reads ISMAE (Ismael?). A memento of the Butler Expedition is wedged between the capital and top drum of Col-

Fig. 24. Temple of Artemis, upper part of column 6 and capital A; showing "dutchman" repair plug in the bottom of the volute.

umn 7 (a zinc plaque inscribed with the name of L. C. Holden, Jr.; see Butler 1925: 145). Fissures and cracks in both columns, especially in the shaft of Column 7 and in Capital A of Column 6, indicate unstable conditions that deserve conservation attention.

BIN TEPE

Tomb of Alyattes

The tumulus conventionally identified as the Tomb of Alyattes (the largest mound at Bin Tepe, locally called Kır Mutaf Tepe) was further explored, both outside and inside the mound.[12] Excavation outside the mound was conducted to determine whether three stone blocks exposed at the foot of the mound on its northwest side belong to a crepis wall. Such a wall is reported for the Tomb by Herodotus (1.93) and for the mound by excavator Spiegelthal in the 1850s (von Olfers 1859: 544–45), but there were no reports of it since Spiegelthal's excavations (Dennis 1878: 388, n. 9; Butler 1922: 9). The blocks are located where the mound meets a modern field and may have become exposed as the result of plowing. Two are of limestone and one of sandstone, both common in Archaic Lydian masonry. All three blocks are appropriately located for a crepis vis à vis the mound, are in rough alignment, and have one or more worked surfaces. One has a worked top surface that is level and a side edge that is vertical, and appears to face away from the mound (as a crepis should); another is tipped forward from what appears to have been the same alignment and orientation.

Excavation of a narrow, 18 m long trench on the line of the blocks exposed four others (all limestone) further north and much limestone rubble behind all seven. Two of the four excavated blocks appear to be *in situ*. They have worked top surfaces that are level at the same elevation; they are joined with an approximately vertical joint, appear to face away from the mound, and are aligned with the most distant of the three blocks first noticed. The blocks that appear to be aligned also seem to make a slight curve, which bows away from the center of the mound; the radius of the curve was roughly estimated to be ca. 155 m, which corresponds to the diameter of the mound at that elevation. The two other excavated blocks have different and separate alignments; the vertical face of one has flat chisel-trimmed side borders and a pick-stippled center. The three blocks that appear to be *in situ* rest on a hard packing of crushed limestone that is roughly level, contains a row of small stones ca. 0.50 m in front of the blocks and roughly parallel with them, and slopes gently down in front of the blocks (fig. 25).

Recovered near the blocks were a small, barrel-shaped block of limestone, dressed with flat, chisel-trimmed borders and pick-stippled center in the style characteristic of Archaic Lydian masonry (S93.7/10101; 0.13 m long, 0.08 m in diameter at the two ends; fig. 26) and approximately a dozen pottery fragments, all of distinctive Archaic Lydian types (e.g., wavy-line vessels, skyphoi).

Although only one course survives and only three of the seven blocks appear to be aligned, the position

Fig. 25. Bin Tepe, Tomb of Alyattes. Stones belonging to the crepis wall of the tumulus; view looking south.

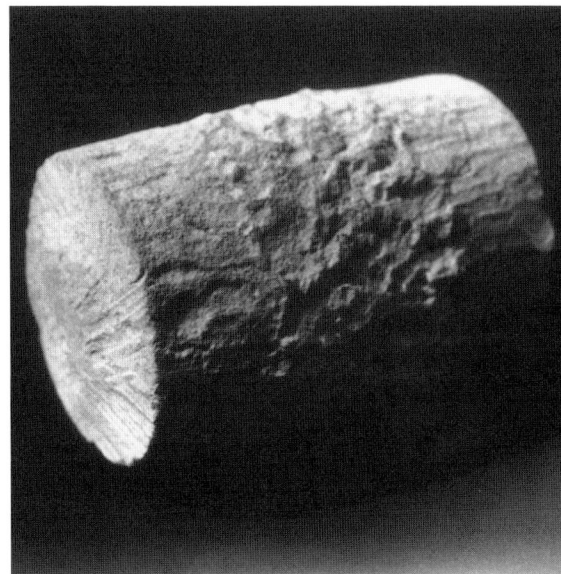

Fig. 26. Barrel-shaped limestone block, from the crepis wall of the Tomb of Alyattes.

and orientation of those three, the general location of the other four, their materials, dressing, and chronological evidence all indicate that the blocks belong to a crepis wall of the Alyattes mound. The elevation drawing published by von Olfers (1859: pl. 2) and his brief account suggest that at the location of the blocks the crepis may have had only one course.

C. Ratté studied interior features of the mound: stratified earth fills exposed in sides of the entrance tunnel dug by Spiegelthal in 1853; construction details of the tomb chamber; and ancient robbers' (or excavators') tunnels that had not been recorded since von Olfers's publication (von Olfers 1859: pl. 3, Tunnels b, l, m, g, and k).

C. H. G., Jr.

KARNIYARIK TEPE

A limited geophysical investigation of Karnıyarık Tepe was begun in 1992. This great burial mound, 220 m in diameter and 50 m high, is one of the largest tombs at Bin Tepe, the vast tumulus cemetery in the Hermus plain north of Sardis. Once, but, it now seems, incorrectly, identified as the tomb of Gyges, Karnıyarık Tepe was the major focus of the Sardis Expedition's work at Bin Tepe in the mid-1960s.

Prior Investigation

Investigation of this tomb began in 1963, and continued until 1966 (Hanfmann 1983: 57–58). The main goal of this investigation was to locate the tomb chamber or chambers presumably buried beneath the mound. In general, tomb chambers in Lydian tumuli are located at ground level at or near the center of the tumulus (McLauchlin 1986: 13–54); they usually are built of squared limestone or marble blocks. The interior dimensions of the largest such chamber (in the tomb of Alyattes) are $3.32 \times 2.37 \times 2.33$ m; most are smaller, on average about $2.5 \times 2 \times 2$ m. The exterior dimensions are harder to determine, but as a rule Lydian tomb chambers seem to have been built of a single thickness of blocks (0.5–1 m in depth) backed only by a light rubble packing; layers of charcoal are sometimes found on top of the chambers, but not the thick layer of rubble present, for example, on top of the chamber in Tumulus MM at Gordion in Phrygia (Young 1981: 94). In many cases, Lydian tumulus tomb chambers are provided with ancillary features such as antechambers and dromoi, but there is no known example of

a Lydian burial mound containing two or more unconnected chambers or chamber complexes.

In 1963, tests were conducted of two different methods—one mechanical, one geophysical—of exploring Karnıyarık Tepe without large-scale excavation (Hanfmann 1964: 53–58). The first method was to try to locate a chamber in the heart of the mound by drilling down from the top, a method used with great success at Gordion (Young 1981: 1–2, 81–83). At Karnıyarık Tepe, however, this method proved ineffective, for in every sounding made, the drill was stopped by pieces of limestone scattered through the fill of the mound. The second method attempted was electrical resistivity testing, used to try to locate the original edge of the mound; the results of that experiment were also inconclusive, in part because of the heterogeneous nature of the tumulus fill—that is, the same characteristic that rendered drilling ineffective—in part because of the limited penetration (not more than 3 m) of the resistivity measurements.

In 1964, work began on the excavation of a tunnel, dug in at ground level from the edge of the mound toward the center (fig. 27). At 60 m from the edge of the mound, the excavators encountered the first of several ancient robber's tunnels (fig. 27, Tunnel "B"), all of which either were dead ends, or appeared to have been intentionally filled in (presumably abandoned, and then filled with the backdirt from other tunnels). Five meters further along, the tunnel intersected a curving limestone wall, apparently the crepis or retaining wall of an earlier and small tumulus, buried beneath the present mound; there are thus at least two major phases in the construction of this mound, raising the possibility (discussed at greater length below) that the mound conceals two or more burial chambers of different periods.

A long section of the curving limestone crepis wall was eventually exposed in branch tunnels dug (in part following an ancient robber's tunnel) to the east and west of the main tunnel (figs. 27, 28). At the same time, the main tunnel was continued to the center of the mound and numerous ancillary tunnels were dug to explore a thick accumulation of rubble northeast of the actual center. But when the tunneling was abandoned in 1966, the tomb chamber or chambers still had not been found.[13]

Renewed investigation of Karnıyarık Tepe began in 1991, when a new elevation drawing of the limestone crepis wall was made so that we could study and record architectural details that seemed to indicate

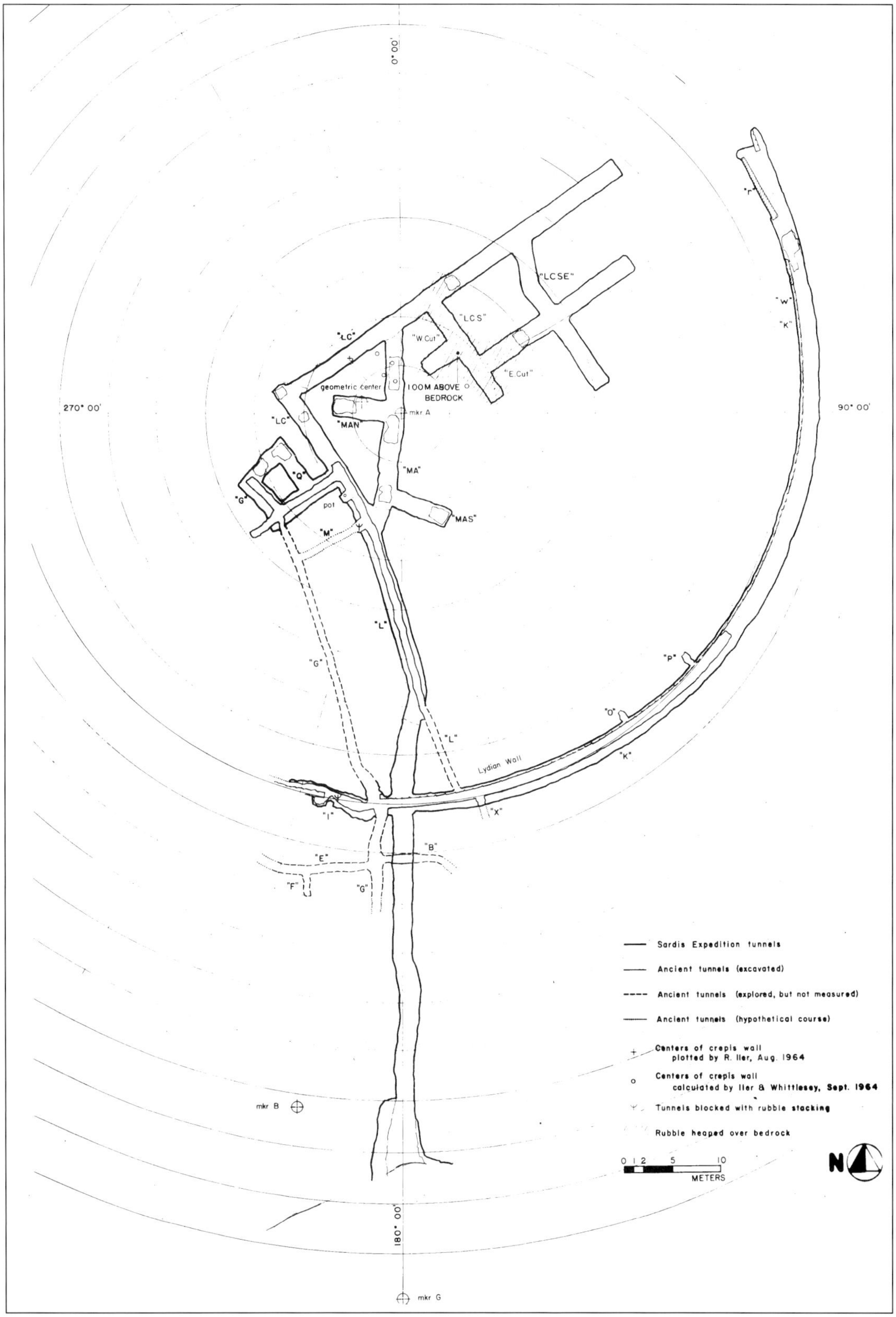

Fig. 27. General plan of Karnıyarık Tepe tunnels.

a date in the early or mid-sixth century B.C.E., and thus to exclude from consideration the identification—based on uncertain textual and epigraphic evidence—of the mound as the tomb of Gyges (Ratté 1994; Greenewalt, Ratté, and Rautman 1994: 28–31). Later that summer, the tumulus was visited and the tunnels were explored by geophysicist X. de Boucaud, who then undertook to develop a program for a new geophysical survey.

Aims and Methods of the Geophysical Survey

From the start, it was agreed that any new geophysical investigation of Karnıyarık Tepe would be confined to certain specific and limited research goals. The main purpose of such an investigation would be to continue to look for a tomb chamber in the central part of the mound, and thus to build directly on previous work. We did not want to tackle the very large problem of trying to locate a chamber in a completely unexcavated mound, but rather, and primarily, to exploit the unusual opportunities afforded by the existence of accessible tunnels in the center of the tumulus. The method or methods of investigation chosen would, moreover, have to be ones that could be used safely in existing conditions, and that would be appropriate to a relatively short (two- to three-season) and inexpensive project.

On deliberation, the method chosen was ground-penetrating radar, to be followed by drilling and coring. The basic principles of the use of ground-penetrating radar are relatively simple and well-known, but it may be useful to review them briefly here (Bevan in McGovern et al. 1995: 88–90). This method depends on the transmission of radar waves into the earth and analysis of the echoes or reflections that return to the surface when the radar pulse strikes a discontinuity underground, such as the seam or interface between two layers. In the course of a survey, an antenna that functions both as a transmitter and as a receiver is pulled slowly along the ground—or pushed along the wall or ceiling of a tunnel—transmitting radar pulses at regular intervals and recording the radar signals reflected back to the surface. The record that results is a continuous cross-section of the discontinuities within the earth, like a stratigraphic profile or (when the radar pulse is transmitted horizontally instead of vertically, as when the antenna is pushed along the scarp of a trench or the wall of a tunnel) a sectional plan. The value of this method is that it provides data of rela-

tively high resolution, in a form familiar to archaeologists. A disadvantage of the method is that the penetration of the radar signal is rather limited, generally varying in archaeological conditions from 1 to 5 m.[14]

Progress of the Survey

The survey, coordinated by de Boucaud and Ratté, was conducted over three weeks in July of 1992. About half of that time was spent preparing for the radar survey, about half on the actual survey. Before the survey could begin, the tunnels had to be cleared as much as possible of rotted wood—remains of the shoring installed during excavation—and fallen earth; although the tunnels were in generally good shape and seemed to be in no danger of collapse, large chunks of earth had fallen from the walls in numerous places. After clearing a path at least 1 m wide through the centers of the tunnels, we then proceeded to carry out a preliminary topographical reconnaissance, measuring the elevations of a number of points on the floors of the tunnels and setting out a series of approximately 60 markers that would be used in the radar survey (below; the locations of the markers are shown by the circled numbers in fig. 28).

The next step was to make a preliminary visual examination of the stratigraphy of the tumulus as exposed in the walls of the tunnels. This had not been possible before, because during excavation wooden boards (held in place by the shoring timbers) had been placed up against the walls and ceilings of the tunnels to protect the workmen from falling debris. Stratigraphic diagrams were made of both walls of almost all the tunnels (a sample diagram is illustrated in fig. 29; note the difference in the horizontal and vertical scales). These diagrams were used to plot contour maps of two very distinctive layers first recognized during excavation: the rubble layer located northeast of the geometrical center of the mound (the "rubble accumulation" in fig. 29), and two layers of very fine, dark brown earth (the "dark chocolate clay" in fig. 29). As seen in fig. 28, it is now clear that the rubble layer has a moundlike or domical shape (the same is true of the dark brown earth layers, of which one is located directly above the rubble layer, the other in the area just southeast of the center of the mound). The possibility that the rubble layer might have been heaped up over a burial chamber originally inspired the

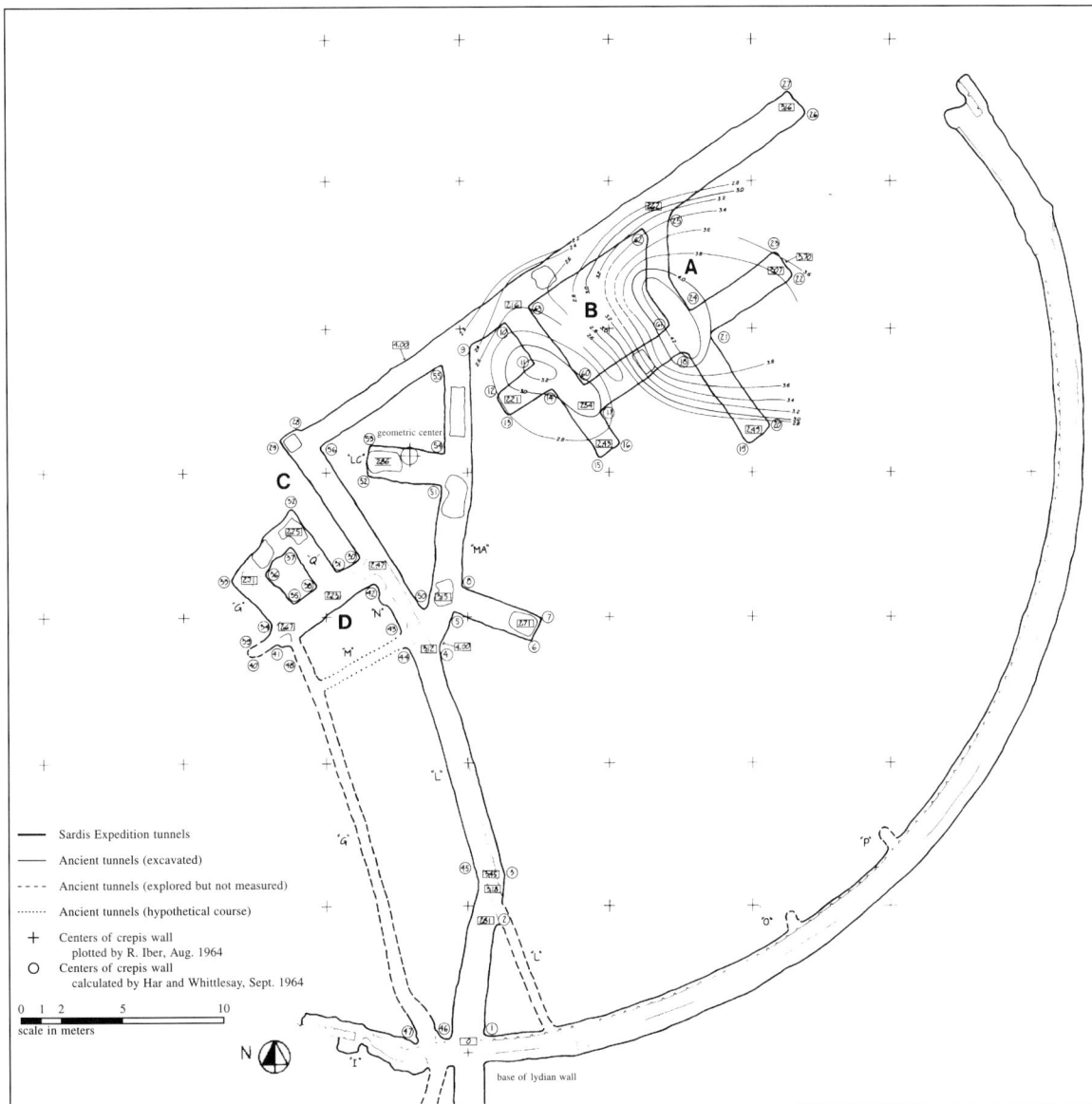

Fig. 28. Plan of central part of Karnıyarık Tepe, showing survey markers, elevations on floors of tunnels, contours of rubble layer, and anomalies detected in the radar survey.

excavation of the network of tunnels in the north-eastern part of the mound, and it remains possible that either or both the rubble and the dark brown earth layers are in fact related to one or more burial chambers. It is also possible that they were deposited for some other reason having to do with the construction of the tumulus, which might have consisted, in its earlier stages, of a group of small mounds eventually united into one.

As already noted, the existence of at least two major phases in the construction of this tumulus—the first associated with the limestone crepis wall, the second associated with the burial of the crepis wall and the enlargement of the mound—raises the possibility that the mound conceals two (or more) unrelated burial chambers. In most known cases, Lydian tumulus tomb chambers are located, as we have seen, at ground level at or near the center of the

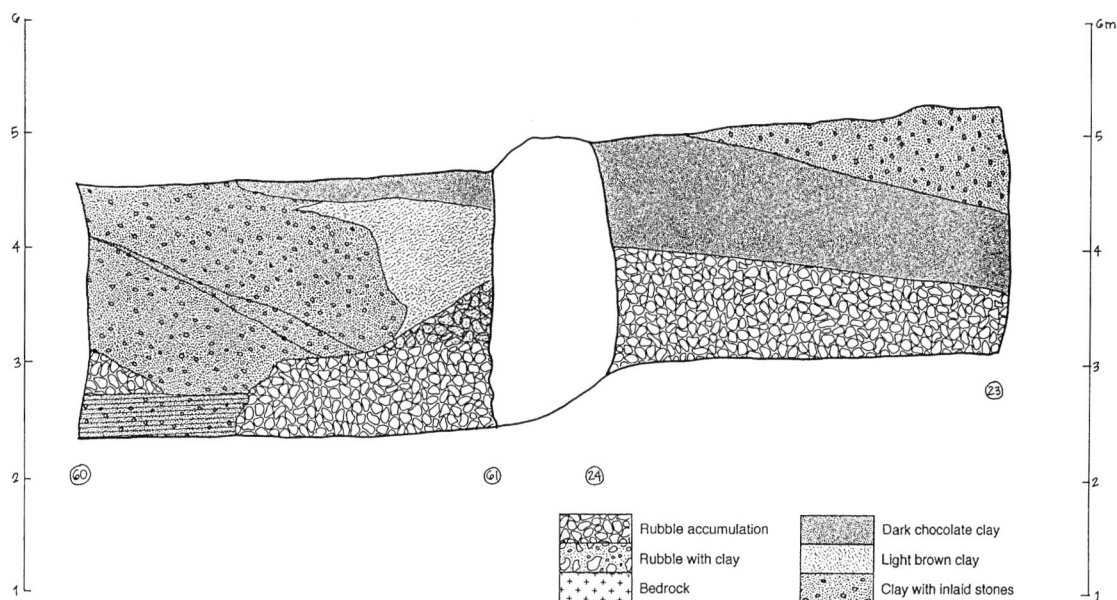

Fig. 29. Stratigraphic diagram of wall of tunnel between survey markers 60 and 23. This is an approximate representation of the walls at the time of the survey, July 1992. Horizontal scale 1 m = 1.3 cm; vertical scale 1 m = 2.6 cm.

mound. This is what we might expect of an earlier burial chamber, if in fact there was one, which is by no means certain since we do not know how far the construction of the mound had progressed before it was enlarged. If, however, the construction of the earlier mound was at least fairly well advanced, then a later burial chamber would have had either to be dug down into this earlier mound or to be placed in a very unusual position, at a much higher than normal elevation on top of the earlier mound, or at ground level outside its perimeter. It is of course also by no means certain that there was a later chamber, since the purpose of the enlargement of the mound may simply have been to make it grander rather than to add another burial. The stratigraphy of the interior of the mound is very complex, and it is not clear whether the layers exposed in the walls of the tunnels belong to the earlier or later phase of construction. But it should be noted that we saw no indication of any intrusion into these layers that might be associated with a secondary chamber dug into the earlier strata.

The actual radar survey began on 22 July and lasted until 30 July. The survey was carried out by S. Geraads of GEOMEGA, a geophysical surveying company based in Paris. The radar system used was

the GSSI (Geophysical Surveying Systems International) SIR (Subsurface Interface Radar) System 10 (fig. 30). The SIR 10 was used in conjunction with three antennas of different frequencies (100, 500, and 900 MHz), several coaxial cables for connecting the antennas to the recording system (total combined length: 70 m), and a graphic recorder for making field records of the survey data. After a day of testing at various spots around Sardis, the equipment was transported to Karnıyarık Tepe (about 10 km as the crow flies from Sardis) on 22 July and kept there until the end of the survey. Power for operating the radar system and two sets of lights (automobile headlights mounted on tripods) was supplied by three 12-volt batteries, recharged every evening.

The immediate goals of the survey were to examine the floors, ceilings, and both walls of all the tunnels in the center of the tumulus (that is, within the circuit of the limestone crepis wall). When the tunnels were excavated in the mid-1960s, they were dug along the surface of the bedrock wherever possible. Where this was not possible, test pits were dug down to bedrock at occasional intervals, to make sure that the level of the bedrock had not changed dramatically; in fact, no such dramatic change was observed.

Fig. 30. Interior of Karnıyarık Tepe, showing condition of tunnels, radar equipment, and survey team in operation.

Nevertheless, it seemed worthwhile to try to use the radar system to obtain a still better understanding of the shape of the bedrock; it also remained possible that one or more of the tunnels had inadvertently passed right over the top of the chamber. We decided to survey the ceilings of the tunnels, largely for the sake of completeness. Surveying of the tunnel walls, on the other hand, would enable us to examine the areas between and beyond the tunnels—and it seemed most likely that a burial chamber would be located in one of these areas, rather than in the areas above or below.

During the survey, the radar system was set up at a series of convenient points in the center of the tumulus. Each linear stretch or segment of each tunnel was then surveyed separately, using the approximately 60 markers that had been set out before the survey began. As seen in fig. 28, these markers were placed on both sides of every tunnel, at every bend or corner in the tunnel walls, so that there was a straight line from each marker to the next; each

marker was assigned a number and these numbers were used to identify each segment or "line" surveyed. The stretch of wall between markers 23 and 24, for example, comprises one such line of the survey (figs. 28 [plan], 29 [stratigraphic diagram], 31, 32 [records of radar surveys]).

The survey was conducted by a team of four. For each part of the survey, one person pulled or pushed the antenna along the stretch of tunnel being surveyed. Another person accompanied the antenna operator to make sure that the cable connecting the antenna to the SIR 10 recording unit did not snag or otherwise interfere with the survey. A third person operated the recording unit, monitoring the data on a computer screen as it was being collected, adjusting the recording parameters so as to improve the quality of the radar signal, and recording the data collected both on paper and on magnetic tape. A fourth person assisted the person operating the recording unit and facilitated communication among the other members of the team.

CP23   CP24

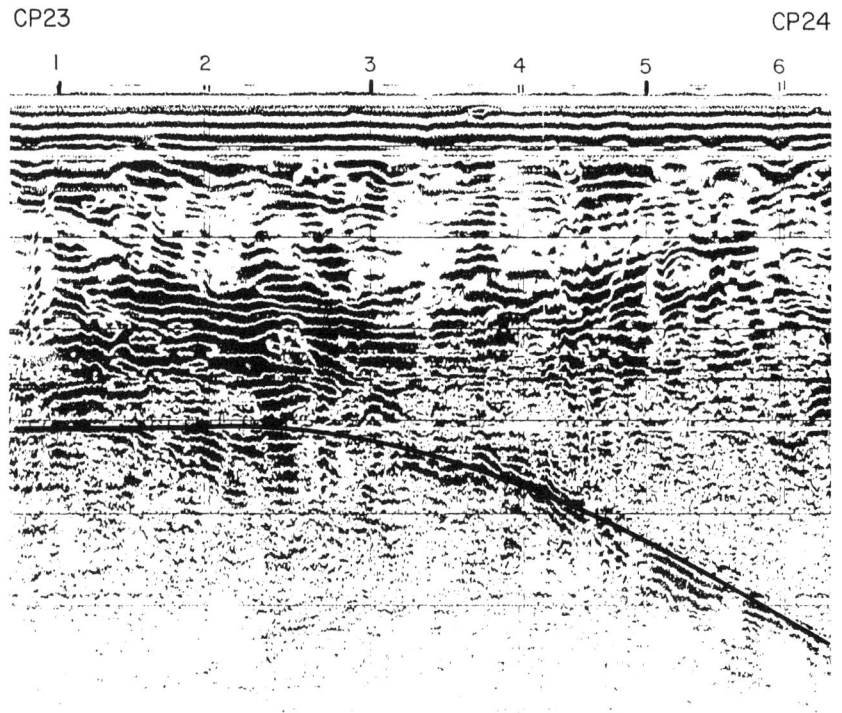

Fig. 31. Record of radar survey of wall of tunnel between survey markers 23 and 24.

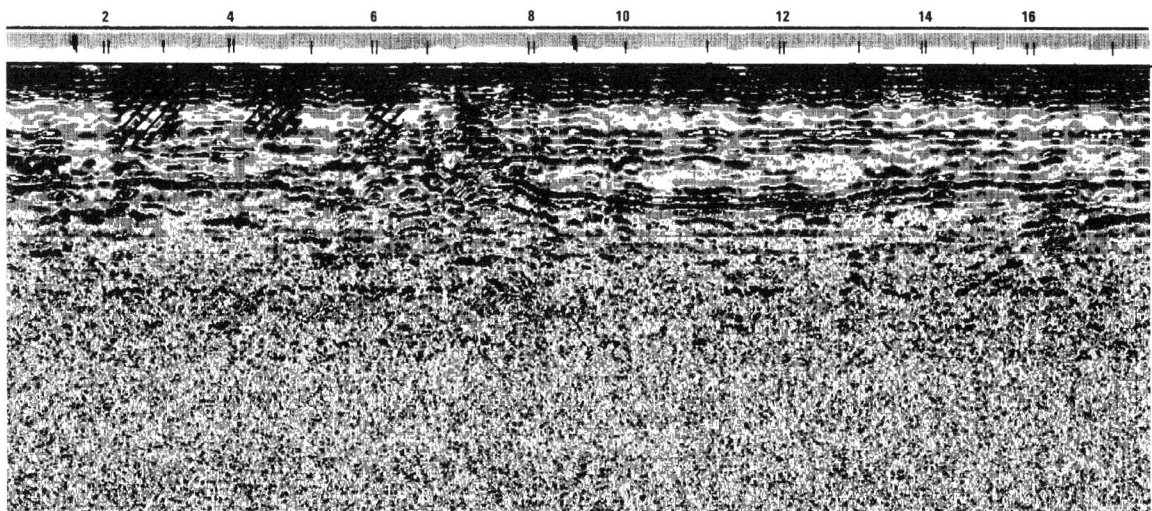

Fig. 32. Record of radar survey of floor of tunnel between survey markers 60-17 and 23-22.

For each segment, we tried to survey every surface of the tunnel with all three antennas, each of which gives information of a different character (the lower the frequency the better the penetration, the higher the frequency, the better the resolution). This was not always possible, but we were able to obtain full coverage with the 900 MHz antenna (shown in fig. 30, the smallest and lightest of the three), nearly full coverage with the 500 MHz antenna, and good coverage of the walls and floors of the tunnels with the 100 MHz antenna (an unwieldy object, approximately 1 m long, 0.5 m wide, and 0.25 m thick). In many instances, we recorded the same line with the same antenna several times, to test different recording parameters. A total (including tests) of 4017 m of linear profiles were recorded in 325 individual records. After the fieldwork was completed, the information recorded on magnetic tape was processed and analyzed by Geraads and de Boucaud at GEOMEGA's headquarters in Paris. Processing was completed in the spring of 1993.

Results of the Survey and Plans for Future Investigation

The main purpose of the data processing was to identify anomalous reflections that might have been caused by a tomb chamber buried beneath the tumulus. Several such anomalies were in fact detected (below). We now plan to investigate these anomalies further by drilling from the tunnels in toward the anomalies with a 50 mm hollow-core drill and then examining the cores retrieved from the drill holes. Since we hope to implement this program of drilling and coring in the near future, it makes little sense to offer speculations about these anomalies now. For this reason, only a brief summary of the results of the survey is presented here.

The particular conditions of the Karnıyarık Tepe tunnels created two serious problems for a radar survey, which became apparent shortly after the survey began. The first was the unevenness of the surfaces of the tunnels, which made for relatively poor coupling between the radar antenna and the ground—a condition that affects the radar data greatly. If the contact between the antenna and the ground is snug, the radar pulse is transmitted from the antenna directly into the ground; but if, on the other hand, the coupling between the antenna and the ground is poor because of bumps or hollows in the ground, much of the radar pulse will fail to penetrate the earth, being reflected instead back to the antenna. This has the double effect of weakening the useful signal (the signal reflected back to the antenna by subsurface discontinuities) and of creating useless signals or noise (the signal reflected directly back to the antenna), which may interfere with or obscure the useful signal.

The second problem also concerns useless signal or noise, in this case caused by the reflection of extraneous radiation off the floor, walls, and ceilings of the tunnels. In a survey conducted out of doors, radar waves that for whatever reason fail to penetrate the earth are quickly dispersed. In the closed space of a tunnel, however, those waves are reflected back repeatedly to the antenna, creating additional noise. The radar waves that fail to penetrate the ground because of poor antenna-to-ground coupling, for example, are reflected back to the antenna not only once but several times as they bounce back and forth between the ceiling and the floor or between opposite walls of the tunnel.

In spite of these problems, the radar seems to have achieved a regular penetration of 1–2 m. Possible subsurface discontinuities, which could be related to a burial chamber, were detected in several places. The most interesting of these anomalous reflections were those recorded during the surveying of the walls of the tunnels. Anomalies of these kinds were recorded at four locations, shown in fig. 28. As an example, one of the records showing one of these anomalies (Anomaly A) is illustrated in fig. 31. This record appears to show a subsurface discontinuity that runs parallel to the wall of the tunnel for the first 3 m of the line (reading from right to left), then slopes sharply away. The nature of this discontinuity is unclear; but it might, for example, be the interface between the dark brown earth and rubble layers visible in the wall of the tunnel (fig. 29).

In addition to the survey of the tunnel walls, the survey of the tunnel floors, while seeming to confirm that the bedrock is generally flat on top, revealed several interesting irregularities. One such irregularity is illustrated in fig. 32, the record of the survey of the floor of the tunnel between points 23–22 and 60–17 (that is, the floor at the base of the tunnel wall illustrated in figs. 29 and 30). This record seems to show that the bedrock is located at or just below "floor level" for the first 7 or 8 m of the line (reading from left to right), after which it apparently steps

down beyond radar-range. When the drilling and coring program is implemented, we will investigate this
and other areas (as well as the anomalies detected by
the survey of the walls), both to check the places
where the radar data seem to indicate that the bedrock is close to the surface and to determine how far
the bedrock lies below the surface in areas where it
was not detected by the radar.

C. R.

NOTES

[1] Excavation and other projects were conducted by the
Archaeological Exploration of Sardis, or Sardis Expedition, which is jointly sponsored by the Harvard University
Art Museums, Cornell University, the American Schools
of Oriental Research, and the Corning Museum of Glass.
The Expedition is supported financially by many corporate
and individual donors. The conservation program is supported by a grant from the Samuel H. Kress Foundation.
Study projects connected with publication of the results
of fieldwork before 1977 are supported by the National
Endowment for the Humanities, a federal agency that supports study in such fields as art history, philosophy, literature, and languages. Field work was authorized in 1992
and 1993 by the General Directorate of Monuments and
Museums, a division of the Ministry of Culture of the Republic of Turkey. Each field season took place during two
and a half summer months.

It is a pleasure to acknowledge fundamental permis-
sions granted by the General Directorate of Monuments
and Museums and the encouragement and support of its
officers; notably Director General Engin Özgen, Deputy
Director Kenan Yurttagül, Excavations Department Chief
Kudret Ata, and Excavations Branch Director Osman
Özbek. The Archaeological and Ethnographical Museum
in Manisa also generously supported, assisted, and encour-
aged Expedition projects; the Expedition is particularly
grateful to Director Hasan Dedeoğlu, Deputy Directors
Fatma Bilgin and Mustafa Tümer, and curators İlhami
Bilgin, Rafet Dinç, and Mehmet Önder. The Government
representatives were Fahriye Bayram (General Directorate
of Monuments and Museums, Ankara) in 1992 and Vahap
Kaya (Museum of Anatolian Civilizations, Ankara) in 1993;
their sound and apt advice, generous support, and unstint-
ing assistance greatly facilitated Expedition programs.

The construction firm of Yapıtek, A.Ş, in Izmir and its
General Manager Teoman Yalçınkaya in 1992 generously
provided scaffolding to permit inspection of two 17.8 m
high columns of the Temple of Artemis, for which the
Expedition is also pleased to record deep gratitude.

Staff members for 1992 and 1993 were the following
(for both seasons where no year is given): C. H. Greenewalt, Jr. (field director; University of California at Berkeley); Teoman Yalçınkaya (administrative officer and agent;
Yapıtek, A.Ş., a division of Çimentaş, Izmir); A. Ramage
(associate director and specialist for sectors HoB and PN
antiquities; Cornell); C. Ratté (assistant director and senior archaeologist in 1992, specialist for Lydian masonry;
Florida State University and Institute of Fine Arts of New
York University); L. Gadbery (associate director, 1993;
Harvard); K. J. Frazer (camp manager; Egypt Exploration
Society); K. J. Severson (senior conservator and conser-
vation consultant; Daedalus, Inc., Boston); P. S. Griffin
(conservator; Smithsonian Institution); I. Tokumaru; M. E.
Thumm (conservators, the latter 1993; both Institute of
Fine Arts Conservation Center, New York University);
T. D. Thompson (senior architect and specialist for site
enhancement, 1993; Woollen, Molzan and Partners, Indi-
anapolis); P. Stinson (architect; RTKL and Associates, Los
Angeles); K. A. Courteau (architect; E. I. Brown Company, Indianapolis); C. S. Alexander (draftsman; Harvard);
M. Daniels; E. Procter (photographers, the former 1992,
the latter 1993; Harvard); A. McLanan (registrar and numismatist, 1992; Harvard); R. E. Leader (registrar, 1993;
Harvard); M. L. Rautman (senior excavator; University of
Missouri–Columbia); G. Umholtz (senior excavator, 1992;
University of California at Berkeley); E. R. McIntosh (excavator and epigraphical recorder; Harvard and University
of Michigan); J. Trimble (excavator, numismatist in 1993;
Harvard and University of Michigan); G. Gürtekin (excavator; Aegean University); C. Chabot (assistant registrar
and excavator; Cornell) J. Cheng (assistant registrar and
assistant for radar survey, 1992; Harvard); M. H. Ramage
(assistant registrar and excavator, 1993; Carleton College);
F. K. Yegül (specialist for graphic recording of Artemis
Temple, 1992; University of California at Berkeley); D. G.
Favro (specialist for Roman architecture, 1992; University
of California at Los Angeles); A. B. Casendino (consultant
for site enhancement, 1992; Casendino, Inc., Boston); X. de
Boucaud (specialist for radar survey, 1992); S. Geraads
(specialist for radar survey, 1992; Geomega, Paris); G. Öza-
ğaçlı (specialist for water pipes, 1993; Aegean University,
Izmir); A. E. M. Johnston (specialist for Greek Imperial
coins, 1993; Cambridge University Press); P. Craddock
(specialist for ancient metallurgy, 1993; British Museum).
The considerable clerical work required by regulations of
the Ministry of Labor and the Social Security Commis-
sion was done efficiently and cheerfully by Celâlettin Şen-
türk (Manisa Museum). To all these for patience, hard
work, high professional standards, and team spirit, heartfelt
thanks.

[2] Conservation, in addition to routine treatments and
field shelters, included the following projects: cleaning of

painted wall and vault surfaces in Late Roman hypogaeum T93.1); stabilization and treatment of Late Roman
wall painting from Sector MMS (Rooms III and VI) and
in situ in Sector MMS/S; testing lightweight backing systems for mosaic pavings from Sector MMS/N; recording
cracks in masonry of the Archaic fortification wall at Sector
MMS and initiating a monitoring system; recording fissures
and cracks in Columns 6 and 7 of the Artemis Temple and
testing an injection system for filling cracks (with epoxy
resin, BICS-unit injectors, and polyester sealant provided
by KORMAL Foreign Trade Construction and Representation Company, Inc., Istanbul, and PAKOR Bouwchemie
B.V., Holland); testing cleaning products (provided by Rol-
land's Company, Baltimore, MD) to remove lichen and
mold from Artemis Temple surfaces.

Other projects included study of Archaic gold refining
installations, including equipment and gold samples, from
Sector PN; planning for reconstruction and site enhancement at Sectors MMS/N, MMS, and MMS/S.

[3] Other graves of the region include the painted *hypogaeum* (Butler 1922: 174); the Tomb of Claudia Antonia
Sabina (Morey 1924); an unpainted *hypogaeum* with *loculi*
(Greenewalt et al. 1990: 161–64); Dedeoğlu and Malay
1991); possibly a monument from which reliefs showing
venatio scenes survive (Hanfmann and Ramage 1978: 121–
24, nos. 147–49).

[4] A third foundation, shallow bedded and located further
north, near LSW, had been removed in 1984 (Greenewalt
et al. 1985: 80, fig. 26).

[5] The cup with intentional red glaze, P93.18/10049,
belongs to a type of the mid-fifth century B.C.E. (see Winter
1978: pl. 5.3). Terracotta revetment tile, T93.8/10102;
one of the glass beads is made of dark blue and yellow
glass, G93.3/10053; bronze handle, M93.4/10048; arrowheads, M93.2/10046, M93.3/10047, M93.8/10067 (trilobate), M93.5/10054 (leaf-shaped); obsidian fragments,
S93.5/10106, S93.6/10107.

[6] For two other phallus tubes, evidently spouts, recovered
from Sardis see Greenewalt 1971: 36, n. 12 and elsewhere
in the article. One of those may belong to an anthropomor-
phic vase similar in shape to a figurine in Athens, National
Museum no. 16455. That identification has been doubted
(Hanfmann 1983: 86–87). For phallus spouts and append-
ages on vessels of conventional shapes and decoration see
Boardman 1974: fig. 177; Gaïdukevic 1958: 208.

[7] For *ketoi* in East Greek and related vase painting, see
Cook 1981: 177 (on a Clazomenian sarcophagus, from
Abdera), Hemelrijk 1984: 46, 121, 211, n. 201 (on no. 29,
Caeretan Hydria, formerly in the Hirschmann Collection).
Although marine life is uncommon in orientalizing vase
painting, inland Sardis has yielded several examples, no-
tably two skyphoi, from a grave in the city cemetery
(Greenewalt 1972: 118–20, 129. The hippocamp also is the
motif of a gold brooch from eastern Lydia, Özgen and Öz-
türk 1996). The capacity was calculated by M. H. Ramage

from an AUTOcad recreation of the interior volume, based
on a drawing of the interior profile by C. S. Alexander.

[8] For a possible touchstone from the same residential
quarter, see Cahill in Greenewalt, Rautman, and Cahill
1987: 68; for touchstones in general, see Moore and Oddy
1985. Large quantities of rock crystal have been recovered
in Archaic occupation levels at Sardis, at sectors HoB and
PN; for the latter, see Hanfmann 1965: 7; fig. 7. For rock
crystal "ear plugs" from Ephesos, see Hogarth 1908: 210–
11; Bammer 1973–1974: 58–61; 1974: 203–4.

[9] For the later Archaic earthwork and "secondary wall,"
see Greenewalt et al. 1990: 143; Greenewalt, Ratté, and
Rautman 1994: 15; fig. 15). The foundation trench on the
east side of the secondary wall was reexcavated in 1992
to determine whether the wall was, as has been generally
supposed, "secondary" to the Archaic fortification that was
destroyed ca. 550 B.C.E. or whether it might be contemporaneous. The nature and deposit of "Brick Fall" in the
trench suggested that the wall was built after the destruction and founded in the truncated stump of the older wall.

[10] While the Roman dump was gradually rising and
covering the late Archaic earthwork surface, the earthwork
surface was gradually eroding and its eroded earth spread-
ing out over the dump. It is not quite certain whether the
earthwork surface exposed in 1993 (fig. 22) includes some
eroded parts that cover edges of the dump. Further excavation can clarify the situation.

[11] Pottery of the fourth century B.C.E. included black-
glaze, palmette-stamped bowl fragments, P92.42/10006,
P92.49/10014, P92.55/10020. Pottery of Archaic styles included fragments with single-letter graffiti, P92.36/9998,
P92.43/10007, and P92.44/10008; and with bichrome and
orientalizing decoration, e.g., P92.34/9996.

[12] For previous investigations by the Harvard–Cornell
Expedition, see Hanfmann 1983: 56 and references therein;
Greenewalt 1978: 71; Greenewalt et al. 1983: 26–27;
Greenewalt, Rautman, and Meriç 1986: 20–22; Ratté 1989:
157–62. The Tomb of Alyattes is the subject of a mono-
graph by C. Ratté, unpublished.

[13] In the years since 1966, the possibility of continuing
to explore Karnıyarık Tepe and other tumuli at Bin Tepe
by geophysical methods has often been discussed. Although none of the methods considered (such as seismic
and radar surveying, microgravity and electrical resistivity
testing, and magnotometry) has seemed appropriate to the
problem of locating—by surveying from the outside—a
small burial chamber in a large conical mound, the existence of a network of tunnels inside Karnıyarık Tepe makes
this a special case, because it is possible to explore this
tumulus not only from the outside, but also from within.

[14] In ideal circumstances, it might have been desirable
to begin a geophysical survey of Karnıyarık Tepe with a
method that sacrificed higher resolution for greater penetration, such as refraction or reflection seismic (comparable in operation to radar, but using sound instead of radar

waves), then to have followed that up with the more precise but more restricted method. We decided against this course of action for reasons of time, expense, and safety (seismic surveys being inherently more dangerous than radar surveys), and because we reasoned that even though more than two-thirds of the central part of the mound remained entirely unexplored, it was worth the gamble that the tomb chamber was located in close proximity to the existing tunnels; if this was the case, we thought we would have a good chance of locating it using ground-penetrating radar alone (followed by drilling and coring, as discussed below), and thereby of avoiding the added expense of a seismic or other type of survey. If the radar survey failed to detect any suggestive features, we could always fall back on a seismic survey of a larger area.

REFERENCES

Argoud, G.
1980   Fours à pain et fours à chaux byzantins de Salamine. Pp. 329–39 in *Salamine de Chypre. Histoire et Archéologie.* Colloques internationaux du C.N.R.S., 578. Paris: Centre National de Recherche Scientifique.

Bammer, A.
1973–   Die Entwicklung des Opferkultes am Altar der
1974   Artemis von Ephesos. *Istanbuler Mitteilungen* 23–24: 53–62.
1974   Recent Excavations at the Altar of Artemis in Ephesus. *Archaeology* 27: 202–5.

Boardman, J.
1974   *Athenian Black Figure Vases, a Handbook.* The World of Art Library. London: Thames.

Brill, R. H., and Cahill, N. D.
1988   A Red Opaque Glass from Sardis and Some Thoughts on Red Opaques in General. *Journal of Glass Studies* 30: 16–27.

Butler, H. C.
1922   *Sardis I, The Excavations Part I, 1910–1914.* Leyden: Brill.
1925   *Sardis II. Architecture, Part 1, the Temple of Artemis.* Leyden: Brill.

Cahill, N. D.
forth- Lydian Houses, Domestic Assemblages, and
coming Household Size. *Biblical Archaeology.*

Cook, R. M.
1981   *Clazomenian Sarcophagi.* Kerameus 3. Mainz: von Zabern.

Crawford, J. S.
1990   *The Byzantine Shops at Sardis.* Sardis Monograph 9. Cambridge, MA: Harvard University.

Davidson, G. R.
1952   *Corinth XII. The Minor Objects.* Princeton: American School of Classical Studies.

Dedeoğlu, H., and Malay, H.
1991   Some Inscribed Cinerary Chests and Vases from Sardis. Pp. 113–20 in *Erol Atalay Memorial*, ed. H. Malay. Ege Üniversitesi Edebiyat Fakültesi Yayınları, Arkeoloji Dergisi Özel Sayı, 1. Izmir: Aegean University.

Dennis, G.
1878   *The Cities and Cemeteries of Etruria.* London: Murray.

Frantz, A.
1988   *The Athenian Agora* XXIV. *Late Antiquity, A.D. 267–700.* Princeton: American School of Classical Studies.

Gaĭdukevic, V. F.
1958   Raskopki Tiritaki i Mirmekiia v 1946–1952 gg. Pp. 149–218 in *Bosporskie Goroda II, Raboty bosporskoĭ ekspeditsii 1946–1953 gg.*, eds. V. F. Gaĭdukevich and T. N. Knipovich. Materialy i Issledovaniia po arkheologii SSSR, 85.

Greenewalt, C. H., Jr.
1971   An Exhibitionist from Sardis. Pp. 29–46 in *Studies Presented to George M. A. Hanfmann*, eds. D. G. Mitten, J. G. Pedley, J. A. Scott. Fogg Art Museum, Harvard University, Monographs in Art and Archaeology, 2. Cambridge, MA: Fogg Art Museum.
1972   Two Lydian Graves at Sardis. *California Studies in Classical Antiquity* 5: 113–45.
1978   The Sardis Campaign of 1976. *Bulletin of the American Schools of Oriental Research* 229: 57–73.
1979   The Sardis Campaign of 1977. *Bulletin of the American Schools of Oriental Research* 233: 1–32.
1990   The Sardis Compaign of 1987. *Bulletin of the American Schools of Oriental Research Supplement* 27: 1–28.
1992   When a Mighty Empire was Destroyed: The Common Man at the Fall of Sardis, ca. 546 B.C. *Proceedings of the American Philosophical Society* 136: 1–24.
1994–   Sea Serpents at Sardis. *Harvard University Art*
1995   *Museums Review* 4, Fall-Winter: 1, 6.

Greenewalt, C. H., Jr.; Cahill, N. D.; and Rautman, M. L.
1987   The Sardis Campaign of 1984. *Bulletin of the American Schools of Oriental Research, Supplement* 25: 13–54.

Greenewalt, C. H., Jr.; Cahill, N. D.; Dedeoğlu, H.; and
    Hermann, P.
  1990   The Sardis Campaign of 1986. *Bulletin of the
          American Schools of Oriental Research Sup-
          plement* 26: 137–77.
Greenewalt, C. H., Jr.; Ramage, A.; Sullivan, D. G.;
    Nayır, K.; and Tulga, A.
  1983   The Sardis Campaigns of 1979 and 1980. *Bul-
          letin of the American Schools of Oriental Re-
          search* 249: 1–44.
Greenewalt, C. H., Jr.; Ratté, C.; and Rautman, M. L.
  1993   The Sardis Campaigns of 1988 and 1989. *An-
          nual of the American Schools of Oriental Re-
          search* 51: 1–43.
  1994   The Sardis Campaigns of 1990 and 1991. *An-
          nual of the American Schools of Oriental Re-
          search* 52: 1–36.
Greenewalt, C. H., Jr.; Rautman, M. L.; and Cahill, N. D.
  1987   The Sardis Campaign of 1985. *Bulletin of the
          American Schools of Oriental Research Sup-
          plement* 25: 55–92.
Greenewalt, C. H., Jr.; Rautman, M. L.; and Meriç, R.
  1986   The Sardis Campaign of 1983. *Bulletin of the
          American Schools of Oriental Research Sup-
          plement* 24: 1–30.
Greenewalt, C. H., Jr.; Sterud, E. L.; and Belknap, D. F.
  1982   The Sardis Campaign of 1978. *Bulletin of the
          American Schools of Oriental Research* 245:
          1–34.
Greenewalt, C. H., Jr.; Sullivan, D. G.; Ratté, C.; and
    Howe, T. N.
  1985   The Sardis Campaigns of 1981 and 1982. *Bul-
          letin of the American Schools of Oriental Re-
          search Supplement* 23: 53–92.
Hanfmann, G. M. A.
  1964   The Sixth Campaign at Sardis (1963). *Bulletin
          of the American Schools of Oriental Research*
          174: 3–58.
  1965   The Seventh Campaign at Sardis (1964). *Bul-
          letin of the American Schools of Oriental Re-
          search* 177: 2–37.
  1983   *Sardis from Prehistoric to Roman Times;
          Results of the Archaeological Exploration of
          Sardis 1958–1975.* Cambridge, MA: Harvard
          University.
Hanfmann, G. M. A., and Ramage, N. H.
  1978   *Sculpture from Sardis: The Finds through
          1975.* Sardis Report 2. Cambridge, MA: Har-
          vard University.
Hanfmann, G. M. A., and Waldbaum, J. C.
  1975   *A Survey of Sardis and the Major Monuments
          Outside the City Walls.* Sardis Report 1. Cam-
          bridge, MA: Harvard University.
Hemelrijk, J. M.
  1984   *Caeretan Hydriae.* Kerameus 5. Mainz: von
          Zabern.

Hirschfeld, Y.
  1992   *The Judean Desert Monasteries in the Byzan-
          tine Period.* New Haven: Yale University.
Hogarth, D. G.
  1908   *Excavations at Ephesus: the Archaic Artemi-
          sia.* London: British Museum.
Jones, F. F.
  1950   The Pottery. Pp. 149–296 in *Excavations at
          Gözlü Kule, Tarsus* I. *The Hellenistic and
          Roman Periods*, ed. H. Goldman. Princeton:
          Princeton University.
McGovern, P. E. *et al.*
  1995   Science and Archaeology: A Review. *Ameri-
          can Journal of Archaeology* 99: 79–142.
McLauchlin, B. K.
  1986   *Lydian Graves and Burial Customs.* Ph.D.
          Dissertation, 1985, University of California
          at Berkeley. Ann Arbor, MI: University
          Microfilms.
Miller, S. G., ed.
  1990   *Nemea, A Guide to the Site and Museum.*
          Berkeley: University of California.
Moevs, M. T. M.
  1973   *The Roman Thin Walled Pottery from Cosa
          (1948–1954).* Memoirs of the American Acad-
          emy in Rome 32. Rome: The American Acad-
          emy in Rome.
Moore, D. T., and Oddy, W. A.
  1985   Touchstones: Some Aspects of their Nomen-
          clature, Petrography and Provenance. *Journal
          of Archaeological Science* 12: 59–80.
Morey, C. R.
  1924   *Sardis V: 1 Roman and Christian Sculpture.
          The Sarcophagus of Claudia Antonia Sabina.*
          Princeton: Princeton University.
von Olfers, J. F. M.
  1859   Über die Lydischen Königsgräber bei Sardes
          und den Grabhügel des Alyattes, nach dem
          Bericht des K. General-Consuls Spiegelthal zu
          Smyrna. *Abhandlungen der Königlichen Akad-
          emie der Wissenschaften zu Berlin* (1858).
          Pp. 539–56.
Özgen, I., and Öztürk, J.
  1996   *Heritage Restored: The Lydian Treasure.* An-
          kara: Ministry of Culture of the Republic of
          Turkey.
Ramage, N. H.
  1986   Two New Attic Cups and the Siege of Sar-
          dis. *American Journal of Archaeology* 90:
          419–24.
Ratté, C. J.
  1989   *Lydian Masonry and Monumental Architec-
          ture at Sardis.* Ph.D. Dissertation, University
          of California at Berkeley.
  1994   Not the Tomb of Gyges. *Journal of Hellenic
          Studies* 114: 157–61.

Rautman, M. L.
  1995   A Late Roman Townhouse at Sardis. Pp. 49–
          66 in *Forschungen in Lydien*, ed. E. Schwert-
          heim. Bonn: Habelt.
Rodziewicz, M.
  1967   Terakotowe kraty okienne z Faras (The Terra-
          cotta Window Grilles of Faras). *Rocznik
          Muzeum Narodowego w Warszawie* 9: 143–74.
Stevens, G. P.; Caskey, L. D.; Fowler, H. N.; and Paton,
      J. M.
  1927   *The Erechtheum*. Cambridge, MA: Harvard
          University.

Waldbaum, J. C.
  1983   *Metalwork from Sardis*. Sardis Monograph 8.
          Cambridge, MA: Harvard University.
Winter, A.
  1978   *Die Antike Glanztonkeramik, Praktische Ver-
          suche*. Keramikforschung III. Mainz: von
          Zabern.
Young, R. S.
  1981   *Three Great Early Tumuli*. University Mu-
          seum Monograph 43. The Gordion Excava-
          tions Final Reports I. Philadelphia: University
          Museum, University of Pennsylvania.

Two Late Roman Wells at Sardis

MARCUS L. RAUTMAN

Department of Art History and Archaeology
University of Missouri
Columbia, MO 65211

Two deep wells were recently excavated at Sardis at Sector MMS. Both were in use during the expansion of a Late Roman residential quarter in the fifth century, one apparently supplying public needs and the other built into a domestic courtyard. Study of the finds suggests that the wells were filled during three phrases in the late fifth, late sixth, and early seventh centuries. These three deposits document the prominence and variety of local wares used at Sardis, as well as the dwindling supply of imported fine wares and amphorae. Among the most important discoveries are a popular local imitation of Late Roman C/Phocaean Red Slip ware and two types of single-handle amphorae, apparently also locally produced.

Sardis lies about 90 km inland from the western coast of Asia Minor, close to where a mountain stream, the Pactolus, descends from the Tmolus range and enters the broad Hermus plain. Following its devastation by an earthquake in 17 C.E., Roman Sardis grew up amidst the legends and physical remains of earlier settlements on the lower terraces and slopes of its steep acropolis. By the fourth century it was one of the largest cities in the province of Asia, filled with monumental buildings, colonnaded streets, and populous neighborhoods (Foss 1976; Hanfmann 1983).

Southeast of the Bath-Gymnasium and Synagogue in the western part of Sardis is a low mound known as Sector MMS. Recent excavations have established that the mound and the south-lying ridge incorporate monumental architecture of Archaic Lydian times (seventh–sixth centuries B.C.E.).[1] During late antiquity these features were covered by a densely built residential quarter. Broad streets with porticoes cut through the area and were flanked by elegant townhouses with colonnaded courts, painted walls, paved floors, and running water (fig. 1; Greenewalt, Ratté, and Rautman 1993: 4–14; Rautman 1995). This world of residential luxury faded around the mid-sixth century C.E., when spaces were gradually partitioned or closed and their furnishings were removed for other purposes. While abandonment was not uniform across the quarter, by the early seventh century the neighborhood's classical lifeways had dramatically changed.

Two wells excavated in this sector help document the quarter's changing fortunes (fig. 2). The Hilltop Well stands near the crown of the MMS mound (at approximately E118/S76 on the "B" grid). With a preserved top at (elevation) *106.9, this well was at least 24.8 m deep. It lacks both wellhead and any clear architectural setting and presumably served general public needs. Most of its length was excavated in eighteen days in 1987 and 1988.[2] The upper 9.7 m are braced by seventeen large, terracotta liners (an eighteenth liner was removed during excavation in 1986). Each of these large, basin-like drums has a diameter of 0.75–0.80 m. A straight 0.5–0.6 m high wall terminates in a heavy triangular rim.[3] Individual drums apparently were fired intact, then sawed in half for installation in the well. Paired footholds were cut in opposite sides of each drum's lower margin. Below *96.6 the shaft consists of lightly mortared schist slabs and fieldstones. Two bands of brick reinforce the lower shaft about 4.5 m and 3.0 m from the bottom. A final uncut terracotta drum, 0.75 m tall and pierced by fifteen small holes arranged in three horizontal rows, rests on a stone surface at *82.1. No ground water was noted at the close of excavation in 1988.

The Courtyard Well was discovered in 1982 in a small residential space approximately 16 m east (ca. E134/S75; fig. 3). It apparently was installed in the early fifth century, at the time when the surrounding rooms were built. Excavation began at floor level of this paved courtyard (elevation *104.0) and reached sterile sand at *81.5 in 1985.[4] The 22.5 m deep well

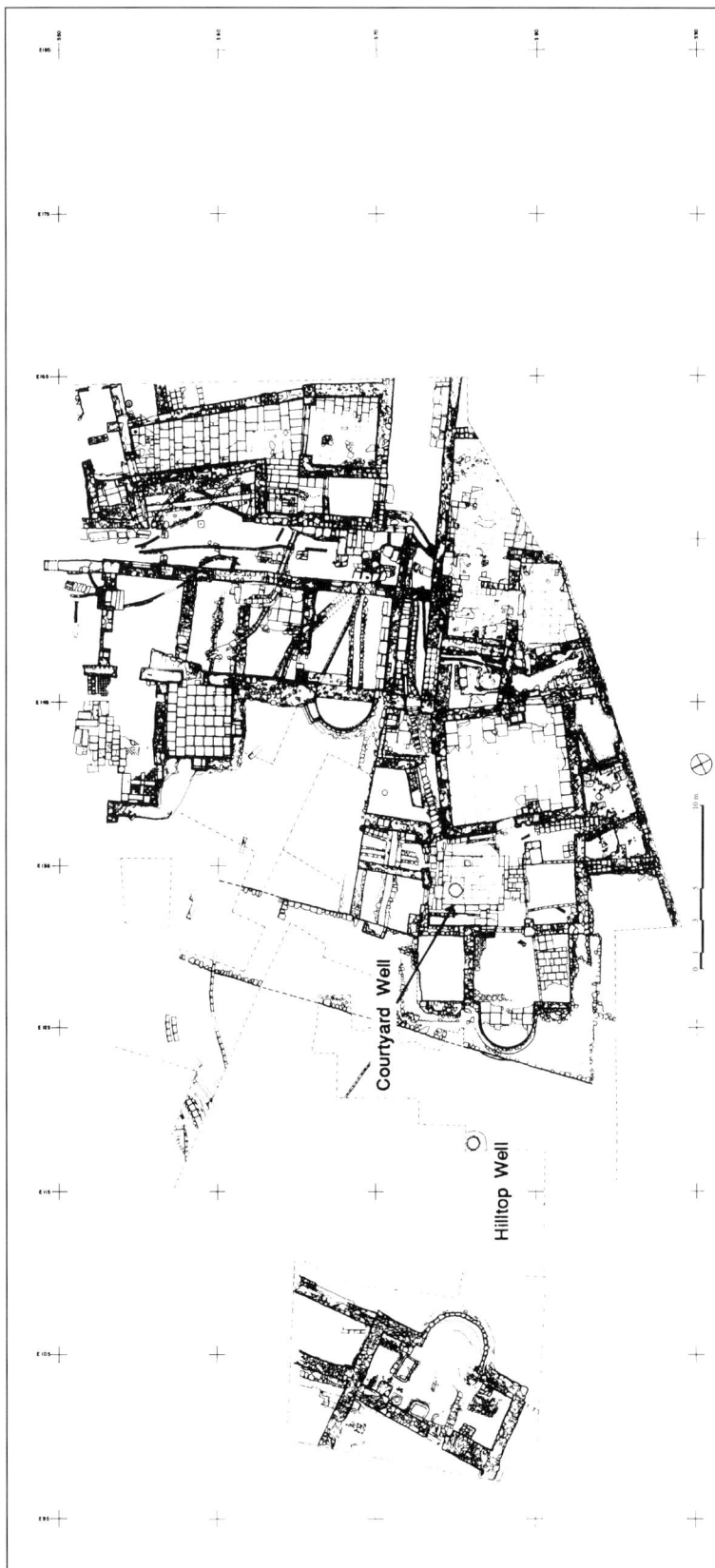

Fig. 1. Sardis, Sector MMS, Late Roman residential complex, plan.

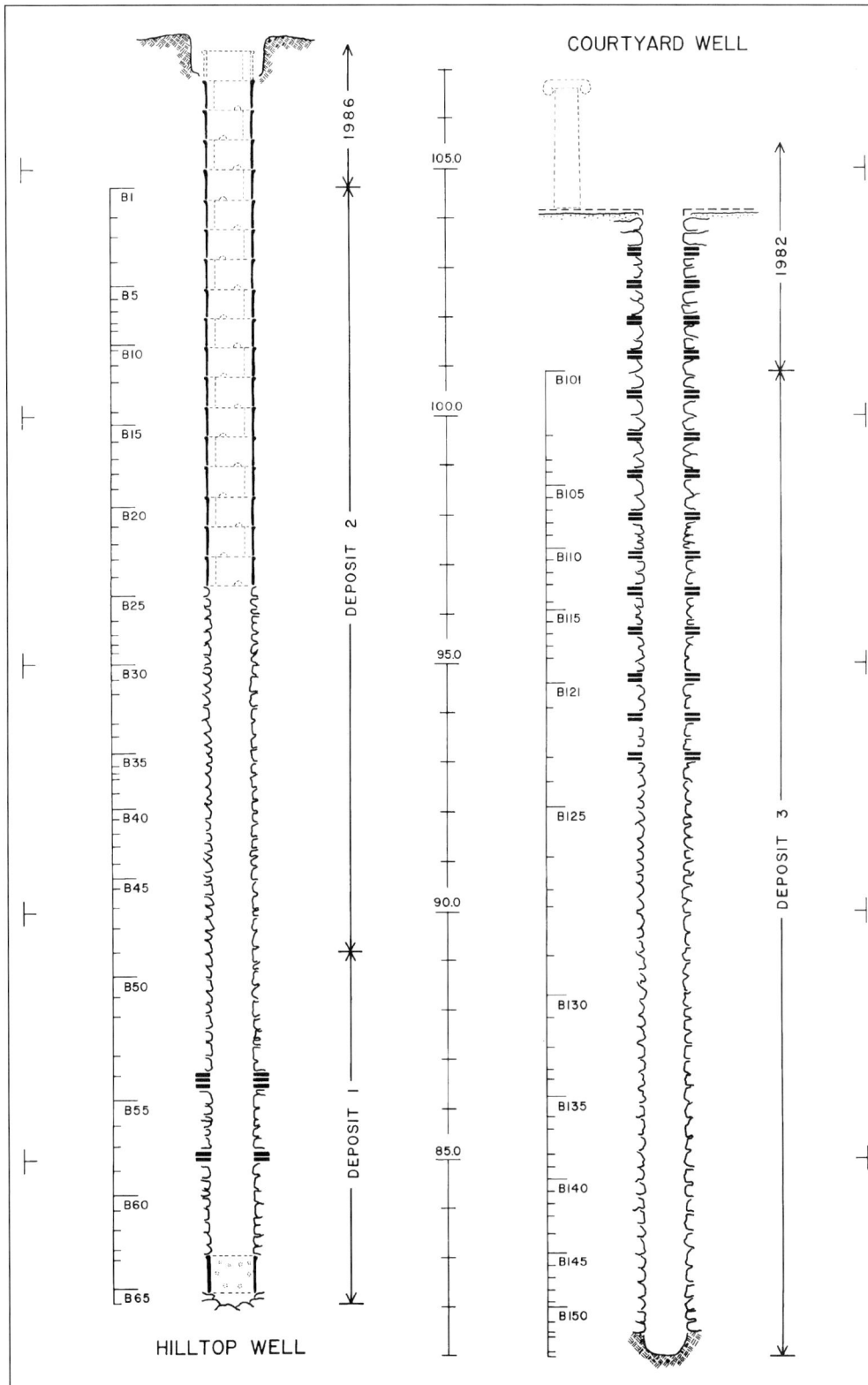

Fig. 2. Sardis, Sector MMS, Hilltop Well and Courtyard Well, schematic sections.

Fig. 3. Sardis, Sector MMS, Late Roman residential complex, courtyard with well; view to north.

was cut through at least 6.0 m of colossal Archaic architecture and 16.0 m of gravel and conglomerate to reach the fifth-century water table. No ground water was noted during excavation in 1985. The 0.88 m wide shaft is lined in its upper 11.0 m with schist blocks alternating with paired courses of mortared bricks. Opposite footholds were cut at ca. 0.8 m intervals but they stop with the final brick band at *93.0, below which continue lightly mortared schist blocks and brick fragments.

Both wells played a role in the residential development of western Sardis. The Hilltop Well's location atop the MMS mound without close relationship to Late Roman features suggests that it was built before the area's fifth-century development. This well was excavated in a series of baskets (B1–65) with changes made at 0.2–0.5 m intervals. The lack of extensive use deposits (such as complete drawing vessels in ceramic or wood) suggests that the well was maintained until the later fifth century, when it first received dumped debris. Most of the shaft was filled with large animal bone, brick, tile, and fieldstone in two heavy layers (ca. *96.8–94.4 and *85.2–83.6). Use of a 0.005 m screen recovered over 118 poorly preserved coins (largely from B8–18 and B44–57); most of the 19 coins that could be approximately identified belong to the fifth century but significantly earlier than the pottery. Ceramics were abundant throughout the well. The distribution of fine wares suggests that the infilling occurred gradu-

ally in two primary phases. The lower 7.1 m (B49–65) includes mostly fifth-century material and no coins or fine wares that date after 500 C.E.; this is discussed as Deposit 1. The upper 15.5 m (B1–48), plus the 2.5 m excavated in 1986, contains material dating through the late sixth century, and is presented as Deposit 2. Approximately 5.5 m below present ground level (B5–8, *102.65–101.75) was a level containing more than 20 amphorae that were apparently dumped at one time. Many of these vessels were substantially represented; a selection was reassembled for drawing and photography.

The Courtyard Well probably was built, together with the house it served, in the early fifth century. It was excavated in 53 baskets (B101–154; no B120). The absence of clear use deposits suggests that the well was cleaned periodically during the fifth and most of the sixth centuries. The bottom surface had risen only 0.30 m when a flat, semicircular piece of marble, apparently half of the court-level cover, entered the well. Most of the shaft was filled with architectural debris, which presumably came from the surrounding rooms. Thirteen coins were recovered (all from the lowest 5.3 m, B133–154), but only five could be approximately dated; the latest is a half-follis of Justinian I. Roughly 65 kg of pottery was recovered, including a few distinctive vessels of the early seventh century. Since some of the latest material comes from the deepest strata with joins occurring among different levels, the contents are treated as a single redeposited group, Deposit 3.

Both wells contained primarily architectural debris and domestic refuse. While moments of deliberate dumping can be detected (e.g., layers of animal bone, mortared rubble, or amphorae), most of the accumulation built up gradually. The differentiation of three deposits is based primarily on study of the fine wares; the coins date consistently earlier than the pottery by several generations. Certain vessel types appear in all levels, attesting their continued popularity at Sardis throughout late antiquity, but they also point to the high proportion of residual material. For these reasons the wells offer a general picture of ceramics used at Sardis rather than closely dated sealed contexts.

Catalog Arrangement

The catalog presents the best-preserved material recovered from the wells. Within each deposit the ceramics are arranged by fine wares, plain wares, amphorae, cooking wares, terracottas, and lamps, generally moving from open to closed forms. A brief list of legible coins and metal artifacts follows; the glass was too fragmentary for publication. The fine wares generally fit into existing typologies but other ceramics represent mostly regional, unreported forms. For this reason the catalog favors vessels that are well represented or familiar from other excavated contexts. Parallels are drawn primarily from other sites in western Asia Minor and the eastern Mediterranean.

Each entry includes the excavation basket and, if inventoried, the expedition number. Except where noted, each vessel is represented by fewer than five joining sherds. Similar unpublished examples within each deposit and published comparanda are noted separately. Fabric descriptions are based on macroscopic study. For convenience the most common inclusions are noted as lime (white particles of varying size), quartz (gray angular quartzite lumps), and mica (particles and flakes of varying size and color). Munsell (1988) readings suggest the average color range of the unslipped fired clay, which often varies considerably within a single vessel. Hardness and texture are noted only when they depart from the usual range of a ware as described below. Dimensions are given in meters. All catalogued objects are stored in the Archaeological and Ethnographical Museum in Manisa or in the expedition depots at Sardis.

African Red Slip Ware. The 28 examples of this well-known fine ware provide the clearest chronological signposts for the two wells. Originating primarily in Tunisia, African Red Slip ware was widely distributed in late antiquity (Hayes 1972; 1980). At Sardis the fabric ranges from rather coarse to moderately fine grained with varying quantities of quartz and lime particles. The fired clay ranges from red (10R 5/6–5/8 to 2.5YR 5/8) to light red (10R 6/6–6/8 to 2.5YR 6/8), and sometimes appears smudged from uneven kiln conditions. Interior surfaces are generally smoothed and covered with a hard red to orange slip that often extends onto the outer rim. In the catalog, vessel forms refer to Hayes's original classification (1972). Of this typology, seven standard shapes and various examples of stamped decoration are present: forms 58, 67, and 68 (e.g., catalog nos. **2.5–7**),* which are presumably residual; and forms 91, 99, and 104 (e.g., **2.8–10**). Two examples of the spiral burnished plate form 109 (**3.4–5**) are among the latest vessels identified at the sector. All assignable forms and stamps are included in the catalog.

Late Roman C/Phocaean Red Slip Ware. As would be expected at any site of western Asia Minor, the most frequently occurring imported fine ware at Sardis is the coastal product known as Late Roman C ware (Hayes 1972; 1980). At Sardis the clay appears uniformly fine grained with slight but varying amounts of lime and mica. The hard-fired fabric occurs through a broad spectrum of pale and weak red (10R 5/4–6/4) to dark grayish brown (10YR 4/2), with most examples appearing light red to reddish yellow (2.5YR 6/8–5YR 7/6). Interior surfaces and rims of these mold-made vessels are smoothed and slipped, leaving bases and exterior walls less finely finished. Interior stamps, exterior rouletting, and firing conditions are those commonly observed for the ware. A production area near Phocaea (Eski Foça) has been suggested for the most widely distributed fabric (Empereur and Picon 1986; Mayet and Picon 1986). The ware occurs at Sardis in two primary vessel shapes: Hayes (1972) forms 3 and 5 (e.g., **1.5–6**). Forty-five examples of the ware occur in the Hilltop Well but none in the slightly later Courtyard

---

*Numbers in bold type correspond to the catalog entries, below.

Well. Fourteen representative examples appear in the catalog.

Imitation Late Roman C Ware.   In all three deposits the standard dish Late Roman C Hayes form 3 also occurs in one or more distinctive fabrics that may originate in the Sardis vicinity (e.g., **1.7–9**).[5] The clay ranges from a fine to moderately coarse-grained texture, but frequently includes a few particles of lime in the body with many small voids on the surface; its distinguishing feature is a large amount of mica that appears in fine particles and occasional large gold flecks. The clay usually fires a little darker than the standard Late Roman C ware to light reddish brown (2.5YR 6/4) or reddish yellow (5YR 7/6–8/6). Like its model, this imitation was usually mold-made. The interior surface often bears marks of wet smoothing rather than a separate slip, while the exterior wall and base are more roughly turned, leaving deep pits and dragged grits across its surface. Unlike the hard-fired Late Roman C ware, these vessels often present a soft, dull, easily scratched surface and occasionally a gray core. The catalog includes 17 of the 149 examples noted.

Other Asia Minor Fabrics.   Possibly related to the Late Roman C ware imitations are light-colored wares found in all three deposits. The variety of fabrics and shapes suggests that this category includes vessels from several sources, but the small number of examples noted here argues against their local production (Hayes 1968; 1972). These fabrics are fine grained, include a little mica and lime, and have small voids scattered through the body. In color the clay typically fires to a light brown to pink (7.5YR 6/4–7/4) or reddish yellow (5YR 7/6). Vessels frequently present sharply angled base and rim profiles and bear grooves or impressed rouletting on visible surfaces (e.g., **1.11, 2.35–40**). Equally distinctive is the light reddish brown slip (about 5YR 6/4) unevenly applied to the interior surfaces. The more complex forms generally occur in the lighter fabrics and have been discussed as "Late Roman Light Colored ware" (Hayes 1992). The thicker and simpler forms with punched decoration may belong to a related production line. Since the range and boundaries of such wares are not yet clear they are not distinguished in the catalog. Of the forty-four recorded examples, eighteen appear below.

Plain Wares.   Other table wares and vessels not intended for use in the hearth are discussed as plain wares. Most of these are basins, bowls, dishes, or jars that share a moderately coarse-grained fabric with frequent lime, quartz, and mica. Different finishing and firing conditions yield a light red (2.5YR 6/8) to reddish-yellow (5YR 7/6) body that often resembles the imitation Late Roman C ware dishes and suggests local production. Plain wares in other unidentified and perhaps imported fabrics can be noted in mortaria, jugs, and fusiform unguentaria. The catalog includes representative examples from each deposit.

Amphorae.   Amphora sherds constitute the bulk of the pottery. Imported amphorae are limited primarily to the large, eastern Mediterranean panel-ridged vessel (LR1, e.g., **3.30**) and the globular jar with conical neck and grooved shoulder (LR2, e.g., **1.34–35**).[6] Apart from a few sherds of Gaza amphorae (LR4, e.g., **2.94**), the Palestinian and Egyptian vessels well-known at coastal sites were conspicuously absent. Representative examples are noted for each deposit in which an imported type occurs. Much more common are two kinds of single-handle vessels. Both vessel types employ a distinctive fabric that is moderately coarse grained and highly micaceous. Small particles of lime occur together with abundant mica in fine particles and large flecks. Uneven firing conditions yield a range of light red or pink (7.5YR 7/4–5YR 7/4) to yellowish brown (10YR 5/6–6/6), frequently with gray cores. The fabric closely resembles certain plain wares and some individual sherds could equally be assigned to basins or similar large forms. Reconstructed amphorae belong to two primary shapes: an elongated ovoid jar (Type A, e.g., **2.85–88**), and a slender fusiform vessel with solid toe (Type B, e.g., **2.89–90**). In fabric and form these vessel types appear related to the micaceous water jar series (LR3, e.g., **3.31–32**). Traces of a resinous interior lining suggest that both vessels may have been used for the storage or transport of wine. Both types occur primarily in the Hilltop Well with relatively fewer examples noted in the later Courtyard Well. Five partially reconstructed vessels are published in Deposit 2; representative rims and shoulders appear in Deposits 1 and 3.

Cooking Wares.   Cooking wares include those vessels manufactured with a high proportion of quartz temper to survive repeated exposure to fire. Such vessels were not abundant in the wells. The most common shape is a globular pot with outturned rim and paired strap handles (e.g., **1.39–40**). Several examples of a shallow frying pan with tubular handle were also noted (e.g., **2.102–103**). The typical fabric is light red (10R 6/6–6/8) to reddish yellow (2.5YR 6/6–5YR 7/6), very micaceous with large quartz-like inclusions. Similar finds from across the site suggest an origin in the Sardis vicinity. The best preserved examples appear below.

Terracottas and Lamps. A few miscellaneous ceramic objects (a loom weight and a possible wick-holder) and mold-made lamps were recovered from the wells. Most of these objects were made in fabrics that resemble local plain wares and they probably were made locally. The lamps belong primarily to the loosely defined category of "Asia Minor lamps," which are known especially from Ephesus but are found at many Aegean sites (Bailey 1988).

All but the most fragmentary objects are included in the catalog.

Metals and Coins. The damp physical environment of the wells took its toll on the metal artifacts, which survived in very poor condition. Apart from a few unidentifiable scraps, six small objects of copper alloy and iron are briefly noted in the catalog. The excavated coins, all bronze, reflect these poor conditions: of 131 coins recovered from the two wells, only 24 (18 percent) were partially legible. Identifiable issues are arranged in approximate chronological order. In addition to basket and expedition inventory numbers, entries include issuing authority, date, denomination, and mint, if known. For each deposit the datable coins predate the pottery by 40 years (Deposit 1) to 80 years (Deposits 2 and 3).

CATALOG

Deposit 1 (B49–65)
Hilltop Well, lower levels, late fifth century

FINE WARES

Residual

1.1. Dish (B53). Fig. 4. Eastern Sigillata A, Hayes 1985, form 6, pl. 2,4. Est. D. rim 0.44. Light fine-grained pink fabric (7.5YR 8/4) with hard, weak red gloss (10R 4/4). Horizontal rim with thickened, grooved lip.

1.2. Cup (B49). Not illustrated. Green glazed cup handle. Light brown fabric (7.5YR 6/4–7/4) with small mica flecks. Curving strap handle (D. 0.017) with two grooves, attached to irregular plain vertical rim, D. uncertain. Glassy green glaze.

African Red Slip

1.3. Bowl (B51). Fig. 4. Hayes form 67, 2nd series, ca. 400–450. D. rim uncertain. Coarse, light red fabric (10R 6/6) with much lime, quartz, and other small inclusions that rupture on surface. Sloping wall with rolled rim. Interior smoothed and slipped; on exterior only rim slipped, outer wall roughly finished. Cf. **2.6**.

1.4. Dish (B59). Fig. 4. Palm stamp on flat base. Medium fine-grained light red fabric (2.5YR 6/6) slightly smudged in firing or later use. Stamped floor with

ovoid palm branch alternating with flanking trefoils; cf. Hayes 1972: 230 fig. 38 type 1 or 3 (late fourth century), 244 fig. 43 type 83 (ca. 400–450).

Late Roman C/Phocaean Red Slip

1.5. Dish (B55). Fig. 4. Hayes form 3C. Est. D. rim 0.27. Fine-grained light red fabric (2.5YR 6/8 to 5YR 7/6), with a little lime and mica. Interior carefully smoothed and covered with good, thick slip. Exterior vertical rim rouletted and slipped, fired slightly darker than wall. Two examples.

1.6. Dish (B57). Fig. 4. Hayes form 5B. Est. D. rim 0.14. Fine-grained reddish yellow fabric (5YR 7/6), with a little fine mica. Broad horizontal rim with flat underside, exterior with irregular groove. Cf. **2.19–20**.

Imitation Late Roman C

1.7. Dish (B61). Fig. 4. Imitation Hayes form 3. Est. D. rim 0.30. Est. D. base 0.15. Dull, light reddish-brown fabric (2.5YR 6/4 to 5YR 7/4) with gray core; abundant gold mica. Heavy, low foot, thick floor and wall with flaring vertical flanged rim. Interior smoothed with three concentric grooves at center of floor; exterior roughly finished with dragged grits, mottled red slip. Similar examples: B55 (est. D. rim 0.22), B58, B62/65. Cf. **1.8, 2.28**. The flanged rim appears loosely based on Hayes form 3 but may have more general antecedents, e.g., Eiwanger 1981: 56 (ware III F, form II).

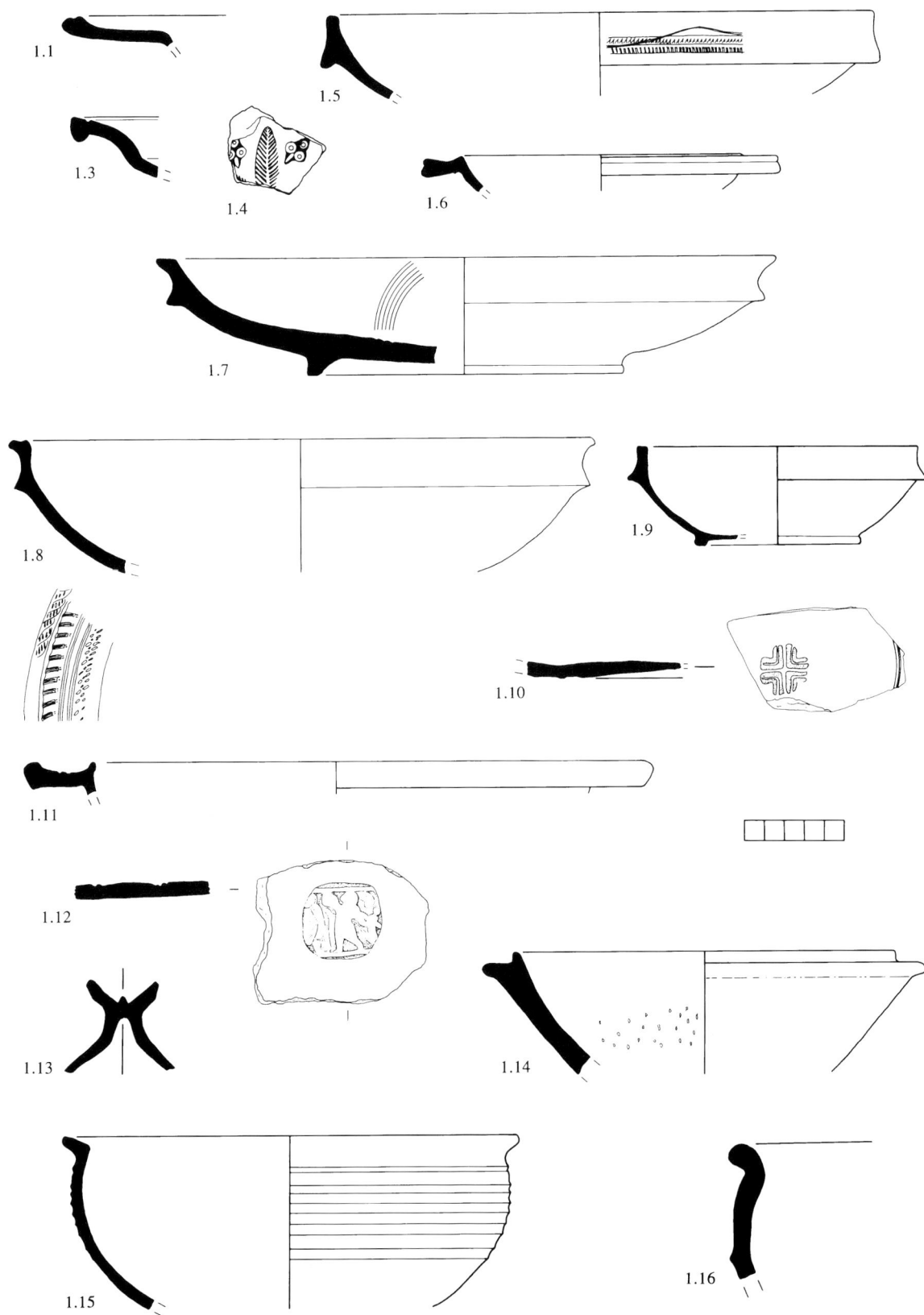

Fig. 4. Hilltop Well, Deposit 1, 1:3 (scale bar=0.05).

1.8. Dish (B53). Fig. 4. Imitation Hayes form 3C. Est. D. rim 0.28. Medium-grained light red fabric (10R 6/6 to 2.5YR 6/6) with dark fired core; rough fracture with many small and some large voids on surface. A little lime and much mica, especially in reddish-yellow slip (5YR 7/6), scratched and flaking.

1.9. Dish (B50). Fig. 4. Imitation Hayes form 3C. Est. D. rim 0.13. H. 0.049. Medium fine-grained fabric ranges from light reddish-brown (5YR 6/4) exterior to light brownish-gray (2.5Y 6/4) interior; very micaceous with many small voids. Interior surface smoothed; exterior wall and base roughly turned with many pits and dragged grits. Traces of thin slip on base and exterior wall.

1.10. Dish (B52). Fig. 4. False foot base with cross stamp on center floor. Micaceous reddish-yellow fabric (5YR 7/6), with little lime but much mica, including large gold flecks on surface. Interior smoothed with fine concentric streaks in weak red slip; bottom roughly finished.

Asia Minor Fabrics

1.11. Plate (B51). Fig. 4. Plate with broad, horizontal rim. Est. D. rim 0.35 (ext). Fine-grained reddish-yellow fabric (7.5YR 6/6–7/4) with a little lime, a few mica flecks, and small voids. Broad rim with flat underside; rolled lip; and raised, slightly inturned inner rim; two grooves and impressed rouletting on upper rim and lip. Uneven slip, thickest (metallic dark reddish-brown) in rouletted hollows, where occasionally cracked and flaking. Cf. **2.40**; Hayes 1968: 211 no. 75 (=1992 fig. 41); Hayes 1992: 94, Deposit 11, no. 10.

1.12. Plate (B54; P88.016/9561). Figs. 4, 5. Dish/plate floor with stamped figural decoration. Medium-grained reddish-yellow fabric (5YR 6/6–7/6), with a little lime, dark grits, and much mica in large gold and silver flecks. Wheel turned; floor 0.007–0.008 thick, unslipped. At center of plate a small, impressed scene (0.041 × 0.038) depicts two standing figures, to the left draped and frontal, to the right (wearing plumed helmet?) striding left; worn.

PLAIN WARES

1.13. Lid (B62/65). Fig. 4. Conical lid handle. D. handle 0.035. Fine-grained, light red fabric (2.5YR 6/6 to 5YR 7/6), very micaceous. Turned handle, spatula-finished with sharp edges. Dull white matt slip on exterior.

1.14. Mortarium (B55). Fig. 4. Shallow mortarium. Est. D. rim 0.19. Coarse, gritty, light red fabric (2.5YR

Fig. 5. **1.12**, stamped plate.

6/6 to 5YR 7/4) with abundant large inclusions including many quartz particles to 0.002. Thick, sloping wall ends in vertical lip with thickened horizontal flange. Interior surface worn smooth; rim and exterior remain gritty, with light wheel marks and flaking yellow slip (2.5Y 7/6). Cf. **2.45–46**.

1.15. Basin/bowl (B62/65). Fig. 4. Hemispherical basin/bowl. Est. D. rim 0.23. Coarse-grained, light red fabric (2.5YR 6/8 to 5YR 7/6) with abundant quartz, mica, and lime often erupting on surface; breaks clean with little splintering. Hemispherical wall with plain, outturned rim; interior smoothed, exterior lightly ridged. Center interior preserves thin white undercoat; upper interior and exterior wall slipped red/light brown, unevenly coated and dribbled. Similar examples: B50, B59.

1.16. Basin (B50/51). Fig. 4. Basin with rounded, outturned rim. Est. D. rim 0.44. Medium coarse-grained reddish-yellow fabric (5YR 7/6) with gray fired core, small lime particles, quartz to 0.003 often rising in lumps beneath smoothed surface, and abundant mica in large gold flecks. Inward curving vertical wall with outturned thickened rim, exterior offset. Thin white slip interior and exterior. Similar example: B59 (est. D. rim 0.34).

1.17. Basin (B55). Fig. 6. Basin with outturned rim. Est. D. rim 0.34. Medium coarse-grained reddish-yellow fabric (5YR 6/6–7/6) with scattered lime particles and large, irregular voids, abundant mica. Straight wall, lightly ridged, rises to vertical lip, horizontal

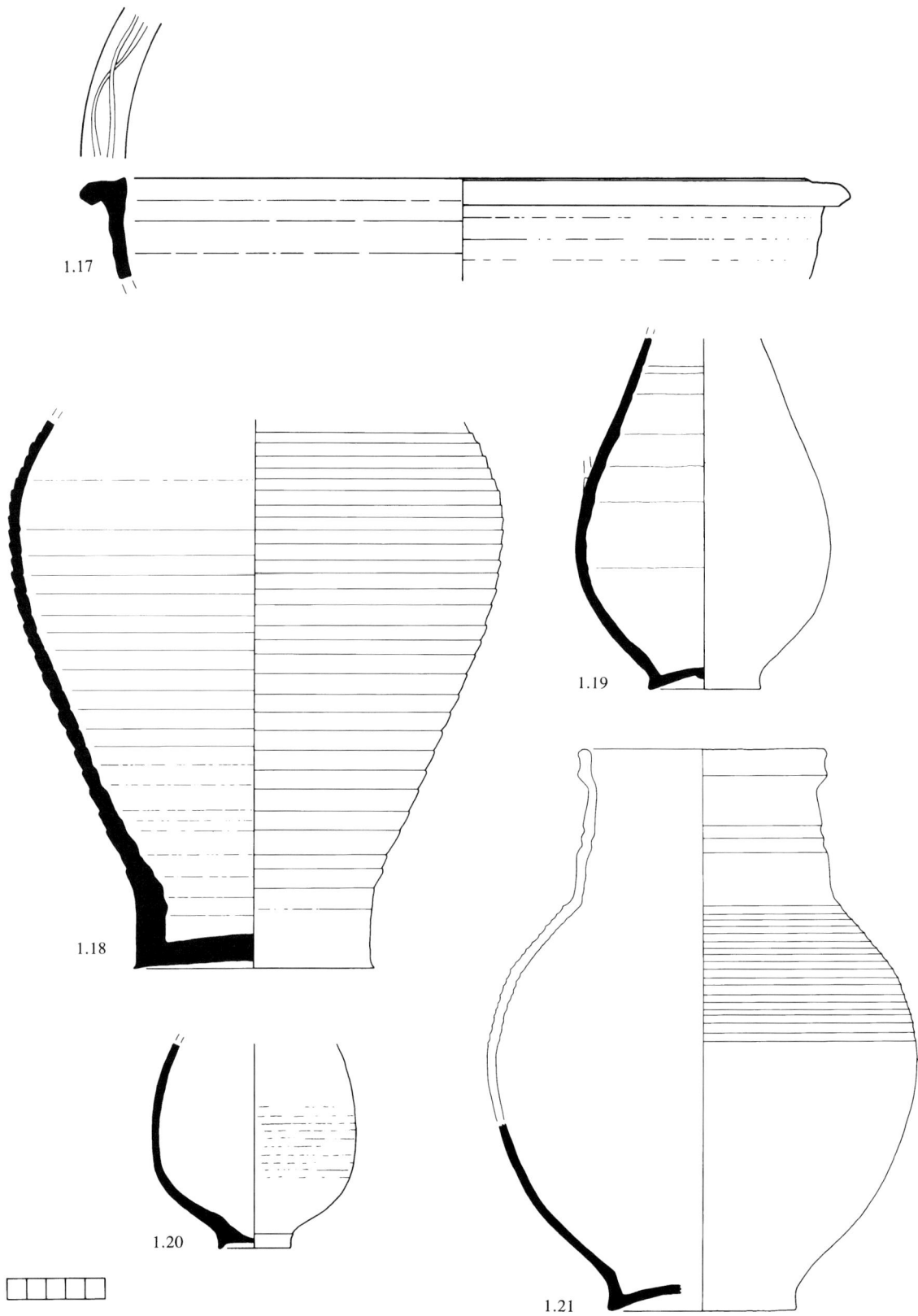

Fig. 6. Hilltop Well, Deposit 1, 1:3 (scale bar=0.05).

and slightly downturned rim; double wavy line incised top of rim.

1.18. Jug (B62/65). Fig. 6. Tall jug with flat base in numerous joining sherds. D. base 0.12. Max. H. 0.27. Medium fine-grained reddish-yellow fabric (5YR 7/6) with abundant lime (to 0.004), mica and small voids in body. Thin wall rises from flat base to high shoulder, partially distorted before firing; exterior sharply ridged. (Cf. Robinson 1959:114 nos. M321, 322.)

1.19. Jug (B62/65). Fig. 6. Spherical jug in ten joining sherds. Max. H. 0.172. D. base 0.055. Max. D. 0.127. Medium-grained light reddish-brown fabric (5YR 6/4 to 7/5YR 6/4) with abundant lime, quartz, and mica, many large grits to 0.003. Spherical jug or pitcher with recessed button base, spherical body, tall neck with handle. Wheelmade body with light interior ridging; exterior smoothed on upper body, base, and lower body roughly finished with deep dragged grits. Splayed root of handle just above mid-body. Similar examples: **1.20**, B49 (est. D. rim 0.06), B59 (est. D. rim 0.08). Cf. **2.80**.

1.20. Jug (B62/65). Fig. 6. Spherical jug base in 13 sherds. Max. H. 0.10. D. base 0.37. Fine-grained light reddish-yellow fabric (5YR 7/6) overfired gray interior (10YR 5/1), with scattered fine lime, quartz, and abundant mica. Thin wall (0.002–0.003) rises from disc base with low foot; exterior lightly ridged. Uneven flaking of mottled, off-white slip. Cf. Mitsopoulos-Leon 1991: 137, no. K27 for a similar example from a disturbed context.

1.21. Jar (B62–65; P88.018/9563). Figs. 6, 7. Spherical jar in numerous joining sherds. H. 0.275. D. base 0.095. Max. D. 0.214. D. rim 0.120. Coarse-grained light reddish-brown fabric (5YR 6/4–7/4) with large particles of lime, quartz (greater than 0.003), other dark grits, and abundant mica. Thin wall rises from probable recessed button base to tall, wide neck and vertical rim with slight flange. Lower exterior body smoothed, upper half covered with regularly spaced shallow ridges, neck with two shallow grooves.

1.22. Jug (B55). Fig. 8. Tall neck of jug in five rim sherds with seven joining sherds and handle root. Est. D. rim 0.11. Very coarse-grained yellowish-red fabric (5YR 4/6–5/6) with darker core, abundant lime, quartz (to 0.0015), and large silver and gold mica flecks. Plain, rounded rim without decoration; single strap-handle root.

1.23. Jar (B51). Fig. 8. Tall neck of jar. Est. D. rim 0.20. Coarse-grained gritty light red fabric (2.5YR 6/6). Slightly outward flaring neck with thickened rim. Exterior covered with black/gray slip.

Fig. 7. 1.21 (P87.018/9563), jar.

1.24. Dish (B57). Fig. 8. Small dish with vertical rim. D. rim uncertain. Medium fine-grained light red fabric (2.5YR 6/8 to 5YR 7/6) with much mica, some splintering at fracture. Outward flaring wall with vertical rim and slight flange; exterior rim combed with five-toothed implement. Cf. de Luca 1984: 10, no. 33 (pl. 25) for similar rim decoration of smaller bowl.

1.25. Pot (B49). Fig. 8. Small hemispherical pot with outturned rim, two handles. Est. D. rim uncertain. Fine-grained light reddish-brown fabric (2.5YR 6/4) with abundant mica, some lime. Thin walled hemispherical bowl with plain outturned rim; roughly finished, with smoothed interior, lightly ridged exterior. Paired strap handles with broad central ridge. Cf. **2.72–73**.

1.26. Cup (B59). Fig. 8. Small, handleless cup. Est. D. rim 0.08. Medium fine-grained red fabric (2.5YR 5/8) with fine quartz particles and abundant mica. Small handleless cup with string-cut base, inturned rim, thickened lip. Light exterior ridging, interior smoothed. Cf. **2.74–75, 3.24**.

1.27. Flask (B61/65). Fig. 8. Large flask in nine joining sherds. Est. D. body 0.18. Est. D. rim 0.06. Medium coarse grained reddish-yellow fabric (5YR 6/6) with lime, large quartz particles to 0.004, and abundant

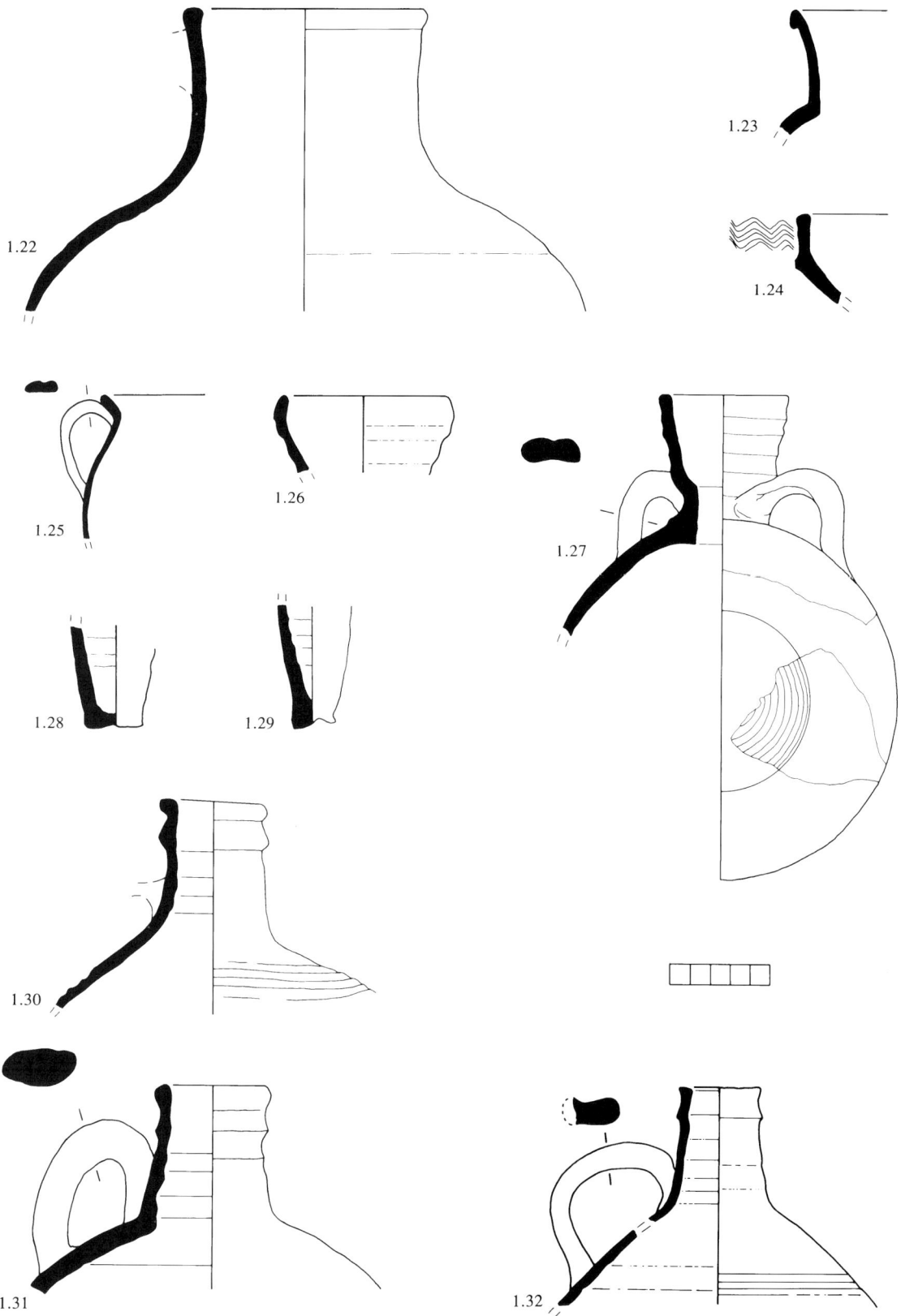

Fig. 8. Hilltop Well, Deposit 1, 1:3 (scale bar=0.05).

mica in large gold flecks; surface easily scratched. Tall spiral ridged neck with rounded lip; spiral grooved face and back; paired strap handles with central shallow ridge. Dull red slip (2.5YR 5/8). Similar examples: B53 and B54. Cf. **2.81**. For similar vessels from Sardis, see Crawford 1990: figs, 258, 259, 372, 420; P88.41/9604 (unpublished, from sector MMS). Cf. Delougaz and Haines 1960: pl. 39, nos. 1–8, pl. 57 nos. 5, 6, 10–12 (asymmetrical Palestinian type); Catling and Dikigoropoulos 1970: 48, no. 13, fig. 3; Williams 1989: 90, no. 545.

1.28. Unguentarium (B59). Fig. 8. Fusiform unguentarium. D. base 0.03. Medium fine grained light-brown fabric (7.5YR 6/4–7/4) with dark red slip dribbled on exterior. Uneven base with straight wheelmade wall, roughly finished. Similar example: B53. See discussion at **2.84**.

1.29. Unguentarium (B49). Fig. 8. Fusiform unguentarium in micaceous fabric. D. base 0.02. Medium fine grained reddish-yellow fabric (5YR 7/6) with a little quartz and much mica. Wheelmade with thin rising walls, uniformly fired. Roughly asymmetrical form with pinched and distorted base, smoothed with light red slip (2.5YR 6/8). Cf. **2.84**; perhaps a local imitation. For similar micaceous variants, see Robinson 1959: 118, no. M369; Hayes 1968: 214; 1992: 99, Deposit 25, no. 6.

AMPHORAE

1.30. Amphora Type A (B62/65). Fig. 8. Jar with tall, ovoid body in five sherds, single strap handle. D. rim 0.048. Very micaceous pink fabric (7.5YR 7/4) with large mica flecks and lime particles to 0.002. Rounded shoulder with vertical neck marked with slight exterior flange, plain rounded lip. Shoulder, neck and handle covered with drab red slip (10R 5/8). Cf. **2.85–88**.

1.31. Amphora Type A (B62/65). Fig. 8. Jar with tall, ovoid body in six sherds, single strap handle, but in different fabric. D. rim 0.048. Medium coarse grained pink fabric (7.5YR 7/4) with dark fired core, little mica but many small, dark inclusions (red, black, and gray) as well as fine lime particles and small voids. Preserved body and neck asymmetrically formed; upper shoulder ridged, preserves traces of pale yellow slip (2.5Y 8/4) that originally covered shoulder and neck. Single splayed strap handle. Incised broken-bar alpha graffito on shoulder.

1.32. Amphora Type B (B61). Fig. 8. Jar with slender, fusiform body in six sherds, single strap handle. D. rim 0.04. Medium fine grained light reddish-brown fabric (5YR 6/4) with moderately large lime parti-

cles to 0.0015, abundant mica in large flecks. Well fired, smoothed. Rim thickened, flattened lip. Handle crudely splayed, with broad central ridge, curving into wide loop. Light red to pink slip (7.5YR 8/4). Cf. **2.89–90**.

1.33. Amphora LR1 (B59). Fig. 9. Panel-ridged amphora. Max. H. 0.075. Sandy reddish-yellow fabric (5YR 7/6) with fine lime and quartz, surface fired yellow (10YR 8/6). Dull red dipinto on lower neck. Similar example: B54. Cf. **2.91, 3.30**. Riley (1979: 212–16) discusses the likely origin of this amphora in Cilicia, north Syria, and Cyprus. For a recent distribution map see Martini and Steckner 1993: 197, fig. 46.

1.34. Amphora LR2 (B52). Fig. 9. Amphora with conical neck. Est. D. rim 0.10. Coarse-grained pink fabric (5YR 7/4) with abundant fine lime and large quartz inclusions but only a few widely scattered mica flecks visible. Many medium to large voids within body and on surface. Riley (1979: 217–19) discusses the likely origin of this amphora in the Aegean and Black Sea region. For a recent distribution map see Martini and Steckner 1993: 197, fig. 46.

1.35. Amphora LR2 (B55). Fig. 9. Basal knob of similar amphora. Floor thickness 0.007. Medium coarse-grained, light red fabric (2.5YR 6/4–6/6) with small quartz particles, abundant lime in widely scattered fine and occasionally large particles (up to 0.005), and a little mica; small and medium voids. Exterior smoothed. Similar example: B59.

1.36. Amphora (B60). Fig. 9. Amphora with high conical neck. Est. D. rim 0.18. Medium coarse-grained light reddish-brown fabric (2.5YR 6/4) with slightly darker fired core; scattered lime, quartz, and fine dark inclusions, highly micaceous; some splintering at fracture. Flaring neck with thickened inturned rim. Cf. Riley 1979: 360, no. 1008 (Deposit 85); Williams and Zervos 1983: 15–16, no. 29, pl. 7 (mid-third century).[7]

1.37. Amphora (B58). Fig. 9. Conical amphora toe. Fine-grained reddish yellow fabric (5YR 7/6), well fired, grayish-purple, with a little lime and mica.

1.38. Amphora (B57). Fig. 9. North African amphora toe. Max. L. 0.14. Coarse-grained pink fabric (5YR 8/4) fired darker toward exterior surface, with scattered small lime particles, small voids. Slightly asymmetrical wheelmade solid toe. Smoothed with light gray to white matte surface (2.5Y 7/2–8/2). Chipped and worn. Similar example: B57 (tapering solid toe in coarse light red fabric [2.5YR 6/8] fired to dark gray core, with quartz, lime and dark grits). For the surface treatment, see Fulford and Peacock 1984: 263–64.

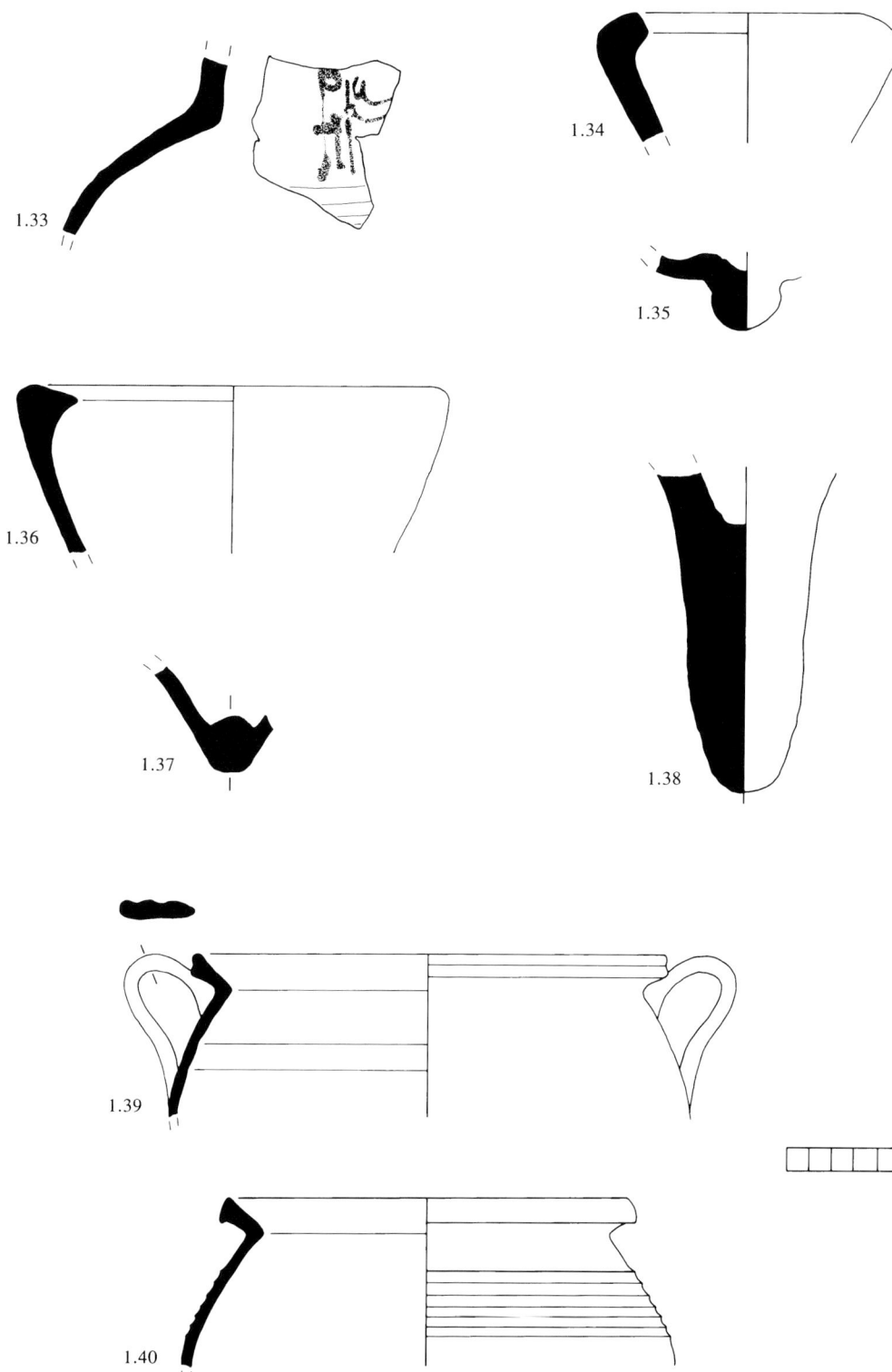

Fig. 9. Hilltop Well, Deposit 1, 1:3 (scale bar=0.05).

COOKING WARES

1.39. Pot (B62/65). Fig. 9. Globular pot with outturned rim and two wide strap handles. Est. D. rim 0.21. Coarse-grained light red fabric (10R 6/6), with many grits, including lime, quartz, large gold and silver mica flecks, and other dark grits. Rounded body with lightly ridged interior wall and plain outturned rim; exterior smoothed. Two wide strap handles with two shallow ridges, roughly splayed and asymmetrically attached. Exterior and lower interior darkened by fire. Similar example: B55 (est. D. rim 0.20). Cf. **2.104–105**.

1.40. Pot (B51). Fig. 9. Globular pot with outturned rim and exterior fine ridging. Est. D. rim 0.18. Coarse-grained, gritty, light red fabric (10R 6/6) with abundant mica, quartz (to 0.002), and other dark grits. Rounded body with outturned thickened rim; exterior marked by fine horizontal ridging. Exterior darkened and smudged. Cf. **3.40**.

OTHER PIECES

Lamp

1.41. Lamp (B53). Fig. 10. Small, mold-made lamp; one-third of disc and wall rim preserved. Max. L. 0.045. Max. W. 0.030. Fine-grained pink fabric (7.5YR 7/4) with abundant mica. Exterior and interior preserve traces of mottled dark red/brown slip, resembling that found on Asia Minor fabric vessels. Disc with radial loops extend from filling hole to raised grooved rim; side of rim decorated with row of raised dots. Cf. Bailey 1988: 387, nos. Q3152–58, pl. 109 (from Ephesus).

Metals

1.42. Ring, cooper alloy (B51). Not illustrated D. 0.021–0.023. Th. 0.0025. Plain hoop without decoration, circular in section. Cf. Waldbaum 1983: 132–33, nos. 862–65; Davidson 1952: 241, nos. 1908–13.

1.43. Cosmetic spoon, copper alloy (B57). Not illustrated Max. L. 0.101. Bowl D. 0.005. Plain elongated shaft, circular in section, with small oval bowl set at slight angle to shaft. Cf. Waldbaum 1983: 105–6, nos. 619–25; Davidson 1952: 181, 184, nos. 1319–24.

Coins

1.44 (B55; 1988.51). Honorius or Arcadius (393–408), AE. Cf. Carson, Hill, and Kent 1960: no. 2580.

1.45 (B51; 1988.31). Arcadius (395–408), AE, Constantinople. Cf. Carson, Hill, and Kent 1960: no. 2580.

Fig. 10. 1.41, lamp.

1.46 (B51; 1988.29). Arcadius (?), AE.

1.47 (B56; 1988.55). Theodosius I or II (379–450), AE.

1.48 (B54; 1988.45). Theodosius II (408–450), AE. Cf. Carson, Hill, and Kent 1960: no. 2214.

1.49 (B51; 1988.27). Theodosius II or Valentinian III (425–450), AE. Cf. Carson, Hill, and Kent 1960: nos. 2004, 2309–10, 2459–61, 2602–6, 2733–35.

Deposit 2 (B1–48)
Hilltop Well, upper levels, late sixth century

FINE WARES

Residual

2.1 Dish (B31). Fig. 11. Dish with straight sloping wall. Est. D. rim 0.32. Medium coarse-grained light red fabric (2.5YR 6/8 to 5YR 7/6) with dark fired core. Abundant mica, fine lime particles, small voids. Wheelmade with external turning marks. Interior with flaking red slip, a shade darker than body; exterior fired light brown to off-white. Cf. Pinkwart and Stamnitz 1983: 138, nos. K208–9; Meyer-Schlichtmann 1988: 118, no. Sa5 Kat. 200, pl. 14 (first–second century).

2.2. Dish (B24). Fig. 11. Shallow dish with incurved rim. Est. D. rim 0.18. H. 0.041. Medium-coarse light red

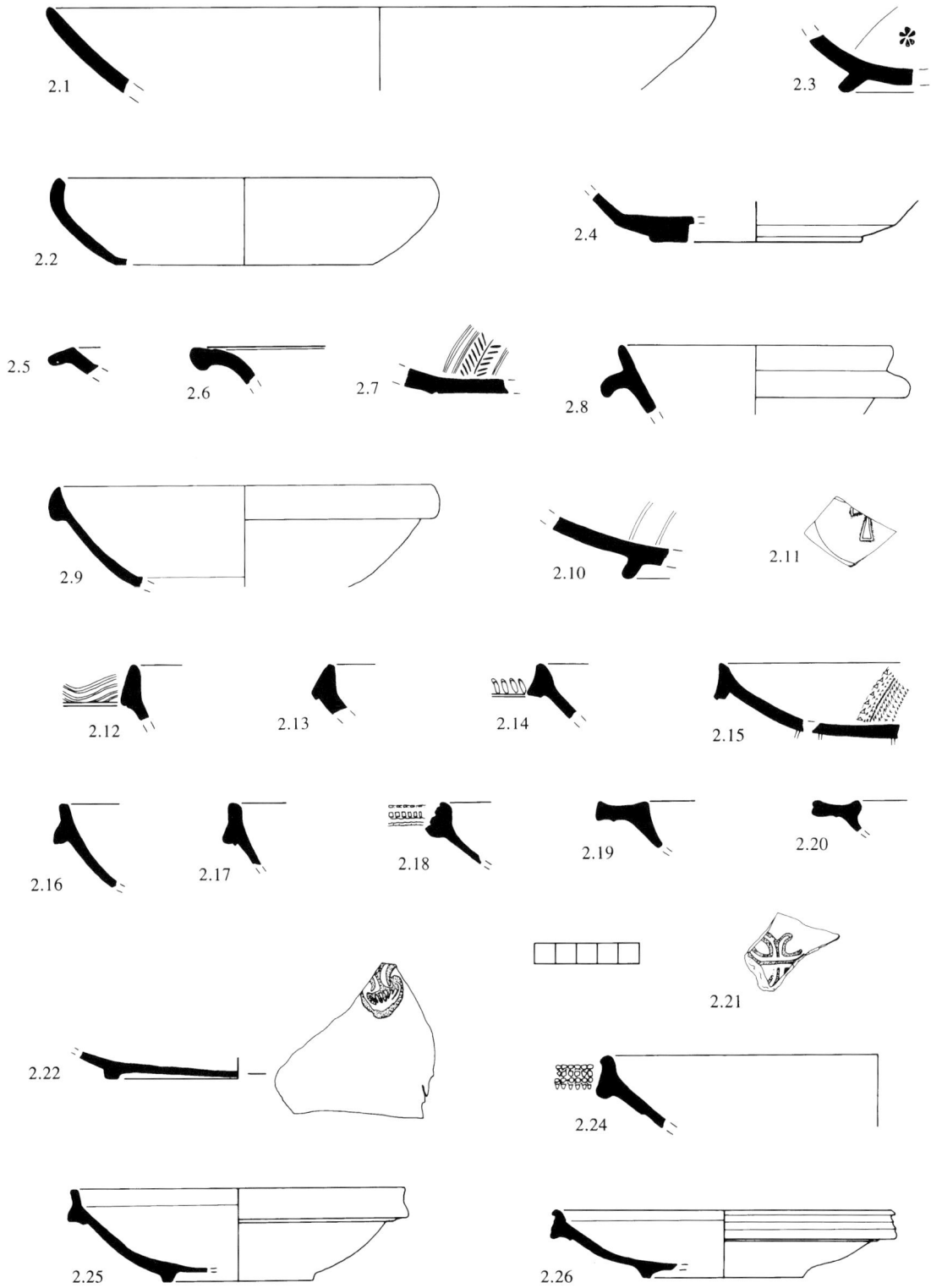

Fig. 11. Hilltop Well, Deposit 2, 1:3 (scale bar=0.05).

fabric (2.5YR 6/8 to 5YR 7/6) evenly fired, with abundant mica in large gold flecks and small lime particles. Interior smoothed and slipped; exterior paddle smoothed, lacking visible slip.

2.3. Bowl (B17). Fig. 11. Small bowl with ring foot base. D. base 0.06. Medium fine-grained pink fabric (5YR 7/4) with small quartz particles, abundant mica in large gold flecks, gray fired core. Interior floor smoothed, with six-petal rosette stamped at center. Asymmetrically formed base, roughly turned with dragged grits across exterior wall and especially base. Flaking dull red slip interior and exterior. Similar example: B36.

2.4. Bowl (B37). Fig. 11. Small bowl in Çandarlı fabric, late second to third century. Est. D. base 0.10. Medium-grained light red fabric (2.5YR 6/6) with a little lime and fine mica particles. Low, heavy foot with squarish section, with sharply rising straight wall. Hard red slip (near 10R 5/6). Cf. Hayes 1972: 318–19, form 1.

African Red Slip

2.5. Bowl (B36). Fig. 11. Variant of Hayes form 58, fourth century. Est. D. rim 0.34. Medium-coarse light red fabric (10R 6/8) with lime, quartz, and small mica flecks. Curved wall with short outturned rim. Interior surface and exterior of rim slipped, flaking.

2.6. Bowl (B10). Fig. 11. Hayes form 67, ca. 360–470. D. rim uncertain. Good quality, medium coarse-grained light red fabric (10R 6/8). Flaring wall with rolled rim. Slipped interior and exterior. Cf. **1.3**.

2.7. Bowl (B32). Fig. 11. Hayes form 68. ca. 370–425. D. base uncertain. Medium fine-grained light red fabric (10R 6/6) with a little lime. Flat floor with grooved base. Floor smoothed with double band rouletting.

2.8. Bowl (B12). Fig. 11. Hayes form 91B/C, sixth century (Hayes 1972: 140–44; Fulford and Peacock 1984: 65). Est. D. rim 0.13. Coarse light red fabric (2.5YR 6/8), scattered lime and quartz. Flaring wall with plain rim, exterior hooked flange. Lightly smoothed and slipped but widely pitted surface; on exterior, only rim and flange slipped.

2.9. Bowl (B10). Fig. 11. Hayes form 99C, ca. 475/500–575 (Hayes 1980: 7–8; Fulford and Peacock 1984: 71). Six body and rim sherds. Est. D. rim 0.18. Medium coarse, light red fabric (10R 6/6) with scat-

tered lime and a few mica flecks. Sloping floor with heavy rolled rim, edge offset. Interior smoothed and completely covered with a high gloss slip; on exterior only rim and upper wall slipped. Cf. **3.3**.

2.10. Dish/bowl (B2). Fig. 11. Hayes form 104A, ca. 500–early seventh century (Hayes 1992:7; Fulford and Peacock 1984: 73–74). Est. D. base 0.16. Medium-grained light red fabric (10R 6/6) with fine lime and quartz. Evenly fired with a high-gloss slip covering the interior. Low ring foot base, thick floor with two concentric inscribed lines above base. Similar example: B30 (with slightly lower foot).

2.11. Bowl (B41). Fig. 11. Stamp with cross in double outline (Hayes 1972: 277, type no. 311, fig. 56e [assigned form 99]; Fulford and Peacock 1984: 96, no. 106).

Late Roman C/Phocaean Red Slip

2.12. Dish (B2). Fig. 11. Hayes form 3B. D. rim uncertain. Fine-grained pink fabric (5YR 7/4), rim fired darker. Fine wavy combing on exterior vertical rim. Cf. Hayes 1972: 330, fig. 67 (=Agora P7636).

2.13. Dish (B44). Fig. 11. Hayes form 3C. D. rim uncertain. Medium fine-grained light red fabric (10R 6/6), thick wall with a little lime and mica. Angular rim profile, with exterior straight, flat beneath; exterior wall paddle smoothed.

2.14. Dish (B32). Fig. 11. Hayes form 3C. Est. D. rim 0.25. Medium fine-grained light red fabric (2.5YR 6/6), with a little lime and mica. Exterior rim roughly rouletted and slipped, fired dark red.

2.15. Dish (B11). Fig. 11. Hayes form 3C. Est. D. rim 0.21. Fine-grained reddish-yellow fabric (5YR 7/6–7/8) with a little mica; mottled light red/orange slip covering interior and exterior surfaces. Nonjoining floor sherd bears band of fine rouletting.

2.16. Dish (B34). Fig. 11. Hayes form 3E. Est. D. rim 0.26. Fine-grained light red fabric (2.5YR 6/6) with a little mica. Well-fired, with small voids on surface; interior smoothed. Curved wall with vertical rim, concave exterior face with pronounced overhang, flat on bottom. Outside of rim blackened in firing.

2.17. Dish (B38). Fig. 11. Hayes form 3E. Est. D. rim 0.26. Medium fine-grained light red fabric (2.5YR 6/8 to 5YR 7/6). Curved wall with vertical rim, concave exterior face with flat bottom, slight offset.

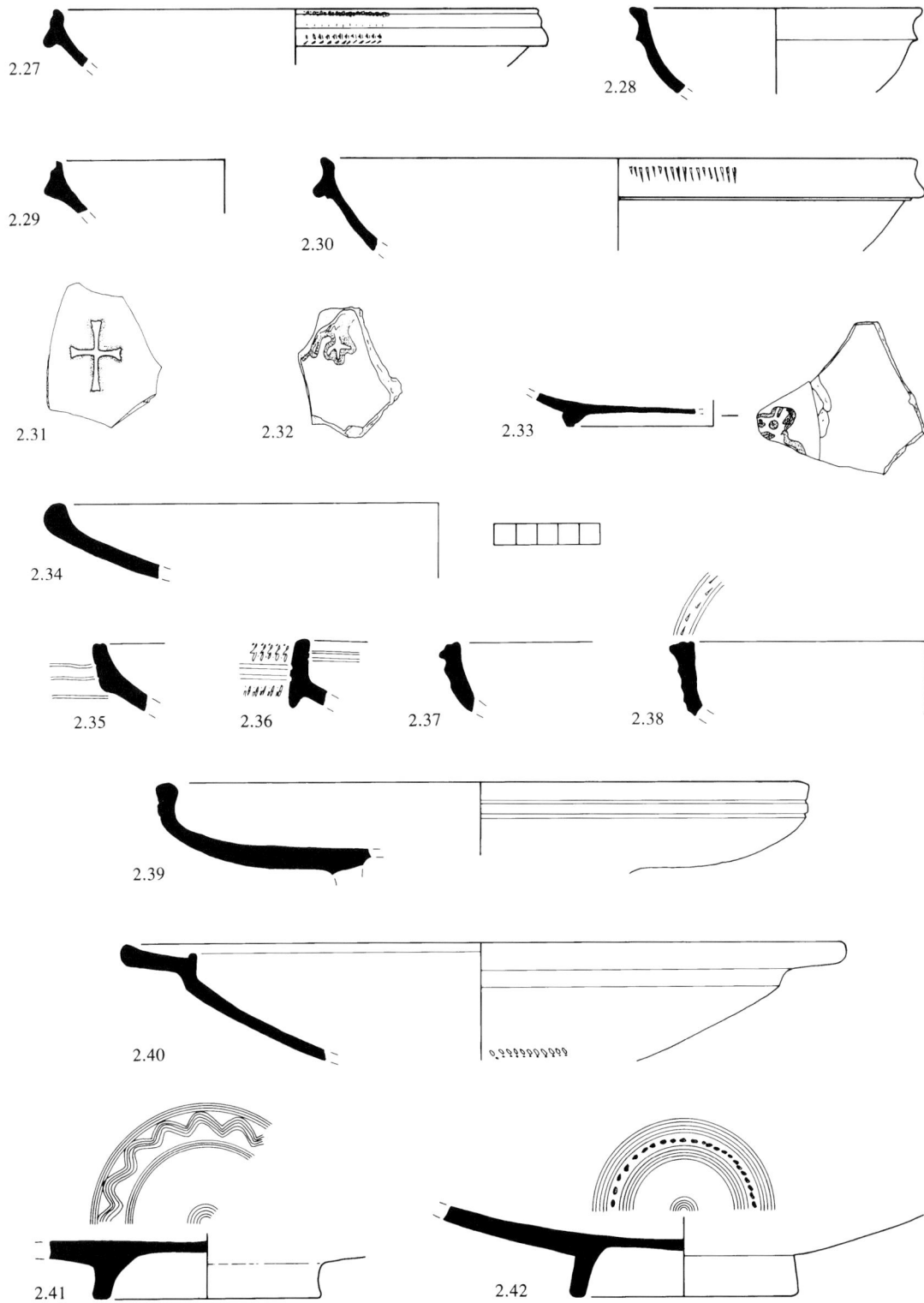

Fig. 12. Hilltop Well, Deposit 2, 1:3 (scale bar=0.05).

2.18. Dish (B45). Fig. 11. Hayes form 3F. Est. D. rim 0.25. Fine-grained light red fabric (10R 6/8 to 2.5YR 6/8) with few inclusions, little mica. Thickened rim, exterior rouletted.

2.19. Dish (B34). Fig. 11. Hayes form 5B. Est. D. rim 0.28. Fine-grained light red fabric (2.5YR 6/8) with scattered mica flecks and a little lime. Broad horizontal rim with beveled lip, slight offset on underside. Slip worn and flaking. Similar examples: B33, B35, B37.

2.20. Dish (B46). Fig. 11. Hayes form 5B. Est. D. rim 0.18. Fine-grained light red fabric (10R 6/6), exterior rim blackened. Broad horizontal rim with inturned lip, slight offset on underside. Similar example: B15.

2.21. Dish (B42). Fig. 11. Double-ribbed Greek cross stamp centered on floor. Cf. Hayes 1972: 364, fig. 78q.

2.22. Dish (B40). Fig. 11. Kantharos stamp on flat base. Est. D. base 0.12. Thin-walled, weak red fabric (10R 5/4–6/4) with fine speckled fracture. Interior smoothed with kantharos stamp at center. Base slightly distorted by stamp pressure, fingerprints and small blobs of clay on exterior. Cf. Hayes 1972: 364, fig. 78a.

2.23. Dish (B40). Not illustrated. Base bearing fragmentary cross stamp with two pendants below arms. Same fabric as **2.22**. Cf. Hayes 1972: 364, motif 67, fig. 78i.

Imitation Late Roman C

2.24. Dish (B45). Fig. 11. Imitation Hayes form 3F. Est. D. rim 0.26. Medium fine-grained light red fabric (2.5YR 6/6), with a little lime and much mica. Interior wall paddle-smoothed leaving broad furrows. Thickened rim slightly concave on exterior and rouletted, fired lighter than wall. Exterior wall roughly finished with deep, irregular diagonal smoothing marks and dragged grits. Similar examples: B9, B45 (both also rouletted).

2.25. Dish (B11). Fig. 11. Imitation Hayes form 3F. Est. D. rim 0.16. H. 0.045. Dull reddish-yellow fabric (5YR 6/6–7/6) with abundant mica, a little lime, and occasional quartz to 0.003. Wall and floor scored by dragged grits. Interior and exterior lightly slipped; exterior surface flaking and easily scratched.

2.26. Dish (B13). Fig. 11. Imitation Hayes form 3F. Est. D. rim 0.16. H. 0.032. Light red fabric (2.5YR 6/6–6/8). Exterior roughly finished with dragged grits and small voids. Interior and exterior slipped.

2.27. Dish (B25). Fig. 12. Imitation Hayes form 3D/F. Est. D. rim 0.23. Medium-grained reddish-yellow fabric (5YR 7/6) with much mica; dull, soft texture. Vertical rim with pronounced flange, outer face slightly concave, top gently rounded with highest point at exterior edge; rouletted. Interior paddle smoothed, exterior scored by dragged grits. Similar examples: B9, B10 (3 examples), B12 (2 examples), B13, B15, B16, B17 (2 examples), B22.

2.28. Dish (B33). Fig. 12. Imitation Hayes form 3. Est. D. rim 0.13. Medium fine-grained light reddish-yellow fabric (5YR 7/6) with fine lime particles and abundant mica, small voids in body. Wheelmade with irregular turning marks; slipped. Similar examples: B9, B12. Cf. **1.7–8**.

2.29. Dish (B33). Fig. 12. Imitation Hayes form 3. Est. D. rim 0.16. Medium-grained light red fabric (2.5YR 6/8 to 5YR 7/6), flaking at surface. Triangular rim with stepped exterior profile, fired off-white.

2.30. Dish (B11). Fig. 12. Imitation Hayes form 3F. Est. D. rim 0.28. Fine-grained reddish-yellow fabric (5YR 6/6) with much mica. Interior paddle smoothed. Rim with pronounced flange, slightly offset on underside; simple rouletting.

2.31. Dish (B18). Fig. 12. Cross stamp on flat base. Light reddish-brown fabric (5YR 6/4), very micaceous, brittle with clean breaks. Smoothed floor with plain, impressed cross with flaring arms; exterior scored by dragged grits. Similar example: B1. Cf. Hayes 1972: 365, no. 71.

2.32. Dish (B40). Fig. 12. Bird stamp on flat base. Light red fabric (2.5YR 6/8), very micaceous with occasional lime erupting on surface. Interior floor smoothed, leaving fine concentric streaks in light orange to light red slip.

2.33. Dish (B17). Fig. 12. Animal stamp on flat base, perhaps depicting a donkey. Est. D. base 0.14. Fine-grained fabric overfired to brown or grayish-brown (7.5YR 5/4 to 10YR 5/2) with many fine voids in body and occasional large lumps erupting beneath surface; highly micaceous, with widely scattered gold and silver flecks. Interior smoothed and slipped. Exterior roughly finished, pitted, and scored by deep dragged grits.

Asia Minor Fabrics

2.34. Dish (B46). Fig. 12. Dish with upturned, thickened rim. Est. D. rim 0.38. Fine-grained reddish-yellow

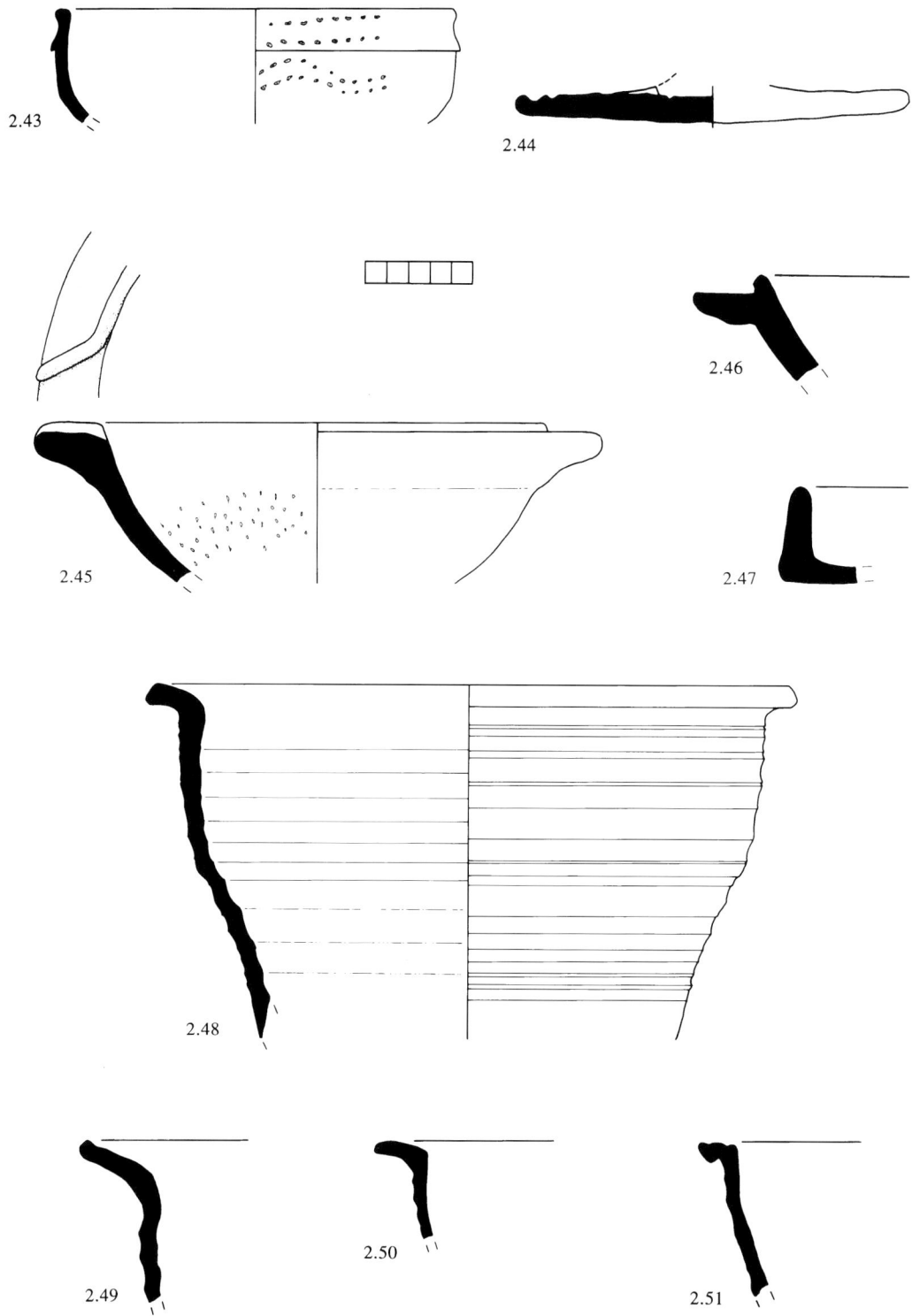

Fig. 13. Hilltop Well, Deposit 2, 1:3 (scale bar=0.05).

fabric (7.5YR 6/6–7/4) with a little lime and mica. Light red/orange slip interior and exterior, worn and flaking, fired reddish yellow (7.5YR 8/6) on exterior. Broadly flaring wall with rounded upturned rim. Interior smoothed; exterior wall scored by dragged grits.

2.35. Dish (B26). Fig. 12. Dish with vertical rim. D. rim uncertain. Medium coarse-grained pink fabric (7.5YR 7/4) with abundant mica, many small dark grits and several large voids. Vertical rim with grooved top, three incised grooves on exterior rim and upper wall. Interior and exterior covered with light reddish-yellow slip, worn and badly flaking. Cf. **3.12**.

2.36. Dish (B47). Fig. 12. Dish with vertical hammerhead rim. D. rim uncertain. Fine-grained light brown fabric (7.5YR 7/4). Sloping wall and vertical rim with sharp exterior offset, exterior rim grooved and rouletted; light reddish-brown slip. Cf. Hayes 1992: 95, Deposit 14 no. 22.

2.37. Dish (B47). Fig. 12. Dish with vertical rim. D. rim uncertain. Fine-grained reddish-yellow fabric (7.5YR 8/6) with fine mica, scattered voids on surface. Sloping wall and vertical rim with grooved top; exterior lightly ridged. Light reddish-brown slip; exterior wall scored by dragged grits. Cf. **3.12**.

2.38. Dish (B2). Fig. 12. Dish with vertical rim. Est. D. rim 0.22. Fine-grained micaceous reddish-yellow fabric (5YR 7/6). Vertical rim with two top grooves and punched decoration. Interior and exterior lightly ridged and covered with slightly metallic light reddish-brown slip.

2.39. Dish (B19). Fig. 12. Dish. Est. D. rim 0.30. Medium fine-grained reddish-yellow fabric (7.5YR 8/6) with scattered lime, quartz particles to 0.0025, abundant mica. Broad sloping floor rises to vertical, rounded rim; two grooves on exterior rim. Interior and exterior smoothed, covered with red slip, badly flaking.

2.40. Plate (B15). Fig. 12. Plate with broad horizontal rim in five joining sherds. Est. D. rim 0.34 ext. Medium-grained pink fabric (5YR 8/4 to 7.5YR 8/4) with a little lime and abundant mica, evenly fired. Straight, sloping wall rises to vertical lip with wide, horizontal rim; faint rouletting on top surface of rim, lower exterior wall. Interior and exterior smoothed and covered with light red slip (10R 6/6 to 2.5YR 6/6), worn and flaking. Similar example: B29. Cf. **1.11**; Hayes 1968: 211, no. 75 (=1992 fig. 41).

2.41. Plate (B1). Fig. 12. Plate with high foot. Est. D. base 0.108 ext. Medium fine-grained reddish-yellow fabric (5YR 7/6) with scattered fine lime particles and

abundant mica; surface and body badly pitted. High foot with flat floor decorated with concentric circles, wavy line combed with five-toothed implement between two straight bands of same. Interior and exterior surfaces slipped light red (7.5R 6/8). Similar example: B51. Cf. **3.15**; Crawford 1990: fig. 419. For general shape, decoration, and perhaps fabric, see Hayes 1992: 106, Deposit 31, no. 25.

2.42. Plate (B5/8). Fig. 12. Plate with high foot in 11 sherds. D. base 0.10. Fine-grained, light reddish-brown fabric (2.5YR 6/4) with a little mica. High foot with flat floor, gently upcurving wall. Floor smoothed, decorated with concentric circles in two bands flanking row of punched holes and central spiral. Dark reddish-brown, mottled slip.

2.43. Bowl (B1/2). Fig. 13. Bowl with vertical rim in five sherds. Est. D. rim 0.18. Medium fine-grained pink fabric (5YR 7/4) with scattered lime and abundant mica. Thickened vertical rim with slight flange. Roughly punched rouletting in two undulating rows of dots on exterior of rim and outer wall. Interior and exterior slipped metallic light brown. Similar example: B5/8.

PLAIN WARES

2.44. Lid (B13). Fig. 13. Flat lid. Th. 0.08–0.09. Est. D. rim 0.18. Coarse-grained micaceous reddish-yellow fabric (5YR 7/6–7/8). Flat circular lid with two shallow grooves near rim and one near center; broad strap handle with splayed ends. Top surface fired off-white; edge blackened. Similar examples: B2 (three examples), B13, B17 (two examples), B26, B38, B43 (two examples). Cf. Crawford 1990: figs. 295–97.

2.45. Mortarium (B19). Fig. 13. Mortarium. Est. D. rim 0.20. Coarse-grained light reddish-brown fabric (2.5YR 6/4–6/6) with scattered lime, quartz, mica, and other small grits. Flaring wall with outturned horizontal rim and raised lip curving to form spout. Interior surface worn; exterior roughly finished and gritty; both with flaking pale yellow slip (2.5Y 8/4). Cf. **1.14, 2.46**.

2.46. Mortarium (B36). Fig. 13. Large mortarium. Est. D. rim ca. 0.50. Coarse-grained pink fabric (7.5YR 7/4) with gray core, lime, quartz (to 0.002), mica, and scattered voids. Gently curving wall with outturned, thickened flange rim with raised lip. Interior smoothed; exterior surface coarse and sandy.

2.47. Tray (B35). Fig. 13. Flat tray with plain vertical rim. Est. D. rim 0.30. Medium coarse-grained reddish-yellow fabric (5YR 7/6) with a little lime, quartz,

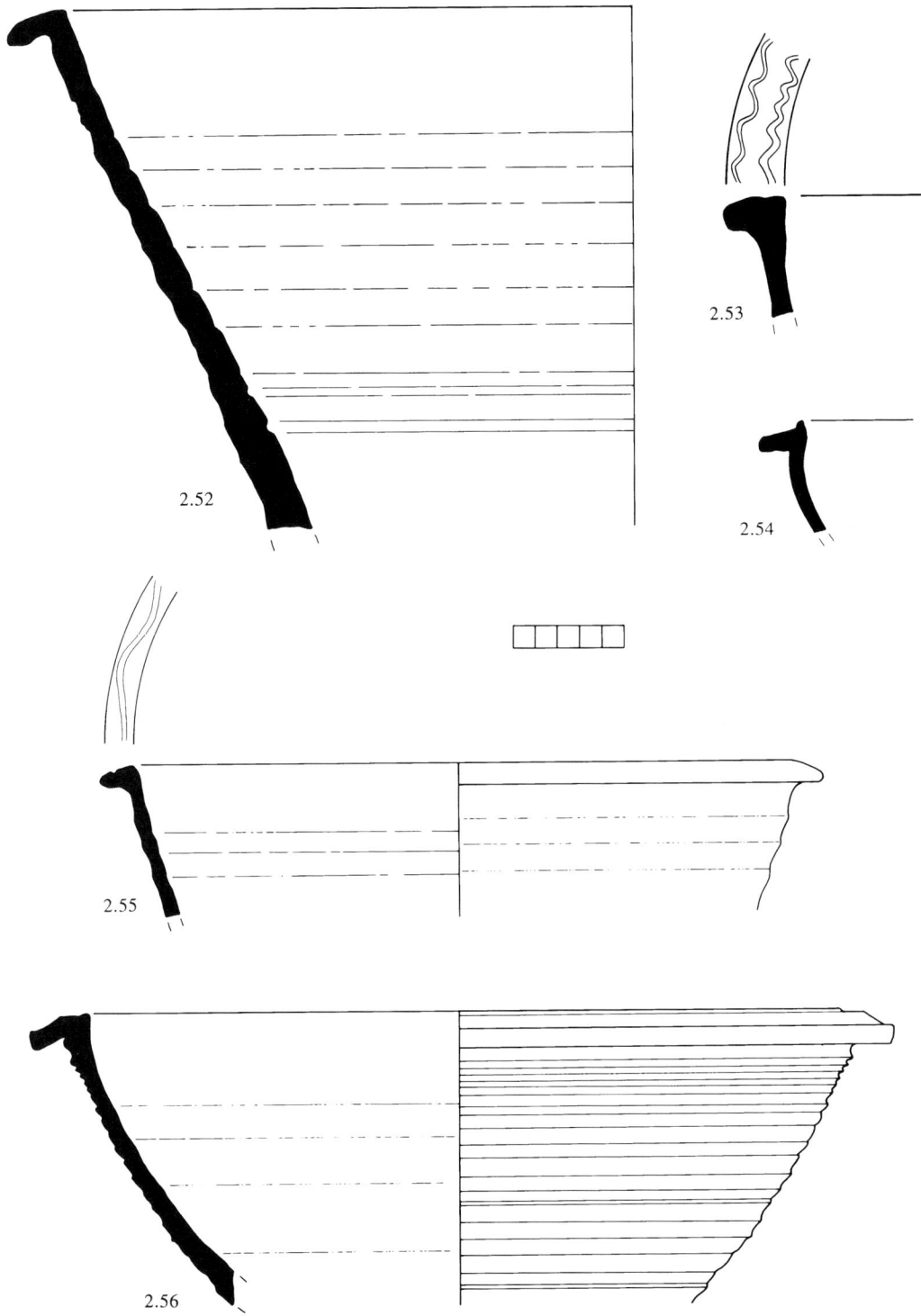

Fig. 14. Hilltop Well, Deposit 2, 1:3 (scale bar=0.05).

and many large gold mica flecks. Interior and exterior covered with light pink matte slip (7.5YR 7/4), flaking. Exterior base very sandy and micaceous. Similar examples: B16 (est. D. rim 0.5), B17 (est. D. rim 0.46), B24 (ext. D. rim 0.4), B30 (est. D. rim 0.5), B35 (est. D. rim 0.3). Cf. Boardman 1989: 105, no. 216.

2.48. Basin (B31). Fig. 13. Basin with outturned rim. Est. D. rim 0.29. Medium coarse-grained reddish-yellow fabric (5YR 7/6–7/8) with lime and much mica. Curving ridged wall rises to thickened outturned rim.

2.49. Basin (B27). Fig. 13. Basin with broad outturned rim. Est. D. rim 0.32. Medium coarse-grained reddish-yellow fabric (5YR 7/6–7/8) with dark fired core, some lime, and much mica. Lightly ridged wall with broad outturned rim. Top of rim and exterior fired light pink to off-white. Similar example: B13.

2.50. Basin (B38). Fig. 13. Basin with outturned rim. Est. D. rim 0.28. Same fabric as **2.49**. Smaller rim, straight and outturned. Similar example: B32.

2.51. Basin (B11). Fig. 13. Basin with horizontal rim. Est. D. rim 0.34. Medium fine-grained reddish-yellow fabric (5YR 7/6) with a little lime and mica. Irregular rising wall with flat outturned ledge rim, top surface decorated with two shallow grooves.

2.52. Basin (B9). Fig. 14. Large basin with outturned rim. Est. D. rim 0.52. Medium coarse-grained fabric with large lime particles (to 0.006), abundant mica and large voids in body. Interior and exterior sharply ridged despite superficial smoothing.

2.53. Basin (B46). Fig. 14. Large basin with heavy rim. D. rim greater than 0.50. Coarse-grained light red fabric (2.5YR 6/8 to 5YR 7/6) with darker core, fine quartz particles and abundant mica. Straight wall with heavy rim incised with two wavy lines. Similar example: B29.

2.54. Basin (B43). Fig. 14. Basin with outturned rim. Est. D. 0.32. Coarse gray fabric (5Y 6/1) with abundant lime, quartz, mica, and other inclusions. Curved wall rises to narrow lip, outturned rim. Similar examples: B11, B26, B31.

2.55. Basin (B41). Fig. 14. Basin with outturned rim. Est. D. rim 0.30. Medium coarse-grained reddish-yellow fabric (5YR 7/6) with scattered lime, abundant mica, and many irregular voids. Straight wall rises to flat outturned rim incised with wavy line. Interior surface and top of rim preserve traces of a dull yellow wash. Similar examples: B31, B45.

2.56. Basin (B19). Fig. 14. Basin with downturned rim. Est. D. rim 0.34. Medium coarse-grained light red fabric (2.5YR 6/6–6/8) with some lime and abundant gold mica. Curving wall rises to narrow lip and downturned rim. Exterior sharply ridged despite superficial smoothing.

2.57. Basin (B19). Fig. 15. Deep basin with thin wall and triangular rim. Est. D. rim 0.33. Coarse-grained light red fabric (2.5YR 6/8) with many large lime particles (to 0.003), often erupting on surface, quartz and other stony inclusions, abundant mica in large gold flecks. Thin wall with slightly hooked lip, plain outturned rim. Interior smoothed; exterior and rim covered with dull white wash.

2.58. Basin (B16). Fig. 15. Basin with flanged rim. Est. D. rim 0.32. Coarse gray fabric (5Y 5/1) with abundant lime, quartz, and mica, many small voids and other inclusions. Thickened vertical rim, downturned and hooked.

2.59. Basin (B35). Fig. 15. Basin with flanged rim. Est. D. rim 0.25. Coarse-grained light red fabric (2.5YR 6/8 to 5YR 7/6) with large lime particles erupting on surface, abundant mica in large gold flecks. Thick, flaring wall with vertical rim, prominent exterior flange. Interior and exterior slipped red to light brown. Similar examples: **2.60**; B10 (est. D. rim 0.24), B42, B43, B44 (two examples, est. D. rims 0.26, 0.28), B45 (est. D. rim 0.38).

2.60. Basin/bowl (B42). Fig. 15. Deep basin/bowl with outturned rim. Est. D. rim 0.22. Coarse-grained fabric (2.5YR 6/8) with many particles lime, quartz (to 0.003), and abundant mica. Hemispherical basin with broad outturned rim. Interior covered by mottled red slip, rim fired yellow/brown/black.

2.61. Pithos (B25). Fig. 15. Storage vat. Est. D. rim 0.30. Coarse light red fabric (2.5YR 6/8 to 5YR 7/6), with scattered lime and abundant mica in large gold flecks. Thick wall rises to heavy knob rim. Yellow slip on exterior wall and rim, dribbled onto interior of mouth; crude, wavy line incised through slip on exterior. A nonjoining but similar sherd from B23 bears a slight exterior offset and a second incised wavy line on the exterior wall.

2.62. Pithos (B25). Fig. 15. Storage vat. Est. D. rim 0.22. Medium coarse-grained light reddish-brown fabric (5YR 6/4) with darker core, large lime particles to 0.003, many large voids, and pitted surface. Straight wall slopes inward to thickened, inturned rim with narrow exterior flange. Interior smoothed; exterior lightly ridged and decorated with at least two zones

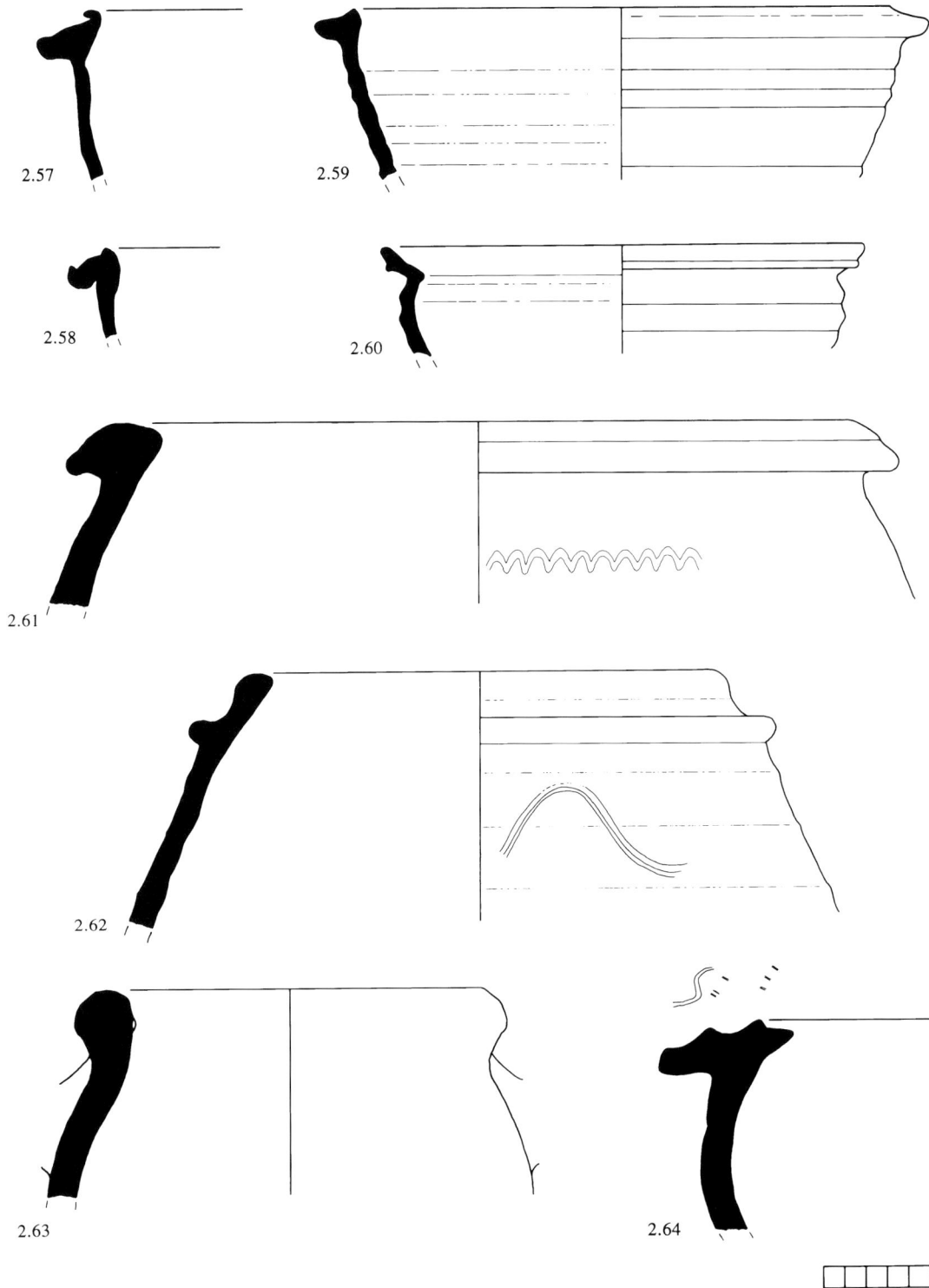

Fig. 15. Hilltop Well, Deposit 2, 1:3 (scale bar=0.05).

of broad incised wavy line pattern (as also rim, by analogy with nonjoining sherds). Similar examples: B5/8 (est. D. base c. 0.40), B13, B15, B34.

2.63. Pithos (B12). Fig. 15. Storage vat. Est. D. rim 0.18. Dense, coarse-grained red fabric (2.5YR 5/8) with fine quartz particles, lime to 0.007, large voids in body but little mica. Rounded, thickened rim, top and interior rim roughly leveled with spatula. Heavy handle root. Related example: flat lid (B43) with incised wavy lines.

2.64. Pithos (B38). Fig. 15. Basin. Est. D. rim uncertain. Medium coarse-grained reddish-yellow fabric (5YR 7/6–7/8) with a little lime, abundant mica, and many voids. Top rim decorated with incised notches, wavy lines. Interior and top rim covered with off-white matt slip; exterior smoothed.

2.65. Dish (B35/37). Fig. 16. Dish with grooved vertical rim. Est. D. rim 0.24. Est. D. base 0.12. Medium fine-grained light red fabric (2.5YR 6/8 to 5YR 7/6) with abundant mica, a little lime, and many irregular voids. Slightly curved wall rises to vertical rim and slight exterior overhang, exterior grooved. Interior smoothed and covered with pink micaceous slip (7.5YR 7/4); exterior pitted and scored by dragged grits and drying cracks. Exterior upper wall blackened. Low foot turned as Hayes form 3; floor preserves single band of rouletting in form of five simple lozenge-shaped impressions. Similar example: B33 (two sherds, charred, perhaps from same vessel).

2.66. Bowl (B16). Fig. 16. Small bowl with outturned rim. Est. D. rim 0.14. Medium-grained light red fabric (2.5YR 6/8) with abundant mica. Small bowl with thick, flaring wall and downturned rim with grooved top. Interior smoothed; exterior score by dragged grits, badly flaking.

2.67. Bowl (B38). Fig. 16. Small bowl with vertical rim and ring foot base. Est. D. rim 0.13. Medium-grained light red fabric (2.5YR 6/6 to 5YR 7/6) with much mica and many small voids. Thick, sloping wall rises from low ring foot to vertical rim. Interior surface smoothed, covered with thin red wash; exterior scored by fine dragged grits; upper wall marked by two incised grooves. Exterior rim fired off-white.

2.68. Bowl (B38). Fig. 16. Small bowl with inturned rim. Est. D. rim 0.10. Coarse-grained light red fabric (2.5YR 6/8) with much lime, quartz, and mica. Small bowl with thickened, inturned rim with small exterior ledge.

2.69. Bowl (B37). Fig. 16. Small bowl with vertical rim. Est. D. rim 0.16. Fine-grained light red fabric (2.5YR 6/6) with few inclusions and clean fracture, light gray core. Small bowl with plain vertical rim, thickened lip with top groove. Interior and upper exterior smoothed and slipped, leaving well-fired, light reddish-brown (2.5YR 6/4) surface with much silver and gold mica. Similar examples: **2.70–71**, B9, B10, B15, B34, B40, B46, B50.

2.70. Bowl (B44). Fig. 16. Small bowl with vertical rim. Est. D. rim 0.15. Shape similar to **2.69, 2.71**, but fabric less well levigated, with abundant mica, several large lime particles, pitted surface. Exterior lower wall fired darker than rim; exterior rouletted.

2.71. Bowl (B26). Fig. 16. Small bowl with vertical rim. Est. D. rim 0.15. Fabric and shape similar to **2.69**, with fine-toothed rouletting on exterior of rim; exterior rim slightly offset from wall.

2.72. Bowl (B15). Fig. 16. Deep hemispherical bowl with outturned rim. Est. D. rim 0.13. Medium fine-grained pink fabric (5YR 7/4–7/6) with small lime particles and many gold mica flecks. Thin-walled bowl with plain, outturned rim; interior smoothed, exterior lightly ridged. Paired strap handles with broad central ridge, asymmetrically attached to rim and upper wall. Similar examples: **2.73**, B9, B37. Cf. **1.25**.

2.73. Bowl (B25). Fig. 16. Deep hemispherical bowl with outturned rim. Est. D. rim 0.13. Similar reddish-yellow fabric (5YR 7/6) to **2.72**. Thin-walled bowl with outturned rim, inward hooked lip; exterior lightly ridged.

2.74. Cup (B15). Fig. 16. Small cup with inturned rim. Est. D. rim 0.07. H. 0.042. Medium fine-grained light red fabric (2.5YR 6/8 to 5YR 7/8) with abundant mica. Small, handleless cup with inturned rim and string-cut base, lightly ridged. Exterior fired light brown (7.5YR 6/4). Similar examples: **2.75**, B5/8 (ten+ examples), B19, B22, B24, B26. Cf. **1.26, 3.24**. For other examples, see Crawford 1990: e.g., figs. 151, 313; Boardman 1989: 105, no. 214 (a low variant); Johnson 1981: 71, nos. 463–66; 77–78, nos. 523–25.

2.75. Cup (B5/8). Fig. 16. Small cup with inturned rim. D. rim 0.073. H. 0.05. Almost complete. Medium fine-grained light red fabric (2.5YR 6/8) with abundant mica. Small, handleless cup with inturned rim and string-cut base, light exterior ridging.

2.76. Jar (B17). Fig. 16. Jar. Est. D. rim 0.11. Fabric as **2.59–60**, medium coarse-grained light red (2.5YR

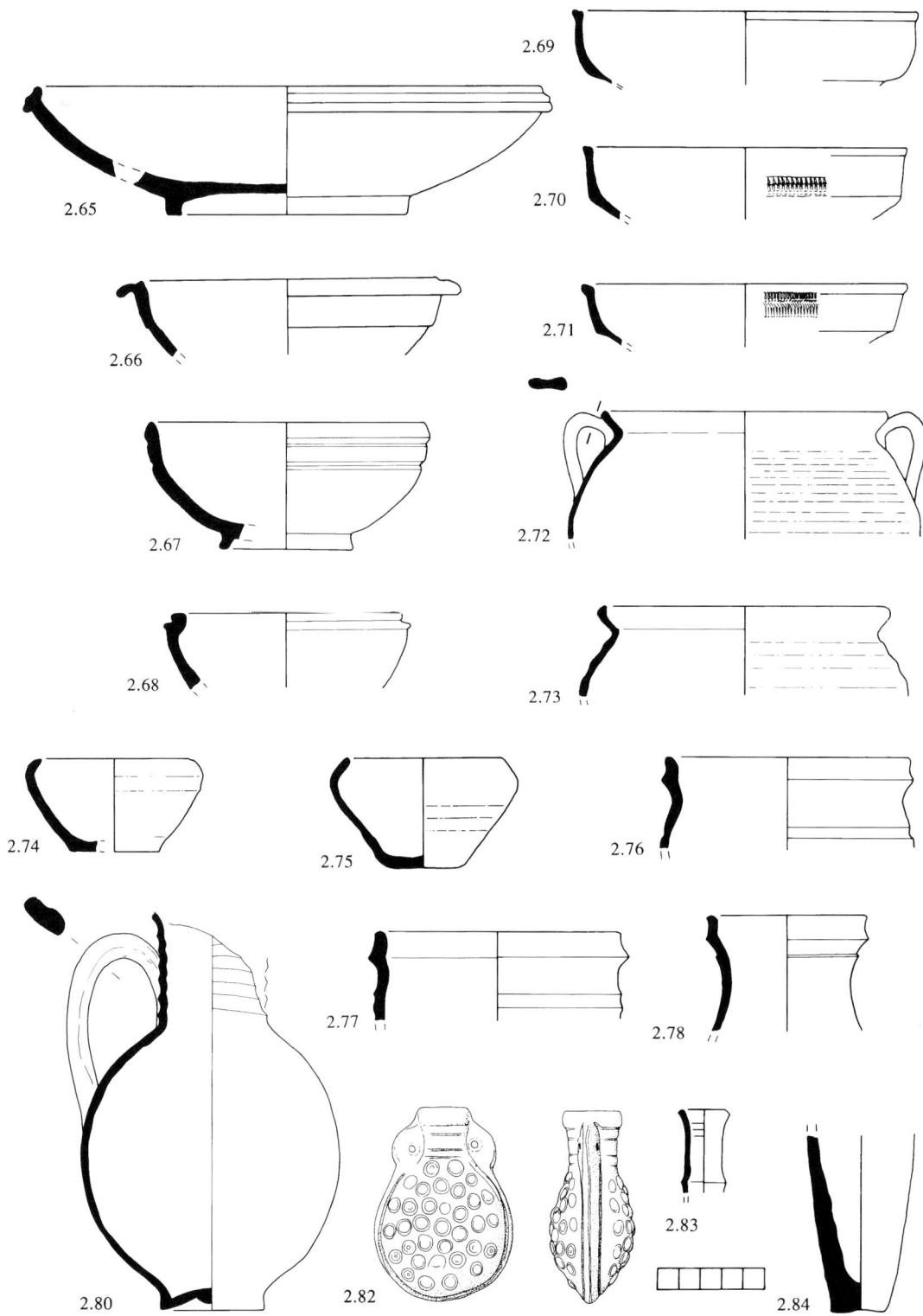

Fig. 16. Hilltop Well, Deposit 2, 1:3 (scale bar=0.05).

6/8 to 5YR 7/6) with lime (to 0.005), quartz (to 0.002), and abundant mica in large gold flecks. Vertical rim with narrow flange; red to black slip covers interior and exterior.

2.77. Jar (B35). Fig. 16. Small jar or pitcher. Est. D. rim 0.11. Coarse-grained olive gray fabric (5Y 4/2) with large lime and quartz particles and mica flecks. Unslipped. Similar example: B144.

2.78. Jar (B14). Fig. 16. Small jar or pitcher. Est. D. rim 0.07. Medium fine-grained dark gray (5Y 4/1) with lime (to 0.002), quartz, and much mica. Unslipped. Cf. Riley 1979: no. 1190 for the form.

2.79. Jar (B42). Not illustrated. Jar sherd with brush rouletting on exterior. Medium fine-grained light red fabric (2.5YR 6/6) with abundant mica. Exterior covered with off-white slip with dark dull red brush rouletting. Similar example: B109.

2.80. Jug (B5/8; P87.009/9390). Figs. 16, 17. Spherical jug in 15 sherds. D. base 0.048. Max. W. 0.125. Max. H. 0.185. Coarse-grained reddish-brown fabric (5YR 5/3) with darker core (10YR 4/2); scattered quartz and mica in large silver flecks (to 0.002) and many large voids in body. Spherical jug with thin wall rising from recessed button base to tall neck and (missing) trefoil rim. Exterior body smoothed, neck lightly ridged. Handle attachments carefully splayed with single off-center ridge. Fired gray with black dribble slip. Similar example: B31 (est. D. base 0.06). Cf. **1.20.** For the base, see Catling and Dikigoropoulos 1970: 47–48, nos. 5, 6, 9, 10; fig. 3; Bass 1982: figs. 8–12, nos. P24–28; Boardman 1989: fig. 33, nos. 199–202. Unlike these late examples, the Sardis bases have a more defined foot, as Crawford 1990: fig. 184; cf. Pülz 1985: fig. 8, no. 56. For the upper body and ridged neck, see Bass 1982: fig. 8–12, no. P29; Abadie-Reynal and Sodini 1992: fig. 19, no. CC105.

2.81. Flask (B33). Not illustrated. Large lentoid flask in 42 sherds. Est. D. body 0.22. W. edge 0.090. Medium-grained reddish-yellow fabric (5YR 6/6) with fine lime, quartz, and mica. A more fragmentary example similar to **1.27**; three broad ridges along center of edge. Similar example: B37.

2.82. Ampulla (B6; P87.001/9381). Figs. 16, 18. Small lentoid flask, intact. Max. W. 0.065. H. 0.089. D. rim 0.027. Light reddish-yellow micaceous fabric (5YR 6/6) with worn reddish brown slip (10R 4/6–4/8). Mold-made lentoid flask with narrow neck and plain rim; two pierced handles. Body decorated with 34 small raised bumps. Cf. **3.29.**

Fig. 17. 2.80 (P87.009/9390), jug.

2.83. Unguentarium (B38). Fig. 16. Fusiform unguentarium. Est. D. rim 0.002. Fine-grained pink fabric (7.5YR 7/4). Thin vertical wall with outturned rim, offset on neck; interior and exterior covered with uneven brown slip. Similar example: **2.84.**

2.84. Unguentarium (B26). Fig. 16. Fusiform unguentarium. D. base 0.025. Generally smooth, fine-grained light red fabric (10R 6/6) with gray core, little lime or mica. Roughly made with thick lower wall and base, small cracks in inner wall, unfinished exterior base; blotting and finger marks on exterior with dark red dribbled slip. No stamps. Many similar examples: B9, B13 (blue-gray), B14, B15, B16, B24, B27, B34 (two examples blue-gray), B53, B59, B149 (two examples blue-gray). Cf. **1.28–29.** For the type and suggested Palestinian origin, see Hayes 1971. For further examples, see Hayes 1968: 212–14; Hayes 1992: 8–9; Riley 1979: nos. 1030–35; Mitsopoulos-Leon 1991: 150, 153, nos. 053–54. Such Late Roman unguentaria belong primarily to the sixth century,

Fig. 18. 2.82 (P87.001/9381), ampulla.

although examples have been reported from 450 (Mitsopoulos-Leon) to 650 (Hayes).

AMPHORAE

2.85. Amphora Type A (B5/8; P88.019/9565). Figs. 19, 20. Jar with tall ovoid body and single handle, largely reconstructed. H. 0.555. Max. W. 0.227. Est. D. rim 0.045. Medium-grained fabric, fired exterior light reddish-brown (5YR 6/4–6/6), interior yellowish brown (10YR 5/6–6/6). Fabric smooth to touch, with few voids, laden with fine lime particles and abundant mica in fine sparkling points as well as large gold and silver flecks. Wall rises from solid toe through pinched waist, rounded shoulder, and conical neck with vertical rim; interior surface lightly ridged and smoothed, tending to laminate. Ridged neck narrows to sharp outward flange; thickened lip with flattened top. Single strap handle with two uneven shallow ridges, splayed to attach at neck and upper shoulder. Upper body decorated with irregu-

larly spaced shallow grooves; an orange to red slip (about 10R 4/8–5/6) covers the upper shoulder and neck, continuing over rim onto interior of mouth. Interior coated with black resin or mastic. Similar examples: **2.86–88**. Cf. **1.30–31**.

2.86. Amphora Type A (B5/8; P88.029/9581). Figs. 19, 20. Jar with tall ovoid body and single handle. H. 0.590. Max. W. 0.240. Est. D. rim 0.050. Fabric as **2.85**, surface tending to laminate. Vessel a little larger and heavier; hollow toe, lower body smoothed, top third lightly ridged. Light red slip covers shoulder and neck, also splashed on lower body. Interior heavily coated with resin or mastic.

2.87. Amphora Type A (B5/8; P88.022/9572). Figs. 19, 20. Jar with tall ovoid body and single handle. H. 0.565. Max. W. 0.225. D. rim 0.040. Fabric as **2.85** but more evenly fired without darker interior; large flecks of gold mica. Similar form but with hollow toe lacking ball plug; upper body not grooved but lightly ridged; strap handle less clearly ridged; flange on rim less pronounced and lip outturned. Light red slip on shoulder and neck (about 2.5YR 5/8–6/8).

2.88. Amphora Type A (B5/8; P88.030/9582). Fig. 21. Jar with tall ovoid body and single handle. H. 0.573. Max W. 0.237. Est. D. rim 0.050. Similar fabric and form. Medium-grained pink fabric (5YR 7/4), evenly fired but leaving a few large voids on surface. Hollow toe, smoothed body partially covered with regular shallow grooving; high rim with sloping flange. Handle marked by two light ridges. No red slip on shoulder; entire exterior covered with a dull very pale brown wash (10YR 7/3) with darker blotches.

2.89. Amphora Type B (B5/8; P87.008/9389). Figs. 20, 21. Jar with slender fusiform body and with single handle. H. 0.044. Max. W. body 0.017. Rim and part of neck missing. Medium coarse-grained light red fabric (2.5YR 6/8) with darker fired interior; smooth to touch, with abundant mica in fine and medium gold flecks, occasional particles of lime. Roughly shaped fusiform body with solid toe tapering to point. Badly distorted and scraped before firing. Interior wall sharply ridged; exterior lower body scored by deep dragged grits, large irregular voids. Upper body smoothed, surface mottled in firing (10R 3/6 to 7/5R 3/4) and occasionally flaking. Short strap handle turned into tight loop, attached to neck with roughly splayed ends. Interior coated with thick layer of resin or mastic.

2.90. Amphora Type B (B5/8; P88.017/9562). Figs. 20, 21. Jar with slender fusiform body and with single handle. H. 0.048. Max. W. body 0.158. D. rim uncertain.

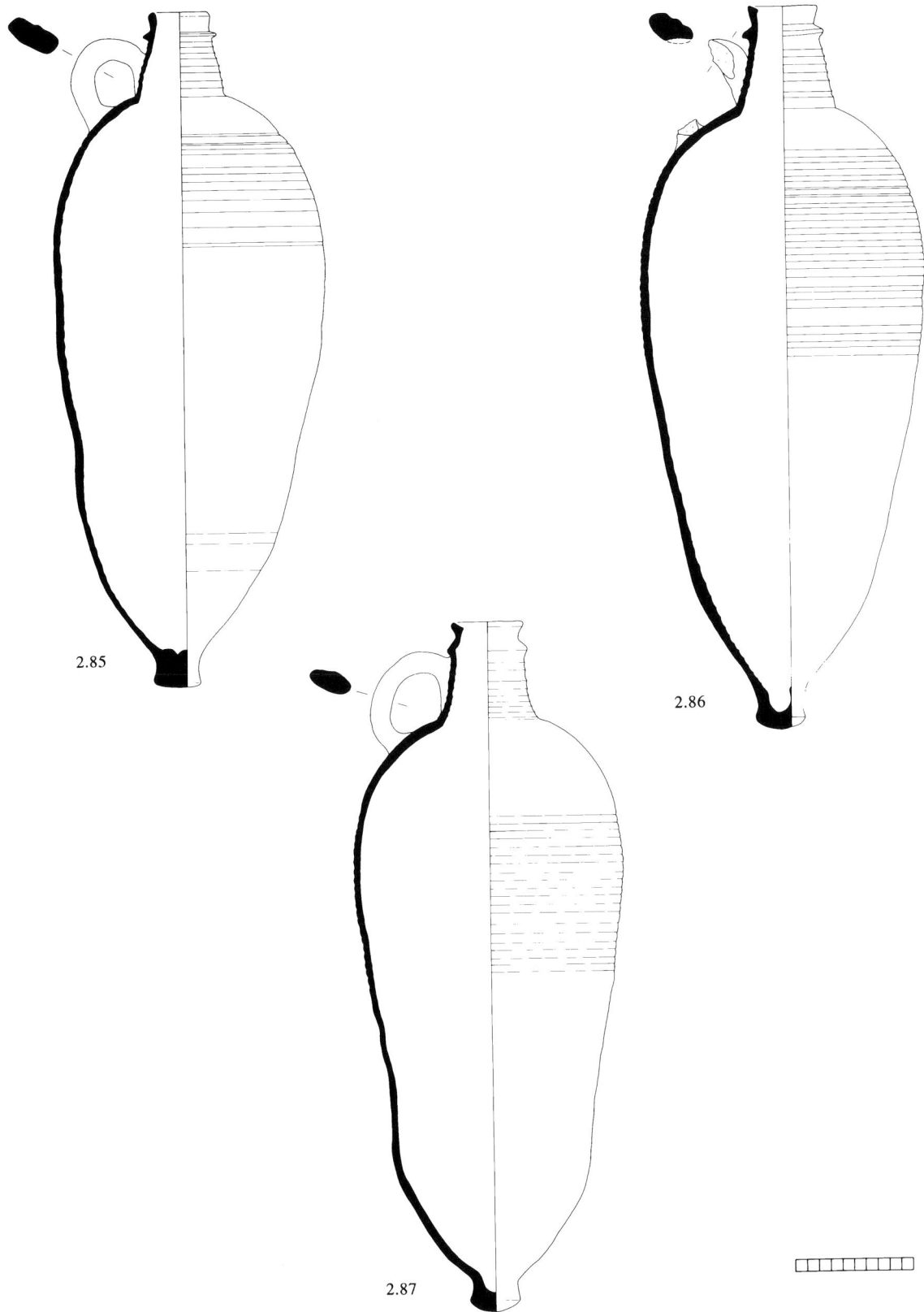

Fig. 19. Hilltop Well, Deposit 2, 1:5 (scale bar=0.10).

Fig. 20. **2.85** (P88.019/9565), **2.86** (P88.029/9581), **2.87** (P88.022/9572) Type A amphorae; **2.89** (P87.008/9389), **2.90** (P88.017/9562) Type B amphorae.

Medium coarse-grained reddish-yellow fabric (5YR 7/6 to 2/5YR 6/6), uniformly fired, with abundant mica and fine lime particles. Fusiform body with thick wall rising from solid toe, becoming much thinner above mid-vessel in tapering shoulder and tall neck with vertical rounded rim. Lower body marked by deep dragged grits, tears, and cracks from drying; upper body carries pronounced, widely spaced ridges spiraling up to neck. Exterior surface smoothed, mottled in firing from light red/pink to yellow/off-white, flaking. Single strap handle with central ridge, splayed attachment. Similar example: **2.90**. Cf. **1.32**.

2.91. Amphora LR1 (B5/8+). Fig. 21. Panel-ridged amphora. Coarse-grained fabric ranging from light red (2.5YR 6/6) core to very pale brown (10YR 8/4) ex-

terior, with fine particles of lime, quartz, and other dark inclusions. Similar examples: B5/8+ (body sherds in related fabrics ranging from yellow, 10YR 8/6 to 2.5Y 8/4). Cf. **1.33, 3.30**.

2.92. Amphora LR3 (B12). Fig. 21. Micaceous water jar. Est. D. rim 0.04. Light red fabric (10R 6/6 to 2.5YR 6/6), very micaceous; exterior dusky grayish-brown (2.5Y 5/2), smoothed. Tapering neck with thickened, slightly inturned rim. Similar example: **2.93**. Cf. **3.31–32**. See Riley 1979: 183–84, 229–30 for the distribution and likely origin of this amphora in western Asia Minor, perhaps in the Maeander Valley.

2.93. Amphora LR3 (B22). Not illustrated. Micaceous water jar with solid foot. D. base 0.03. Light red fab-

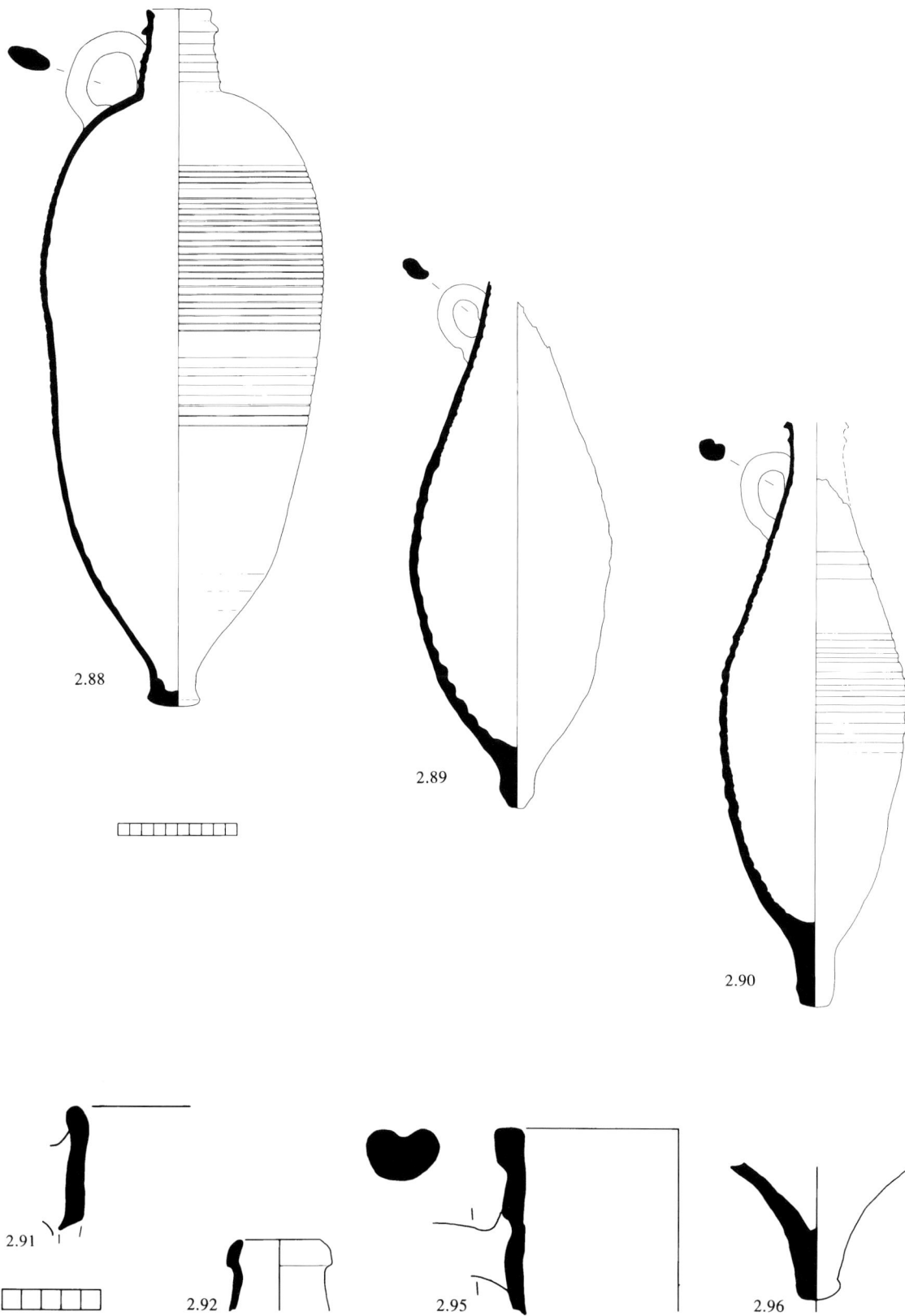

Fig. 21. Hilltop Well, Deposit 2, **2.88–2.90** 1:5 (scale bar=0.10); **2.91–2.96** 1:3 (scale bar=0.05).

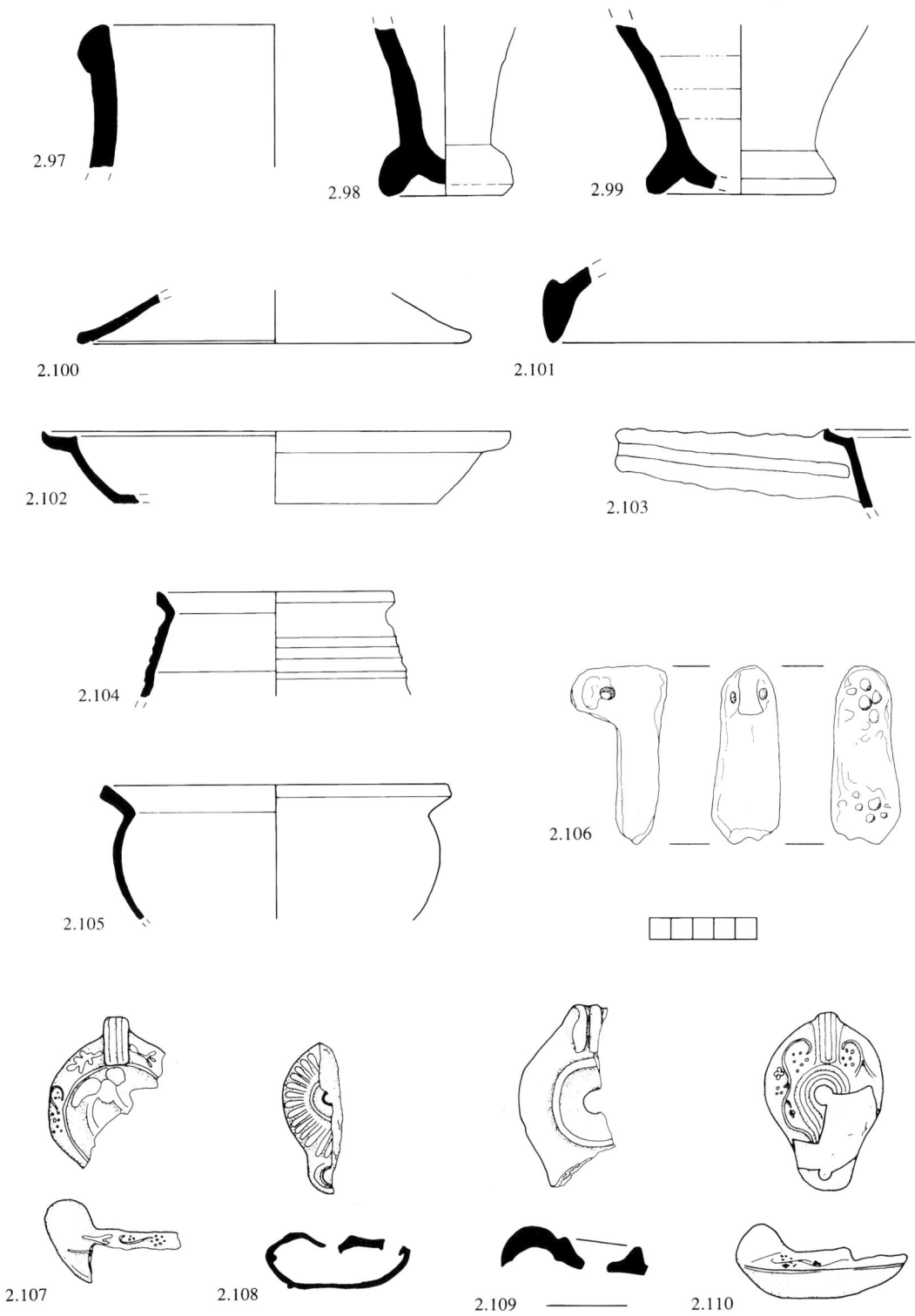

Fig. 22. Hilltop Well, Deposit 2, 1:3 (scale bar=0.05).

ric (2.5YR 6/8), very micaceous with a little lime. Roughly formed body with turning marks and deep dragged grits. Dribbled red slip exterior.

2.94. Amphora LR4 (B36). Not illustrated. Fragment of large cylindrical amphora, probably from the Gaza region. Coarse-grained dull light reddish-brown fabric (5YR 6/4–6/6) with scattered quartz and lime. Shoulder fragment with rough exterior grooving. See Riley 1979: 219–22 for the distribution and likely origin of this amphora.

2.95. Amphora (B25). Fig. 21. Amphora with thickened vertical rim. Est. D. rim 0.16. Coarse-grained pink fabric (7.5YR 7/4–8/6) with many large particles lime, quartz, black inclusions, and abundant mica in large gold flecks; sandy texture. Wide mouth with vertically thickened rim. Ovoid rolled handle with deep central groove. Related example: **2.96**.

2.96. Amphora (B25). Fig. 21. Conical amphora base. Same fabric as **2.94**; solid toe with flaring wall.

2.97. Amphora (B48). Fig. 22. North African amphora. Est. D. rim 0.16. Coarse-grained light red fabric (2.5YR 6/8) with darker core; small particles lime, quartz, scattered flecks of mica, and small voids. Thickened vertical rim. Surface roughly smoothed, with thin white matte wash. Similar example: B9. Cf. **1.37**.

2.98. Amphora/jar (B19). Fig. 22. Amphora/jar with ring foot base. Est. D. base 0.053. Medium-grained light reddish-brown fabric (5YR 6/4–7/8), unevenly fired, with a little lime, quartz, and fine mica. Low ring foot base with steep wall. Red dribbled slip exterior. Similar example: **2.99**.

2.99. Amphora/jar (B38). Fig. 22. Amphora/jar with ring foot base. Est. D. base 0.075. Very micaceous light red fabric (2.5YR 6/6); dark red dribbled slip on exterior and bottom floor of interior.

COOKING WARES

2.100. Lid (B11). Fig. 22. Conical lid in cooking fabric. Est. D. rim 0.18. Medium-grained reddish-yellow fabric (5YR 7/6). Sloping lid with straight conical side, rounded lip offset by slight interior groove.

2.101. Lid (B12). Fig. 22. Large conical lid in cooking fabric. Est. D. rim 034. Medium-coarse light red fabric (2.5YR 6/8) with large lime and quartz particles. Rounded rim offset from wall.

2.102. Pan (B12). Fig. 22. Frying pan with horizontal ledge rim. Est. D. rim 0.22. Coarse-grained red fabric

(2.5YR 4/6 to 5YR 4/6) with many large gold mica flecks and abundant quartz. Flat floor rises in low wall to horizontal ledge rim with slight inner and outer ridges; hollow tube handle (missing) probably attached as **2.103**. Similar examples: B15, B18.

2.103. Pan (B29). Fig. 22. Frying pan with horizontal ledge rim, tube handle. D. rim uncertain. Fabric and form similar to **2.102**; hollow tube handle, lightly ridged. Similar examples: B16, B29. Cf. Crawford 1990: fig. 536.

2.104. Cooking pot (B42). Fig. 22. Small pot with out-turned rim and fine exterior ridging. Est. D. rim 0.18. Coarse-grained gritty red fabric (2.5YR 4/6) with lighter core, abundant mica and quartz, other dark grits. Sloping wall with outturned rim; fine exterior ridging. Similar examples: B10, B25, B26, B35/38, B43. Cf. **1.39–40**.

2.105. Cooking pot (B11). Fig. 22. Small globular pot with outturned rim. Est. D. rim 0.16. Medium-grained light red fabric (2.5YR 6/8) with large quartz particles (to 0.002) and large gold mica flecks. Curved wall with broad outturned rim, slight exterior groove.

Terracotta

2.106. Loom weight (B36). Fig. 22. Loom weight with pierced handle. L. 0.079. Max. W. 0.031. Preserved weight 55 g. Coarse-grained light red fabric (2.5YR 6/8) with large quartz inclusions and small dark grits. Elongated weight with raised, pinched handle, pierced; back side scored with small round impressions.

OTHER PIECES

Lamps

2.107. Lamp (B15). Fig. 22. Mold-made lamp, part of handle and disc preserved. Fine-grained light brown fabric (7.5YR 6/4–7/4) with much mica. Disc with grooved rim enclosing winged genius(?) facing right, arm extended; shoulder decorated with leaves and vine with grapes; solid handle three grooves; fishtail on base. Dark red/black exterior slip. Cf. Bailey 1988: 383, no. Q3111, pl. 105 (from Ephesus) for the shoulder.

2.108. Lamp (B14). Fig. 22. Mold-made lamp, almost half preserved. Max. L. 0.069. Max. W. 0.028. Max. H. 0.026. Fine-grained light reddish-brown fabric (7.5YR 6/4 to 5YR 6/4) with a little lime and abundant mica. Plain disc with raised rim; sloping shoulder with long radiate petals or bars; underside

Fig. 23. 2.111, lamp.

offset by paired ridges; base rim with *planta pedis*.
Cf. Perlzweig 1961: no. 362, pl. 11; Bailey 1988:
417, no. Q3332, pl. 124 (sixth century).

2.109. Lamp (B20). Fig. 22. Mold-made lamp, slightly
over half of top preserved. Max. L. 0.084. Max. W.
0.052. Max. H. 0.020. Fine-grained pink fabric
(5YR 7/4–7/6), very micaceous, with traces of dark
red/black slip exterior. Deep-set, plain disc with tall,
raised collar rim, projecting spout; large hollow
handle with two sections preserved.

2.110. Lamp (B5/8). Fig. 22. Mold-made lamp, most of
bottom, top, and handle preserved. L. 0.082. W.
0.055. H. 0.035. Fine-grained reddish-yellow fabric
(5YR 6/6) with fine mica. Disc plain, with groove
extending around rim to spout; shoulder decorated
with vine scroll with leaves and grape clusters; solid
handle with three grooves; base ring with paired
ridges beneath spout, four ridges beneath handle.

2.111. Lamp (B11). Fig. 23. Mold-made lamp, half of top
preserved. Max. L. 0.047. W. 0.049. Fine-grained
light red fabric (10R 6/6) with abundant mica,
unslipped. Disc plain, with groove around rim,
continuing to spout and nozzle; rim decorated with
rows of raised, widely spaced dots; at least two
pairs of loops extend from nozzle to body.

Coins

2.112 (B18; 1987.46). Obscure, 383–395, AE4.

2.113 (B11; 1987.16). Obscure, 383–395, AE4. Cf. Carson, Hill, and Kent 1960: 89.

2.114 (B48; 1988.10). Honorius or Theodosius II (395–
450), AE. Cf. Carson, Hill, and Kent 1960: no. 2223;
Buttrey et al. 1981: no. 934.

2.115 (B15; 1987.25). Arcadius, Honorius, or Theodosius II (400/402), AE4. Cf. Carson, Hill, and Kent
1960: no. 2210–2212.

2.116 (B46; 1988.64). Leo (457–74), AE4, monogram 2.
Cf. Carson, Hill, and Kent 1960: 110.

2.117 (B17; 1987.17). Leo (457–74), AE4, standing lion.
Cf. Carson, Hill, and Kent 1960: no. 2258.

2.118 (B46; 1988.66). Zeno (474–91), AE4, monogram.
Cf. Carson, Hill, and Kent 1960: no. 2281; Buttrey
et al. 1981: no. 1107.

2.119 (B19; 1987.52). Anastasius (?), AE4.

2.120 (B17; 1987.38). Anastasius (?), AE, monogram?

2.121 (B15; 1987.23). Anastasius (491–517), AE, monogram. Cf. Carson, Hill, and Kent 1960: no. 2288.

2.122 (B15; 1987.29). Anastasius (491–517), AE4, monogram. Cf. Carson, Hill, and Kent 1960: no. 2288.

2.123 (B9; 1987.11). Anastasius (491–517), AE4,
monogram.

2.124 (B1; 1987.5). Obscure, sixth century, penta-
nummium.

Deposit 3 (B101–154)
Courtyard Well, early seventh century

FINE WARES

Residual

3.1. Dish (B144). Fig. 24. Dish with straight flaring wall.
Est. D. rim 0.38. Fine-grained light red fabric (10R
6/6) with clean break, little mica. Hard, weak red
slip interior and exterior (10R 4/4–4/6). Cf. Pinkwart and Stamnitz 1983: 138, no. K216 (second
century); Meyer-Schlichtmann 1988: 128, no. Sa27a
Kat. 235–37.

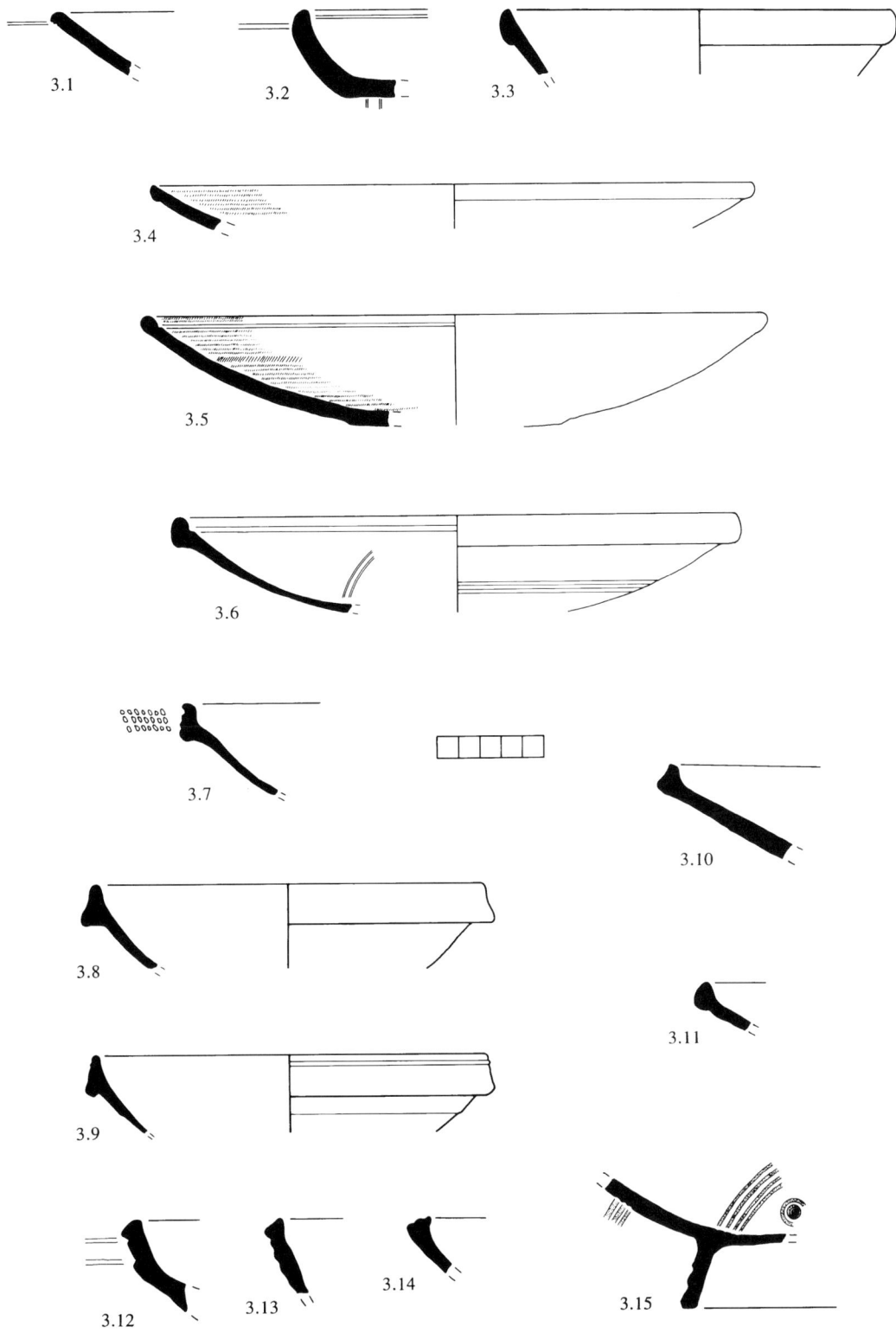

Fig. 24. Courtyard Well, Deposit 3, 1:3 (scale bar=0.05).

3.2. Plate (B104). Fig. 24. Broad plate with inturned vertical rim. Est. D. rim 0.34. Medium fine-grained light reddish-brown fabric (2.5YR 6/4) with fine silver mica in body. Worn red slip (10R 5/8) on interior and top of rim. Interior and exterior wall smoothed with a few large voids on surface; exterior more roughly finished.

African Red Slip

3.3. Bowl (B141). Fig. 24. Hayes form 99C, early sixth century. Est. D. rim 0.18. Medium-grained red fabric (2.5YR 5/8) with scattered lime and dark grits. Cf. **2.9**.

3.4. Dish (B106). Fig. 24. Hayes form 109, ca. 610/20–700 (Hayes 1992: 4). Est. D. rim 0.28. Medium-grained red fabric (2.5YR 5/8) with scattered lime and dark grits. Sloping wall with rounded lip and exterior offset. Rim and interior slipped and spiral burnished, badly pitted. Exterior wall smoothed, unslipped.

3.5. Dish (B146/150). Fig. 24. Hayes form 109 in 12 joining sherds. Est. D. rim 0.29. Coarse-grained red fabric (10R 5/6–5/8) with a little lime, quartz, and rare mica. Flat base, thick curving wall and plain rounded rim, set off by interior groove. Interior thickly slipped and spiral burnished, slightly pitted. Exterior rim irregularly slipped, lower exterior wall paddle smoothed and unslipped. Cf. Hayes 1968: 208, nos. 41–43 (in abundance).

Imitation African Red Slip

3.6. Dish (B146/149). Fig. 24. Imitation Hayes form 104C in nine joining sherds. Est. D. rim 0.24. Fine-grained reddish-yellow fabric (5YR 6/6) with abundant silver mica, fired gray core with a few small voids, dull texture and light density. Shallow, curving wall with thickened vertical rim, offset by interior groove. Interior and exterior covered with dull red slip (close to 10R 4/6), easily scratched. Two incised lines on floor, four lines on exterior wall.

Imitation Late Roman C

3.7. Dish (B152). Fig. 24. Imitation Hayes form 3F. D. rim uncertain. Medium fine-grained light red fabric (2.5YR 6/6) with some lime, quartz, and much mica. Sloping wall with rouletted rim. Interior smoothed, exterior scored by deeply dragged grits; rim fired slightly darker than wall.

3.8. Dish (B147). Fig. 24. Imitation Hayes form 3. Est. D. rim 0.18. Medium-grained reddish-yellow fabric (5YR 7/6) with lime, much mica, and large irregular voids. Sloping wall with rounded, thickened rim. Interior and exterior covered with dull red slip, badly flaking.

3.9. Dish (B150). Fig. 24. Imitation Hayes form 3F. Est. D. rim 0.18. Fine-grained reddish-yellow fabric (5YR 7/6) with a little lime and much mica. Sloping wall thickens to rounded lip with exterior flange. Slip light reddish-brown on interior; exterior fired to dull black and off-white, flaking.

Asia Minor Fabrics

3.10. Dish (B144). Fig. 24. Dish with straight wall and upturned lip. Est. D. rim 0.35. Medium fine-grained light red fabric (2.5YR 6/8 to 5YR 6/4) with abundant mica. Interior smoothed, slipped. Exterior less finely finished, covered with brown slip (about 7.5YR 5/8). Cf. Crawford 1990: fig. 253.

3.11. Dish (B145). Fig. 24. Dish with vertical rim. Est. D. rim 0.24. Medium fine-grained light reddish-brown fabric (2.5YR 6/4) with abundant mica. Rounded, thickened rim. Red slip interior; exterior rim and wall fired off-white.

3.12. Dish (B109). Fig. 24. Dish with vertical rim. Est. D. rim 0.22. Medium-coarse pink fabric (7.5YR 7/4) with abundant mica, many small, dark grits and several large voids. Straight wall continues into vertical rim with two exterior grooves. Light reddish-yellow slip interior and exterior, worn and flaking. Cf. **2.37**.

3.13. Dish (B151). Fig. 24. Dish with vertical rim. Est. D. rim 0.18. Medium-grained reddish-yellow fabric (7.5YR 8/6) with little mica. Plain vertical rim with raised lip, three ridges on exterior wall; mottled dark red slip.

3.14. Dish (B134). Fig. 24. Dish with vertical rim. Est. D. rim uncertain. Medium fine-grained light reddish-brown fabric (2.5YR 6/4) with abundant mica. Rim thickened, top grooved. Light red slip interior and top rim; thin wash exterior.

3.15. Dish (B151). Fig. 24. Dish with tall foot. Est. D. base 0.20. Medium-grained light reddish-yellow micaceous fabric (5YR 7/6); lime in fine particles, occasionally erupting through interior surface. Tall foot supports broad sloping floor, smoothed, decorated with circular stamp and concentric grooves. Exterior wall decorated with concentric grooves, scored by dragged grits. Base roughly made, with lightly ridged exterior. Similar example: B147. Cf. **2.41–42**; Hayes 1972: 409 fig. 92, 6 for floor grooving.

PLAIN WARES

3.16. Lid (B119). Fig. 25. Saucer-shaped lid with raised knob. D. rim uncertain. Coarse-grained light red fabric (2.5YR 6/6) with gray core; small particles lime, quartz, other grits to 0.003, and abundant mica in large gold flecks. Roughly made with curving wall and string-cut base; spindle knob handle with cracks around base. Interior and exterior smoothed. For similar lids see Crawford 1990: figs. 262, 537, 552; Jones 1950: fig. 210D–F; Hayes 1968: 214, no. 107; Bass 1982, 175, nos. P41, 42; Boardman 1989: 110 nos. 262–64; Williams 1989: 74–75, nos. 434–440).

3.17. Lid (B147). Fig. 25. Domed lid with hollow handle. D. handle 0.04. Medium fine-grained pink fabric (5YR 7/4) with scattered lime and mica. Incurving walls with hollow vertical handle. Thin off-white wash on exterior. Cf. Crawford 1990: fig. 107; Williams 1989: 73, no. 430.

3.18. Basin (B147). Fig. 25. Basin with outturned rim. Est. D. rim 0.38. Medium-grained pink fabric (5YR 7/4). Undulating vertical wall, lightly ridged, rises to plain outturned rim. Interior wall slipped, flaking.

3.19. Basin (B151). Fig. 25. Large basin with triangular rim. Est. D. rim 0.56. Medium-grained pink fabric (5YR 7/4–7/6) with abundant mica. Roughly made with many small voids in body. Heavy triangular rim decorated with incised wavy line.

3.20. Basin/bowl (B134). Fig. 25. Small basin/bowl with downturned rim. Est. D. rim 0.26. Medium-grained reddish-yellow fabric (5YR 7/6) with fine lime particles and abundant mica. Thin, flaring wall, externally ridged; slightly incurving rim with downturned flange.

3.21. Bowl (B150). Fig. 25. Small bowl with outturned rim. Est. D. rim 0.14. Medium coarse-grained reddish-yellow fabric (5YR 7/6) with abundant mica and fine lime particles. Steep wall with plain outturned rim. Interior smoothed; exterior deeply scored by dragged grits and small voids.

3.22. Bowl (B130). Fig. 25. Small bowl with vertical rim. Est. D. rim 0.16. Fine-grained light red fabric (2.5YR 6/8) with fine lime particles and abundant mica. Straight wall continues into slightly thickened vertical rim. Interior and exterior smoothed and lightly slipped.

3.23. Bowl (B150). Fig. 25. Small bowl with outturned rim. Est. D. 0.13. Medium-grained light reddish-brown fabric (5YR 6/4) with small lime particles and much gold mica. Rounded body narrows to short neck with outturned lip and downturned flange. Exterior wall lightly ridged and covered with light red slip.

3.24. Cup (B151). Fig. 25. Small cup with inturned rim. Est. D. rim 0.09. H. 0.055. Fine-grained light red fabric (2.5YR 6/6–6/8) with abundant mica and lime particles to 0.003. Small handleless cup with inturned rim, thickened lip. Interior smoothed; exterior ridged. Exterior base roughly cut with drawn string. Surface mottled by firing. Similar example: B147. See **2.74** for other examples.

3.25. Jar (B144). Fig. 25. Tall neck of large jar. Est. D. rim 0.13. Gritty grayish-brown fabric (10YR 5/2) with lime, quartz, and large gold mica flecks. Vertical wall with thickened rim; flattened strap handle.

3.26. Jar (B128). Fig. 26. Jar with outturned rim. Est. D. rim 0.15. Coarse-grained light red fabric (2.5YR 6/8) with lime, quartz, and gold mica flecks. Short neck with exterior ridge, plain rim.

3.27. Jug (B130). Fig. 26. Tall neck of jug. D. rim 0.035. Medium-grained light reddish-brown fabric (2.5YR 6/4) with abundant mica. Slender tapering neck with bowl-shaped rim and outturned lip; small strap handle attached at mid-neck. Exterior smoothed; interior and lip partially covered with dribbled black resin or mastic.

3.28. Unguentarium (B149). Fig. 26. Fusiform unguentarium. Est. D. rim 0.025–0.029. Fine-grained weak red fabric (10R 5/4) with fine lime particles, fired grayish and covered with darker slip. Cf. **2.83**.

3.29. Ampulla (B152). Fig. 26. Small lentoid flask with cross decoration. D. rim 0.022. Max. H. 0.063. Dull pale yellow fabric (2.5Y 8/4) with a little mica. Mold-made lentoid flask with two small, pierced handles; relief cross with circles between arms set within circle with raised dots. Dark slip poorly preserved on exterior. Cf. **2.82**; Crawford 1990: figs. 43, 155, 156; de Luca 1984: 35, nos. 300–303; Wintermeyer 1980: 159, no. 247, pl. 67.

AMPHORAE

3.30. Amphora LR1 (B151). Fig. 26. Est. D. rim 0.018. Coarse, sandy fabric, pale yellow (2.5Y 8/4 to 5Y 8/4). Many small, dark grits as well as lime (to 0.005) and quartz. Plain rounded rim. Thick grooved handles with splayed attachments. Dipinto at base of neck and shoulder. Cf. **1.33, 2.91**.

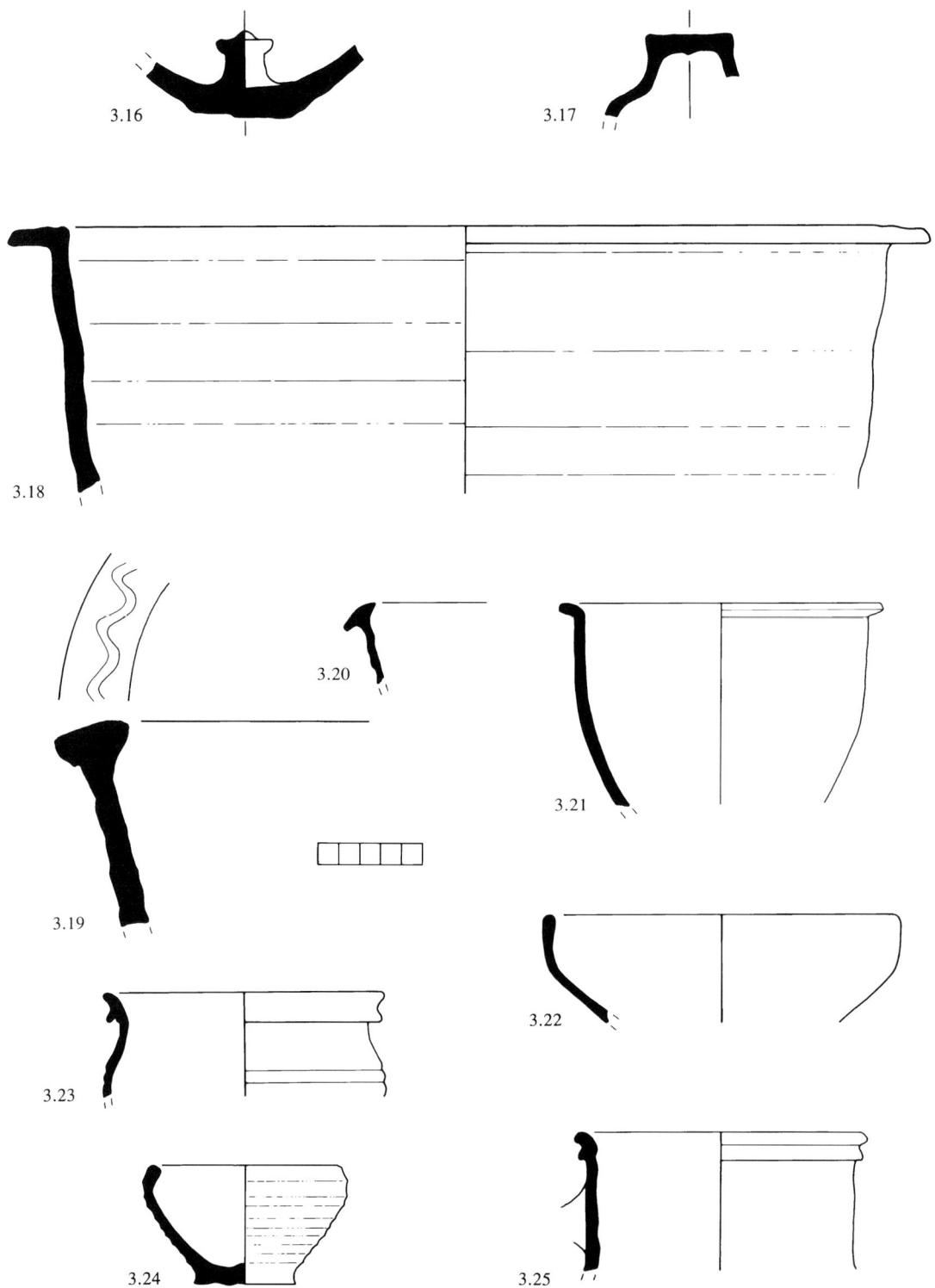

Fig. 25. Courtyard Well, Deposit 3, 1:3 (scale bar=0.05).

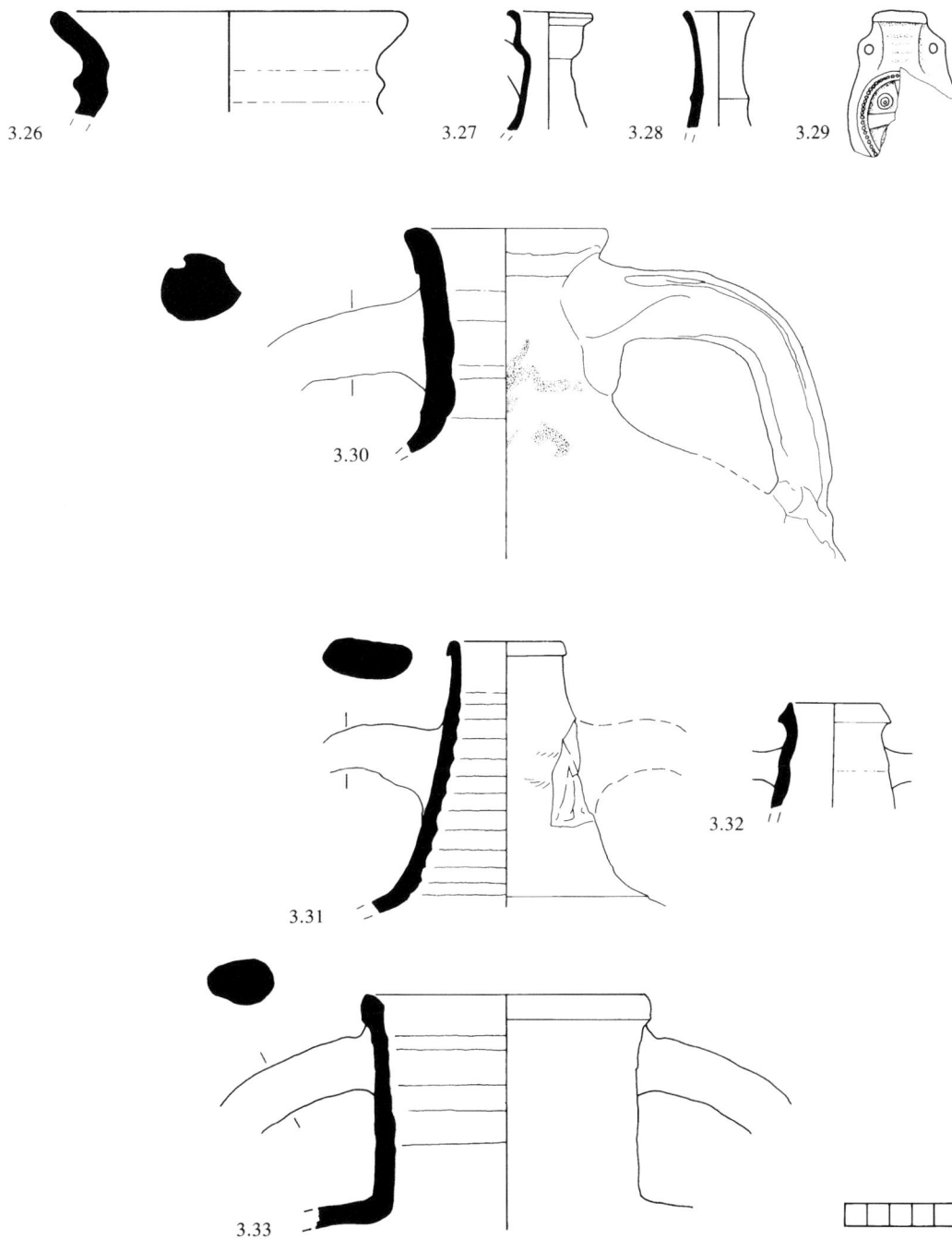

Fig. 26. Courtyard Well, Deposit 3, 1:3 (scale bar=0.05).

3.31. Amphora LR3 (B151). Fig. 26. Micaceous water jar. Est. D. rim 0.045. Soapy textured fabric, dark gray interior (5Y 4/1–4/2) to olive exterior (5Y 5/2–5/3); medium fine grained with only a little lime but abundant mica, including large silver flecks. Roughly made with sharp interior ridging, smoothed exterior.

Conical neck, plain lip, two splayed strap handles. Similar example: **3.32**. Cf. **2.92–93**.

3.32. Amphora LR3 (B111). Fig. 26. Micaceous water jar. Est. D. rim 0.04. Medium fine-grained light red fabric (2.5YR 6/6) with abundant mica. Tapering neck,

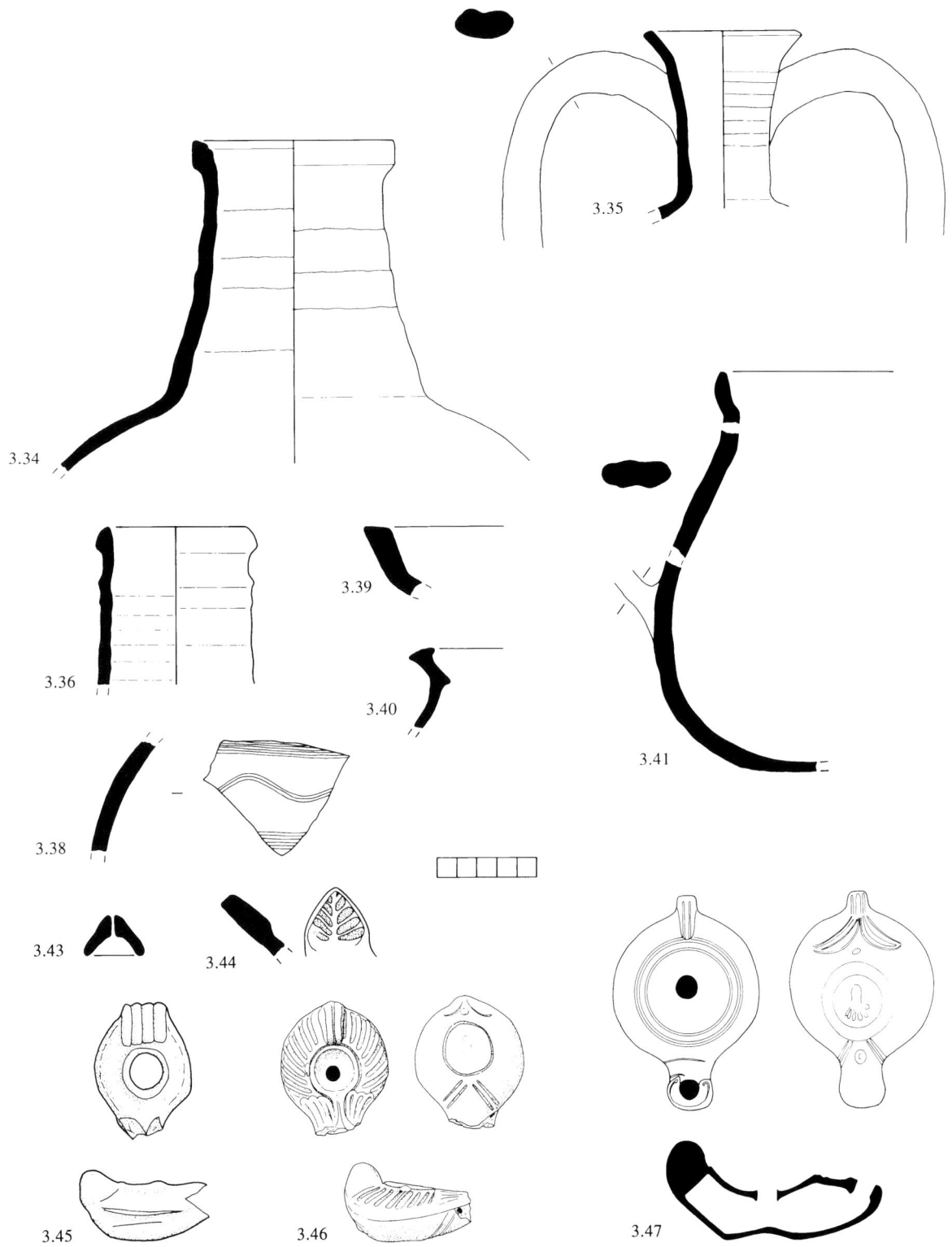

Fig. 27. Courtyard Well, Deposit 3, 1:3 (scale bar=0.05).

thickened rim, with splayed strap handle. Exterior smoothed, fired darker.

3.33. Amphora (B111). Fig. 26. Amphora with tall neck. Est. D. rim 0.12. Coarse light red fabric (2.5YR 6/8 with darker core), with abundant lime, quartz, dark grits to 0.002, and abundant mica especially on surface; uneven fracture with irregular voids in body. Interior lightly ridged; exterior smoothed with traces of a light off-white wash. Tall neck with thickened rim, highest at outer edge. Rolled handle ovoid in section. Three associated sherds suggest gently recessed bottom with broad curving wall. Similar examples: **3.34**, B106 (est. D. rim 0.07), B129 (est. D. rim 0.08).

3.34. Amphora (B111). Fig. 27. Amphora with tall neck. Est. D. 0.10. Same fabric as **3.33**. Slightly taller neck, lacking handles.

3.35. Amphora (B111/113). Fig. 27. Amphora with flaring mouth. Est. D. rim 0.07–0.08. Coarse-grained light red fabric (2.5YR 6/4) with lime, quartz, and dark grits to 0.002, and much mica on surface; clean fracture. Exterior smoothed. Lightly ridged neck flares to plain outturned rim; high handles with central groove.

3.36. Amphora/jar (B106). Fig. 27. Amphora/jar with vertical rim. Est. D. rim 0.07. Medium-grained light reddish-brown fabric (2.5YR 6/4) with lime, quartz, and abundant mica. Vertical neck with thickened rim; lightly ridged interior, smoothed exterior.

3.37. Amphora/jar (B154). Not illustrated. Amphora/jar with wavy line incised decoration. Coarse pink to light reddish-brown fabric (5YR 6/4–7/4) with scattered lime, quartz, and mica. Thick wall, smoothed exterior with horizontal three- to five-toothed combed bands spaced 0.005–0.015 apart. Similar example: **3.38**.

3.38. Amphora/jar (B109). Fig. 27. Amphora/jar with wavy line incised decoration. Medium-grained light red fabric (2.5YR 6/8) with lime particles to 0.002, fine dark grits and mica flecks. Shoulder fragment with combed decoration: two horizontal bands flank a three-toothed wavy pattern.

COOKING WARES

3.39. Dish (B106). Fig. 27. Thick walled vessel with vertical rim. Est. D. rim 0.40. Fabric and slip resemble Pompeian Red Slip ware. Very coarse-grained pink fabric (5YR 7/4) with a little mica and many large irregular grits in body, including lime, quartz, and

voids to 0.003. Straight wall with vertical rim. Smoothed interior with darker finish; flaking red slip interior, top an exterior of rim.

3.40. Pot (B143). Fig. 27. Globular cooking pot. Est. D. rim 0.18. Coarse-grained light brown fabric (7.5YR 6/4) with gray core, quartz particles to 0.002, and abundant mica. Outturned thickened rim with interior ledge. Interior and exterior covered with gray/black slip. Similar examples: B147, 151. Cf. **1.40**.

3.41. Glazed pot (B109/112). Fig. 27. Globular cooking pot with lead glaze interior in 18 sherds. D. rim uncertain. Coarse-grained red fabric (10R 5/6), mostly darkened by use; uneven fracture, with quartz and silver and gold mica flecks. Rim outturned with slight interior ledge. Rounded bottom with thick rising wall; root of strap handle suggests a central groove or ridge. Interior fully covered with vitreous yellow-green glaze, running to dark purple and black where thickest; a few splashes of glaze also on exterior wall. Positive laboratory test for lead. Similar example: **3.42**. Cf. Hayes 1968: 205, no. 19.

3.42. Glazed pot (B107). Not illustrated. Cooking pot with lead glaze interior. D. rim uncertain. Medium coarse-grained pale red fabric (10R 6/4) with small voids, a little lime and quartz, and large gold mica flecks. Interior surface covered with a thick coat of dark brownish-yellow glaze fired to a hard finish, with a single splash on exterior.

OTHER PIECES

Terracotta

3.43. Wickholder? (B146). Fig. 27. Pierced conical object. Max. D. 0.030; H. 0.019. Medium-grained light red fabric (2.5YR 6/6) with scattered quartz and abundant mica. Similar example: B147. Variously identified as counters, gaming pieces, weights, or wickholders, similar objects appear frequently at Sardis (Crawford 1990: e.g., 37, fig. 125) and other sites.

Lamps

3.44. Lamp (B109). Fig. 27. Mold-made lamp handle. Max. L. 0.035. Fine-grained light reddish-yellow fabric (7.5YR 8/6) with abundant mica. Mold-made palmette handle; uneven red slip. Cf. Wintermeyer 1980: 158, nos. 243–44, pls. 66, 67; Vitelli 1982: 190–91, nos. L1–3, figs. 9-2, 9-4; Bailey 1988: 392–93, nos. Q3204–5, Q3208, pl. 114 (from Ephesus).

3.45. Lamp (B144). Fig. 27. Mold-made lamp, missing nozzle and handle fragment. Max. L. 0.066. Max.

Fig. 28. **3.46** (L85.011/9006), lamp.

Fig. 29. **3.48**, chisel head; **3.49**, hook; **3.50**, revetment pin?

W. 0.05. H. 0.035. Medium-grained light red fabric (2.5YR 6/8 to 5YR 7/6) with a little lime and abundant mica. Large open filling hole with raised rim, plain wall; molded handle with four ribs; base ring with faint *planta pedis*, much worn. Cf. Crawford 1990: fig. 264; Bailey 1988: 395, no. Q3216, pl. 114 (from Sardis).

3.46. Lamp (B127; L85.011/9006). Figs. 27, 28. Mold-made lamp, missing nozzle. Max. L. 0.065. Max. W. 0.055. H. 0.040. Fine-grained light red fabric (2.5YR 6/8) with fine mica. Plain disc with raised rim extending to spout; sloping shoulder with long radiate petals or bars, three paired loops extend toward nozzle; base ring with *planta pedis*; paired ridges under spout.

3.47. Lamp (B152; L85.026/9051). Fig. 27. Mold-made lamp, intact. L. 0.014. W. 0.073. H. 0.048. Fine-grained light red fabric with fine mica. Plain disc with raised grooved rim and undecorated sloping shoulder; projecting spout with heart-shaped nozzle; handle solid with three grooves and fishtail on base;

base ring with six-toed *planta pedis*; paired ridges and dotted circle under spout. Light red slip.

Metals

3.48. Small chisel head, iron (B108). Fig. 29. Max. L. 0.039. Head W. 0.018. Symmetrically splayed, flattened head with curved edge, originally continuous with shaft (broken). Cf. Waldbaum 1983: 52, no. 154.

3.49. Small hook, iron (B108). Fig. 29. Max. L. 0.062. Max. W. 0.027. Th. 0.005. Irregularly shaped suspension hook with rounded ends. Cf. Waldbaum 1983: 81 for various steelyard parts; Davidson 1952: 194, nos. 1450–51 for lamp hooks (copper alloy).

3.50. Revetment pin(?), iron (B108). Fig. 29. Max. L. 0.082. Max. W. 0.01. Irregular shaft, square in section, tapering to flattened points at either end. Cf. Waldbaum 1983: 55.

3.51. Shaft, iron (B151). Not illustrated. Max. L. 0.34. Straight shaft, squarish section, with flattened attachment (for suspension hook?), very corroded. Probably beam from steelyard set. Cf. Waldbaum 1983: 80–81, nos. 435–37; Davidson 1952: 207–8, 214–16, nos. 1661–69 (copper alloy).

Coins

3.52 (B154; 1985.205). Obscure, fifth century, AE4, monogram.

3.53 (B154; 1985.204). Obscure, fifth/sixth century, AE.

3.54 (B146; 1985.174). Obscure, sixth century, decanummium.

3.55 (B147; 1985.177). Obscure, sixth century, decanummium?

3.56 (B150; C85.16). Justinian I (527–538), half-follis, Constantinople. Cf. Bellinger 1966: 81, no. 33c.2.

CONCLUSIONS

The two wells at Sector MMS preserve important evidence concerning life in one quarter of Late Roman Sardis. The fine ceramic wares, supported to a limited extent by the coins, offer a consistent chronological framework for distinguishing three deposits among their contents. Clearly residual sherds appear only sporadically, and a broad range of fine, plain, and coarse wares includes imported objects as well as vessels of regional or local origin.

The value of the wells as archaeological deposits naturally is conditioned by their context. Deep wells offer linear deposits with potentially good stratigraphy and minimal contamination. Excavation of these two wells yielded more than 11,000 sherds in addition to a dump of partially reconstructable amphorae. The lack of complete drawing vessels from use levels and the multiple joins noted among different baskets, however, demonstrate that the contents are substantially redeposited and probably highly localized. Study of the pottery took place over eight years using different recording procedures, which have left some gaps in the quantified data. As is often the case with well deposits, moreover, reconstructable vessel types tend to be overrepresented in the summary counts and weights. Legible coins are few and date significantly earlier than the pottery. Despite these limitations, comparison of the three deposits suggests basic patterns in the ceramics used at Sardis in late antiquity.

In all three deposits, African Red Slip ware provides the firmest chronological benchmarks. Discounting earlier survivals, the contexts of individual sherds generally agree with accepted chronologies.

TABLE 1. Fine Ware, by Count

Ware	Deposit 1 No.	Deposit 1 %	Deposit 2 No.	Deposit 2 %	Deposit 3 No.	Deposit 3 %
African Red Slip	5	18	19	9	4	10
Late Roman C	7	25	38	19	0	0
Imitation Late Roman C	14	50	116	59	19	48
Asia Minor fabrics	2	7	25	13	17	42
Total	28	100	198	100	40	100

Only Hayes form 67 appears in the late fifth century deposit (**1.3**), but the later sixth-century levels include multiple forms extending down to 91, 99, and 104A (**2.8–10**). The distribution of this very small number follows previously suggested patterns of supply in the eastern Mediterranean, which apparently rebounded in the sixth century with Justinian's campaigns in North Africa (Hayes 1972; Abadie-Reynal 1989). The ware not only continued to reach the site through the late sixth century but it also spawned regional imitations of familiar forms in a dull, unevenly fired micaceous fabric with a thick red slip (**3.6**). The Courtyard Well contained two examples of the spiral burnished dish form 109 (**3.4–5**), which appears to have been primarily a seventh-century form (Hayes 1992).

The only other imported fine wares appear to be western Anatolian products. Late Roman C ware, which was produced along the coast, seems to have arrived at Sardis a little ahead of the more distant African Red Slip products. The appearance in the lower Hilltop Well of the dish with slightly offset horizontal rim (Hayes form 5B, **1.6**) points to an origin for the form by the later fifth century. The Hilltop Well's late sixth-century upper levels present a wide variety of the form 3 dish, with the later forms 3E–F occurring together with the large forms 3B–C, which are probably survivals by this time (**2.12–18**). Yet the unmistakable form 10, widely distributed from 570 (e.g., Waagé 1948: 53; Hayes 1968: 208 [=1992 Deposit 30]; Williams 1977: 190; Wintermeyer 1980: 155–56; Bass 1982: 167; Boardman 1989: 92–94) is altogether absent from this late sixth-century deposit (and uncommon at Sardis as a whole), while the early seventh-century Courtyard Well produced no Late Roman C ware at all. The ware's disappearance in the early seventh century is usually attributed to Persian and Arab campaigns in the eastern Mediterranean; at Sardis its eclipse occurs earlier and for unrelated reasons.

Late Roman C ware seems to have been challenged at Sardis by local imitations, which outnumber the standard fabric in all three deposits and across the site (Table 1). The most popular vessels include a series of shallow dishes, frequently rouletted, in endless variation of Hayes form 3 (**1.7–10, 2.24–33, 3.7–9**). The distinctively fine-grained micaceous fabric closely resembles Archaic through Hellenistic and late Byzantine pottery found at the site and appears consistent with the local geology, whose metamorphic schists and gniesses reveal in thin section particles of quartz, chert, schist, and abundant muscovite and biotite (Scott and Kamilli 1981; Hughes, Leese, and Smith 1988: 479). Superficially similar examples have been reported at other Aegean sites, although not in this number (e.g., at Ephesus; Mitsopoulos-Leon 1991: 141). It seems that these vessels took over the local market with one standard shape in the 500s. After the middle of the sixth century Late Roman C and African Red Slip wares appear less frequently at Sardis.

The wells also produced a few scattered examples of other regional fabrics. These light textured wares remain poorly understood, lacking typology, dates, and likely proveniences. Their variety suggests several production centers. The relative infrequency of Late Roman Light Colored wares points away from Sardis as a likely source. Only the horizontal rim with elaborate rouletting appears in the late fifth-century deposit (**1.11**). It is joined by curved rim and vertical forms in the later sixth-century levels (**2.34–40**). In the early seventh-century Courtyard Well deposit appeared a tall footed dish with stamped decoration (**3.15**), similar to the champlevé plates found below sixth-century floors nearby (cf. Greenewalt, Rautman, and Cahill 1987: 62, fig. 6).

The abundant plain and cooking wares changed little from the late fifth through the early seventh centuries. Certain forms appear in all three deposits: a small cup with string-cut base (e.g., **2.74–75**), a small, thin-walled, frequently rouletted bowl (e.g., **2.69–71**), a hemispherical jug with recessed, molded base (e.g., **2.80**), and a globular cooking pot with everted rim (e.g., **1.39–40**). All are made of very micaceous fabric with much lime and quartz. Deep basins occur in all contexts and exhibit only minor changes in rim form; for example, incised wavy line patterns (e.g., **2.53, 2.55**) occur in all three deposits, but plain outturned

rims (e.g., **2.48–50**) tend to be earlier and down-turned rims later (e.g., **2.56–58**). Imported Late Roman unguentaria (e.g., **2.83–84**) appear in all levels (and in other fifth-century contexts at Sardis), suggesting that they may have originated a little earlier than is usually suggested. Most are of the standard type: wheelmade with flat base, thick wall, thin neck, and an irregularly dribbled exterior slip; none of the well examples is stamped. The fabric is typically reddish or overfired to slate blue-gray. One base, crudely made in a soft orange-red micaceous fabric, may belong to a local variation.

Of particular interest are fragments of two cooking pots with glazed interiors found in the Courtyard Well (**3.41–42**). The origin of lead-glazed pots remains unsettled but is generally assigned to the mid-seventh century (Hayes 1968: 216; Bass 1982: 165–67; Williams 1989: 68). At Sardis this date is reinforced by the appearance in the same deposit of two examples of a late African Red Slip ware dish (Hayes form 109, **3.4–5**), which occurs throughout the 600s. These late forms are exceptional in the well, however, and the lack of mid-seventh-century coins at the sector argues for a somewhat earlier date. On the other hand, no lead-glazed cooking pots were observed in the extensive debris of the nearby Byzantine Shops, which were destroyed in the early 600s. Too little is known of provincial seventh-century ceramics to answer the question.

Amphorae formed the largest part of the contents of both wells. Present in all strata, they constitute a special assemblage in the upper Hilltop Well, where about thirty examples of two distinctive types were dumped in the late sixth century. These vessels appear related in fabric and form. Both are single-handle jars made in a highly micaceous fabric. Type A is a large ovoid vessel in a dull dark fabric, often formed with a hollow toe, and whose exterior body is partially grooved and slipped (e.g., **2.85–88**). The fabric of Type B appears harder and lighter, and was less carefully potted into a more slender fusiform shape with solid toe (e.g., **2.89–90**). In all three deposits Type B appears to have been five to fifteen times more common than Type A (Table 2). Considered together, these two vessel types comprise at least a third of all amphorae from the wells.

The closest parallel to these two vessel types is the well-known micaceous water jar LR3. Yet single-handle versions of this vessel flourished much earlier and were superseded elsewhere by double-handle jars

TABLE 2. Amphorae, by Count and Weight

Type	Deposit 1				Deposit 2*			Deposit 3			
	Count		Weight		Count		Weight	Count		Weight	
	No.	%	Kg.	%	No.	%		No.	%	Kg.	%
Type A	100	3	2.1	3	233	4	NA	148	7	2.6	7
Type B	1327	40	28.4	44	1770	30	NA	809	36	11.5	33
LR1	431	13	11.6	18	233	4	NA	28	1	0.6	2
LR2	27	1	1.9	3	2	trace	NA	2	trace	trace	
Other	1447	43	19.8	31	3959	62	NA	1271	56	20.2	58
Total	3332	100	63.8	100	5812	100	NA	2258	100	34.9	100

*Excludes amphora deposit in B5/8, which rim/handle tallies indicate comprised at least nine examples of Type A (23.1 kg) and at least 20 examples of Type B (37.3 kg).

in the late fourth or early fifth century (Lang 1955; Robinson 1959: 17; Riley 1979: 183). It seems reasonable to suggest that both of the well types were produced near Sardis. The fabric closely resembles earlier local wares and both forms are common at the site, although unreported elsewhere. On the other hand, the continuity of large single-handle transport jars down through the sixth century departs from the experience of most Aegean sites, where such vessels usually are considered residual by this date. As if to reinforce the point, the Courtyard Well yielded the neck of a LR3 jar with two handles in its distinctive dark gray fabric (**3.31**). Its presence in standard fabric and shape emphasizes the relative scarcity of this important vessel type near its suggested source in the Maeander Valley, which stood separated from Sardis by the towering Tmolus range (Riley 1979: 183–84; Peacock and Williams 1986: 188–90).

Other imported amphorae occur less frequently and mostly in Deposit 1, the lower Hilltop Well (Table 2). In these late fifth-century levels, identifiable imports account for almost 20 percent of all amphorae. The most frequent visitor is the sandy panel-ridged vessel (LR1, e.g., **3.30**) now associated with Cilicia, north Syria, and Cyprus (13 percent by count, 18 percent by weight). Next is the funnel necked, spiral grooved jar (LR2, e.g., **1.34–35**), which is widely reported among Aegean and Black Sea sites (1 percent by count, 3 percent by weight). North African amphorae are represented by several large fragments (e.g., **1.37, 2.97**), while a few sherds of Gaza amphorae (e.g., **2.94**) attest limited contact with Palestine. Only LR1 appears in any significant quantity in the later levels: 4 percent by count in Deposit

2, and 1 percent by count (2 percent by weight) in Deposit 3. Even though the sample is significantly affected by the presence of single vessels, the three deposits suggest a drop in the distribution of these vessels that corresponds to the quantified data from other sites (e.g., Carthage, Benghazi, Argos, Thasos, Constantinople). Sardis' inland location, far removed from major sea lanes, likely increased its dependence on local vessels for table and transport.

Further study will show how representative these wells are of Sardis as a whole. Redeposited material need not preserve the best record of contemporary use, of course, but the larger patterns of fine wares and amphorae seem appropriate for the site's location. The prominence of distinctive local forms illustrates both how great a variety can exist among neighboring centers and how little is known of the region's pottery.

Considered together, these two wells add further depth to our understanding of Late Roman Sardis. Their installation records two moments in the life of a neighborhood, one predating the area's systematic development and the other forming an important part of one local residence. The reasons for abandonment remain speculative. The Hilltop Well was closed during a time of urban prosperity, its role apparently taken over by public fountains. Several of the quarter's houses were rebuilt in the late fifth century, and the completion of work may have lessened local demand. The accumulation of animal bone and building debris makes clear the well's purposeful infilling and may reflect the area's general cleanup. Settling of contents or resumed activity led to further dumping in the late sixth century, at a time when the city's water supply had apparently failed and the surrounding houses were being abandoned. The amphora deposit seems to reflect the sector's changed circumstances, as does the industrial reuse of a nearby residential space (Greenewalt, Ratté, and Rautman 1993: 11).

By contrast, the Courtyard Well may have functioned until its house was finally abandoned in the early seventh century (Rautman 1995: 62–63). As an independent source of water it may have attracted

the quarter's last residents after the municipal supply had ceased. By this time earlier domestic routines had given way to haphazard occupation of isolated rooms, stripped of furnishings and cluttered with debris. When the well was finally closed the pottery at hand was relatively sparse and included mostly regional vessels long used at the site. Only a couple of late African plates and glazed cooking pots reached this corner of Sardis to mark the arrival of the seventh century and the city's post-classical age.

NOTES

[1] Sardis has been the subject of excavation and study by the joint Harvard–Cornell expedition since 1958. Work has been carried out at Sector MMS since 1977 under the direction of Crawford H. Greenewalt, Jr., whom I thank for allowing me to excavate and study these wells and for patiently awaiting this report. My thanks also go to Andrew Ramage, Kathleen Warner Slane, and Jane Ayer Scott for discussing the pottery with me and commenting on an earlier draft of this article. For preliminary identifications of the coins I am indebted to several expedition numismatists, especially Katherine Welch and Mary Jane Rein. Expedition draftsperson Cathy Alexander produced several of the more complex drawings, including the six reconstructed amphorae, and advised me in drawing many others.

[2] The well was cleared to *104.7 in 1986, to *95.25 in 1987, and to *82.1 in 1988; see Greenewalt 1990: 8–9; Greenewalt, Ratté, and Rautman 1993: 11.

[3] Similar terracotta liners are known in earlier contexts especially in Athens; e.g., Robinson 1959: 73 (De-

posit F19:1), 82 (Deposit M17:1); Gruben 1970: 122, fig. 6.

[4] The top 3.1 m were cleared in 1982. Excavation in 1985 took 14 days; see Greenewalt, Rautman, and Cahill 1987: 60–61.

[5] A local source for some forms was suggested by Hayes 1972: 336, 370. The fabric resembles local pottery produced in Archaic and Middle Byzantine times. Other imitations of LRC may have been produced along the coast and have been noted elsewhere: Eiwanger 1981: 38 (Demetrias); de Luca 1984: 21 (Pergamon); Boardman 1989: 90–96 (Emborio); Williams 1989: 52–53 (Anemurium).

[6] The most common eastern Mediterranean amphorae are conveniently identified by the Michigan Carthage series (Riley 1981; Abadie-Reynal 1989), although other, more complex typologies also have been proposed (Peacock and Williams 1986; Hayes 1992).

[7] I thank Kathleen Warner Slane for suggestions about this piece.

REFERENCES

Abadie-Reynal, C.
  1989 Céramique et commerce dans le bassin égéen du IVᵉ au VIIᵉ siècle. Pp. 143–59 in *Hommes et richesses dans l'empire byzantin I. IVᵉ–VIIᵉ siècle.* Paris: P. Lethielleux.
Abadie-Reynal, C., and Sodini, J.-P.
  1992 *La céramique paléochétienne de Thasos.* Études Thasiennes 13. Paris: de Boccard.
Bailey, D. M.
  1988 *A Catalogue of the Lamps in the British Museum III. Roman Provincial Lamps.* London: British Museum.
Bass, G. F.
  1982 The Pottery. Pp. 155–88 in *Yassi Ada I. A Seventh-Century Byzantine Shipwreck,* eds. G. F. Bass and F. H. van Doorninck. College Station, TX: Texas A and M University.

Bellinger, A. R.
  1966 *Catalogue of the Byzantine Coins in the Dumbarton Oaks Collection and in the Whittemore Collection I. Anastasius I to Maurice, 491–602.* Washington: Dumbarton Oaks.
Boardman, J.
  1989 The Pottery. Pp. 86–142 in *Excavations in Chios 1952–1955. Byzantine Emborio,* M. Ballance, J. Boardman, S. Corbett, and S. Hood. British School at Athens Supplement 20. Athens: British School.
Buttrey, T. V.; Johnston, A.; MacKenzie, K. M.; and Bates, M. L.
  1981 *Greek, Roman, and Islamic Coins from Sardis.* Archaeological Exploration of Sardis Monograph 7. Cambridge, MA: Harvard.

Carson, R. A. G.; Hill, P. V.; and Kent, J. P. C.
  1960   *Late Roman Bronze Coinage.* London: Spink.
Catling, H. W., and Dikigoropoulos, A. I.
  1970   The Kornos Cave: An Early Byzantine Site in
          Cyprus. *Levant* 2: 37–62.
Crawford, J. S.
  1990   *The Byzantine Shops at Sardis.* Archaeological
          Exploration of Sardis Monograph 9. Cam-
          bridge, MA: Harvard.
Davidson, G. R.
  1952   *The Minor Objects. Corinth XII.* Princeton:
          American School of Classical Studies at Athens.
Delougaz, P., and Haines, R. C.
  1960   *A Byzantine Church at Khirbat al-Karak.* Ori-
          ental Institute Publications 85. Chicago: The
          Oriental Institute of the University of Chicago.
de Luca, G.
  1984   *Das Asklepieion 4. Teil. Via Tecta und Hallen-
          strasse. Die Funde. Altertümer von Pergamon
          XI.* Berlin: de Gruyter.
Eiwanger, J.
  1981   *Demetrias IV. Keramik und Kleinfunde aus
          der Damokratia-Basilika in Demetrias.* Bonn:
          Habelt.
Empereur, J.-Y., and Picon, M.
  1986   A propos d'un nouvel atelier de 'Late Ro-
          man C.' *Figlina* 7: 143–46.
Foss, C.
  1976   *Byzantine and Turkish Sardis.* Archaeological
          Exploration of Sardis Monograph 4. Cam-
          bridge, MA: Harvard.
Fulford, M. G., and Peacock, D. P. S.
  1984   *Excavations at Carthage: The British Mission I,
          2. The Avenue du President Habib Bourguiba,
          Salammbo: The Pottery and Other Ceramic
          Objects from the Site.* Sheffield, Eng.: University
          of Sheffield.
Greenewalt, C. H., Jr.
  1990   The Sardis Campaign of 1987. *Bulletin of the
          American Schools of Oriental Research Supple-
          ment* 27: 1–28.
Greenewalt, C. H., Jr.; Ratté, C.; and Rautman, M. L.
  1993   The Sardis Campaigns of 1988 and 1989.
          *Annual of the American Schools of Oriental
          Research* 51: 1–43.
Greenewalt, C. H., Jr.; Rautman, M. L.; and Cahill, N. D.
  1987   The Sardis Campaign of 1985. *Bulletin of the
          American Schools of Oriental Research Supple-
          ment* 25: 55–92.
Gruben, G.
  1970   Der Dipylon-Brunnen B1. Lage und Befund.
          Datierung des Dipylon. *Athenische Mittei-
          lungen* 85: 114–28.
Hanfmann, G. M. A.
  1983   *Sardis from Prehistoric to Roman Times.*
          Cambridge, MA: Harvard.

Hayes, J. W.
  1968   A Seventh-century Pottery Group. Pp. 203–
          16 in R. M. Harrison and N. Firatli. *Ex-
          cavations at Saraçhane in Istanbul: Fifth
          Preliminary Report, Dumbarton Oaks Papers*
          22: 195–216.
  1971   A New Type of Early Christian Ampulla. *An-
          nual of the British School at Athens* 66: 243–48.
  1972   *Late Roman Pottery.* London: British School
          at Rome.
  1980   *Supplement to Late Roman Pottery.* London:
          British School at Rome.
  1985   Sigillate Orientali. Pp. 1–96 in *Enciclopedia
          dell'arte classica e orientale. Atlante delle forme
          ceramiche II. Ceramica fine romana nel bacino
          mediterraneo.* Rome: Instituto della enciclope-
          dia italiana.
  1992   *Excavations at Saraçhane in Istanbul II. The
          Pottery.* Princeton, NJ: Princeton University.
Hughes, M. J.; Leese, M. N.; and Smith, R. J.
  1988   The Analysis of Pottery Lamps Mainly from
          Western Anatolia, Including Ephesus, by Neu-
          tron Activation Analysis. Pp. 461–85 in *A Cat-
          alogue of the Lamps in the British Museum III.
          Roman Provincial Lamps,* ed. D. M. Bailey.
          London: British Museum.
Johnson, B.
  1981   *Pottery from Karanis. Excavations of the Uni-
          versity of Michigan.* Ann Arbor: University of
          Michigan.
Jones, F. F.
  1950   The Pottery. Pp. 149–296 in *Excavations at
          Gözlü Kule, Tarsus I. The Hellenistic and Ro-
          man Periods,* ed. H. Goldman. Princeton, NJ:
          Princeton University.
Lang, M.
  1955   Dated Jars of Early Imperial Times. *Hesperia*
          24: 277–85.
Martini, W., and Steckner, C.
  1993   *Das Gymnasium von Samos. Das frühby-
          zantinische Klostergut. Samos XVII.* Bonn:
          Habelt.
Mayet, F., and Picon, M.
  1986   Une sigilée phocéenne tardive (Late Roman C
          ware) et sa diffusion en Occident. *Figlina* 7:
          129–42.
Meyer-Schlichtmann, C.
  1988   *Die Pergamenische Sigillata aus der Stadt-
          grabung von Pergamon. Pergamenische For-
          schungen 6.* Berlin: de Gruyter.
Mitsopoulos-Leon, V.
  1991   *Die Basilika am Staatsmarkt in Ephesos,
          Kleinfunde. 1 Tiel. Keramik hellenistischer
          und römicher Zeit. Forschungen in Ephesos
          IX 2/2.* Vienna: Österreichisches Archäolog-
          isches Institut.

Munsell Soil Color Charts
1988   Baltimore, MD: Munsell Color.

Peacock, D. P. S., and Williams, D. F.
1986   *Amphorae and the Roman Economy: An Introductory Guide.* London: Longman.

Perlzweig, J.
1961   *The Athenian Agora VII. Lamps of the Roman Period.* Princeton: American School of Classical Studies at Athens.

Pinkwart, D., and Stamnitz, W.
1983   *Die Peristylhäuser westlich der Unteren Agora. Altertümer von Pergamon XIV.* Berlin: de Gruyter.

Pülz, S.
1985   Studien zu einzelnen Fundgruppen. Kaiserzeitliche Keramik aus dem Heroon III. Pp. 77–115 in W. Müller-Wiener, Millet 1983–1984, *Istanbuler Mitteilungen* 35: 13–138.

Rautman, M. L.
1995   A Late Roman Townhouse at Sardis. Pp. 49–66 in *Forschungen in Lydien*, ed. E. Schwertheim. Asia Minor Studien 17. Bonn: Habelt.

Riley, J. A.
1979   The Coarse Pottery from Benghazi. Pp. 91–467 in *Excavations at Sidi Khrebish, Benghazi (Berenice) 2*, ed. J. A. Lloyd. Libya Antiqua Supplement 5. Tripoli: Department of Antiquities of Libya.
1981   The Pottery from the Cisterns 1977.1, 1977.2, and 1977.3. Pp. 85–124 in *Excavations at Carthage 1977 Conducted by the University of Michigan VI*, ed. J. H. Humphrey. Ann Arbor: University of Michigan.

Robinson, H. S.
1959   *The Athenian Agora V. Pottery of the Roman Period.* Princeton: American School of Classical Studies at Athens.

Scott, J. A., and Kamilli, D.
1981   Late Byzantine Glazed Pottery from Sardis. Pp. 679–96 in *Actes du XVe congrès international d'études byzantines, Athènes 1976 II. Art et archéologie.* Athens: Vivliotheke tes en Athenais Archaiologikes Hetaireias.

Vitelli, K. D.
1982   The Lamps. Pp. 189–201 in *Yassi Ada I. A Seventh Century Byzantine Shipwreck*, eds. G. F. Bass and F. H. van Doorninck. College Station, TX: Texas A and M University.

Waagé, F.
1948   *Antioch-on-the-Orontes IV, 1. Ceramics and Islamic Coins.* Princeton, NJ: Princeton University.

Waldbaum, J. C.
1983   *Metalwork from Sardis: The Finds Through 1974.* Archaeological Exploration of Sardis Monograph 8. Cambridge, MA: Harvard.

Williams, C.
1977   A Byzantine Well-deposit from Anemurium (Rough Cilicia). *Anatolian Studies* 27: 175–90.
1989   *Anemurium. The Roman and Early Byzantine Pottery.* Subsidia Mediaevalia 16. Toronto: Pontifical Institute of Mediaeval Studies.

Williams, C. K., and Zervos, O.
1983   Corinth, 1982: East of the Theater. *Hesperia* 52: 1–47.

Wintermeyer, U.
1980   Katalog ausgewählter Keramik und Kleinfunde. Pp. 122–60 in K. Tuchelt, Didyma. Bericht über die Arbeiten der Jahre 1975–1979, *Istanbuler Mitteilungen* 30: 99–176.

Idalion, Cyprus: Conquest and Continuity

PAMELA GABER and WILLIAM G. DEVER
Department of Near Eastern Studies
University of Arizona
Tucson, Arizona 85721

Theories of conquest and collapse of ancient societies have been discussed in anthropological theory for decades. It is rare to find a site on which to test these theories, but Idalion on Cyprus may be a site suited to testing them. Somewhere in the middle of the fifth century B.C. it was conquered. Excavations in the elite structures of the western acropolis have uncovered massive buildings destroyed in the course of violent conflict, leaving 1.5 to 2 m of destruction debris, and walls constructed of huge blocks completely destroyed. In the domestic and industrial sectors of the Lower City, however, excavations have revealed continuous, undisturbed, apparently prosperous occupation beginning sometime in the seventh century B.C., and continuing down through the Roman period.

INTRODUCTION

Near Eastern historical archaeologists traditionally have sought to explain cultural change by invoking notions of "invasions," particularly when written records imply catastrophic events accompanying large-scale military campaigns or movements of peoples. Such models inevitably stress abrupt and sweeping change at the expense of cultural continuity. Examples of oversimplistic reconstructions based on invasion hypotheses might include the end of the Early Bronze Age in Palestine ("Amorites"); the end of the Late Bronze Age ("Israelites"); the end of the Bronze Age throughout the Levant and in Cyprus ("Sea Peoples" and others) and even in Greece (the "Dorian Invasion"). These models rarely do justice to the complexity of the archaeological record as it becomes increasingly clear, and in any case they possess little explanatory power.

CONQUEST AND COLLAPSE

Recently, sophisticated "collapse" models have been advanced, often employing General Systems Theory, to analyze the multiple factors that may "trigger" the entropy of social, like biological, systems. Seminal treatments, with many cross-cultural examples, have been published recently by Tainter (1989) and Yoffee and Cowgill (1989). The emphasis

in those papers is on indigenous, systemic change; on technical-ecological factors; on socioeconomic rather than "political" history—in short, on the continuities rather than the discontinuities. This current trend in anthropology was already anticipated by Braudel and the *annales* school of historians, who spoke eloquently of *la longue durée*. On the surface of history—"the froth on the crest of the waves"—are superficial accounts of public events and the deeds of great men. Underneath the waves, however, are great, slow swells, the deep undercurrents of events, in large part anonymous and often environmentally determined, measured only in millennia (Bintliff 1991; Knapp 1992). Yet neither of these newer approaches to the understanding of the past has had much measurable impact on Near Eastern archaeology (Dever 1985; 1988).

One of the principles noted by both Tainter (1989) and Yoffee and Cowgill (1989) is Simon's principle of "near-decomposability" (1965), which posits that when complex societies collapse (or even when they are affected by partial destructions) they rarely break down completely into their original constituent parts. Rather, as subsystems collapse, societies sink down to simpler levels of integration; there they find a new equilibrium, they survive, and gradually they begin a new upward spiral. Here again, it is the *continuities*, not always so obvious, that the social historian (and archaeologist) should seek to comprehend.

CYPRUS AND THE EASTERN
MEDITERRANEAN

Excavated Domestic Architecture

The large Cypriot site of Idalion is an ideal site at which to do an archaeological test of a "conquest–collapse" model. Ample evidence exists for a major destruction at Idalion somewhere between 470 and 450 B.C.: allusions in literary records; a change in the numismatic record; the ascendence of the city-state of Kition over Idalion; and the actual picture of massive destruction of defenses and other monumental architecture, especially on the acropolis, that scattered earlier soundings brought to light. Yet the Joint American Expedition, working through 1977 with more modern stratigraphic methods, found that in the domestic quarters in the Lower City there is virtually no evidence of mid-fifth century B.C. disturbance, and occupation at Idalion continues to the present with scarcely a break. How can one reconcile the apparent discrepancies? How might the situation at Idalion, if properly clarified, fit into what we know of the larger picture of first millennium B.C. settlement patterns in the eastern Mediterranean? These questions are especially critical for the periods of Greek colonization, of Phoenician maritime expansion, of the wars between the Greeks and the Persians, and finally of the Neo-Assyrian empire.

Iron Age Sites in Cyprus.
One might expect that Iron Age urban sites comparable to Idalion would have been properly excavated on Cyprus itself, along the southern Turkish coast, and in particular up and down the Phoenician coast. In Cyprus, however, excavation of the major Iron Age city kingdoms has been greatly hampered by the continuation of settlement into the modern day. Kition is overlain by modern Larnaca, and Marion is overlain by modern Polis. At both sites excavators have uncovered monumental architecture, and at Kition port facilities, in discontinuous areas free of modern architecture. The Princeton expedition to Polis, indeed, has found some pre-Roman, nonmonumental architecture; but it is overlain by Roman structures. Then, too, the areas available for excavation are restricted to vacant lots between modern town structures. At Kition (e.g., Yon and Sznycer 1992: 157), no continuous area of domestic architecture was uncovered. At Amathus, adjacent to modern Limassol, the picture is somewhat different. In addition to the monumental architecture uncovered by the French mission on the

Acropolis (e.g., Petit 1989 and references therein) the Cypriot Department of Antiquities has excavated the late agora and numerous tombs. Ancient Paphos is known amply through ancient texts; but it exists in two disparate archaeological sites, Kouklia and Kato Paphos, neither of which has yielded any domestic precincts of the Persian or Cypro-Classical period (e.g., Maier 1985; Daszewsky 1992: 215–54; Hohlfelder 1992: 255–56). The relevant levels may well underlie modern Paphos. Ancient Salamis, whose monumental city core was excavated up through the early 1970s, might one day yield such a domestic precinct; but right now it is in occupied territory and beyond scientific exploration. The site of ancient Kourion, too, thus far has yielded only monumental structures in excavations. The "Royal" necropolis at Tamassos has yielded many tombs (e.g., Buchholz 1990 and references therein), as has Golgoi, but no domestic areas. The only remaining city kingdoms of Iron Age Cyprus mentioned in the Assyrian texts are Kerynia, Lapithos, Soloi, and Chytroi in Turkish occupied Cyprus; Ledra, which lies under modern Nicosia; and Idalion (for references see Karageorghis 1982). Even in the latest compendia of archaeological work on Cyprus, the sorts of questions we are asking here are simply not considered (Karageorghis 1985; 1986; Tatton-Brown 1989).

Domestic Architecture Elsewhere in the Eastern Mediterranean.
Virtually no systematic excavation or even exploration of contemporary sites has been done in southern Turkey. Along the Levantine coast (modern Syria, Lebanon, and Israel) several Phoenician and even Greek sites have been investigated, including Al-Mina (Woolley 1938), Tell Sukas (Lund 1986), Tabbat al-Hammam, Byblos, Sidon, Sarepta (Pritchard 1975), Tyre, Achziv, and Tell Dor (Stern 1993). None of the excavations, however, has produced much more than finds from cemeteries, scattered surface remains, and (not surprising, considering the excavators' objectives) soundings with pottery sequences. As Bikai (1990) observes in surveying some of this material recently, the Phoenicians are recognized all over the Mediterranean through objects, but they remain poorly known in their own homeland—that is, through proper excavation of domestic remains. Again, excavators have concentrated on political history, at the expense of socioeconomic history.

The Danish excavations at Tell Sukas from 1958 to 1963, which have been published in nine volumes thus far, produced the largest exposure of domestic

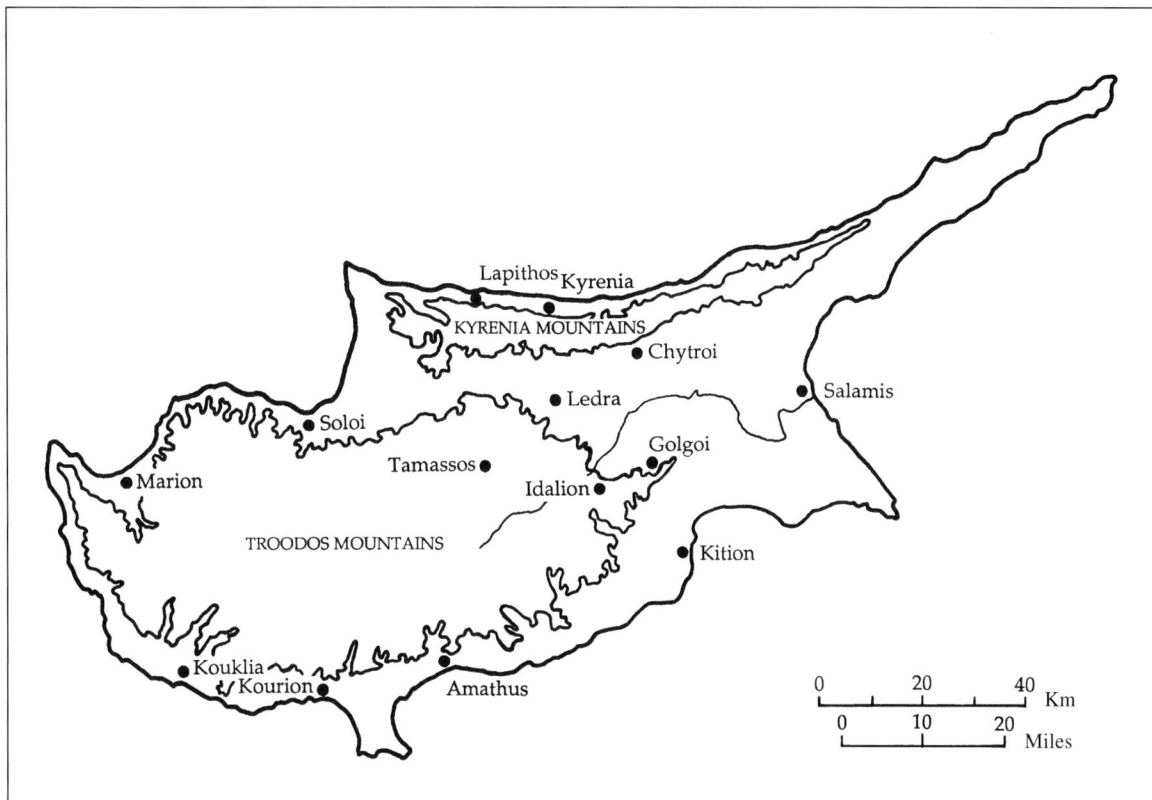

Fig. 1. Cyprus in the Iron Age; Troodos mountains and foothills are outlined.

remains (Lund 1986, with reference to wider literature). After a destruction of Period H1, ca. 677 or 671 B.C., probably by Assarhaddon, the city was rebuilt. According to the excavators, there followed three levels of "Greek domination": Period G3, destroyed ca. 588 B.C.; rebuilt in Period G2, then destroyed again ca. 553–552 B.C.; partially rebuilt in Period G1, then destroyed finally in ca 498 B.C., followed by a century or more of abandonment. The transitions from Period G3 to G2, and from Period G2 to G1, could in theory help to test our "conquest-collapse" model; but the excavators appear to have had more limited objectives, especially clearance of the "Sanctuary" and the "Phoenician High Place" and the documentation of early Greek wares (again typical of more traditional approaches).

THE SITE OF IDALION

Topography and History

History of the city. Idalion was one of the city kingdoms of ancient Cyprus. Its urban center was

situated beside the Yialias River as it entered the Mesaoria Plain out of the foothills of the Troodos Mountains. There Idalion sat astride the crossroads of the routes to the east and south coasts, and thus it had access to the international trade channeled through the port cities. Almost certainly the copper trade in which the ancient city-states engaged accounted for the wealth and growth of ancient inland urban centers like Idalion. The city lies just within the limestone belt, a location that is far hotter in summer than those higher altitudes in the igneous Troodos foothills where copper was found. It must have been the natural confluence of coastal routes, mentioned above, that determined the original placement of the city at some distance from the mines (fig. 1).

The city was famous in Roman times for its two acropoleis, two limestone hills known today as Ambelleri (the western acropolis), and Mouti tou Arvili (the eastern acropolis). Idalion appears to have grown up in the eighth, or possibly the ninth, century B.C., on the western acropolis. The Swedish Cyprus Expedition excavated a complex of structures there

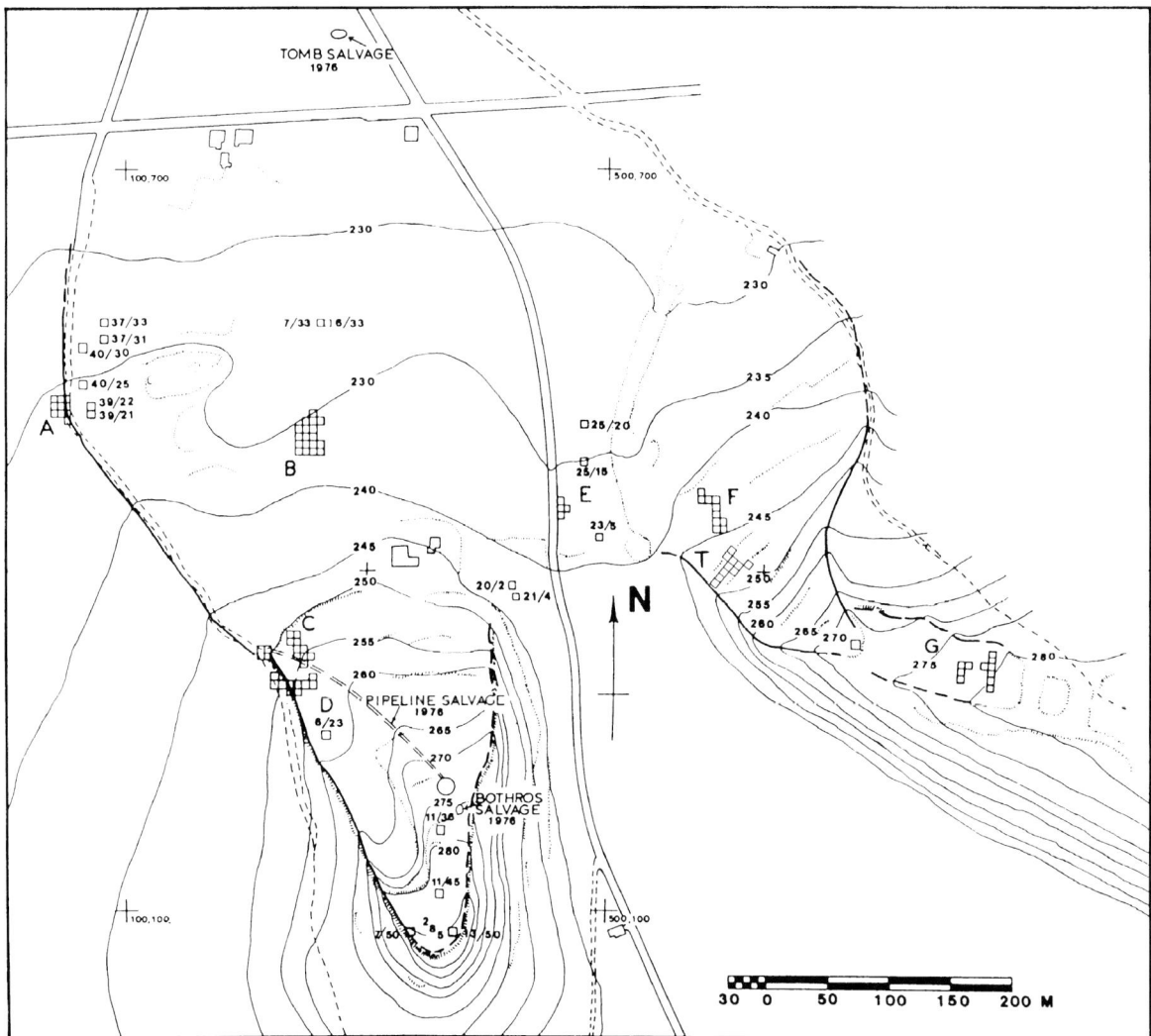

Fig. 2. Plan of Idalion, showing excavation areas. Note especially Areas B and T.

between 1929 and 1931 that may date to that period (Gjerstad et al. 1935: 460–641, Plan 5). The architecture they excavated is certainly a continuous series of Iron Age buildings. There appear to have been twelfth-century tombs underlying those Iron Age remains. The Swedish excavators broke through to the floors of two of those tombs and photographed the characteristic intact tomb deposits *in situ* (Gjerstad 1935: 593). There is no trace as yet of Late Bronze Age occupation on the site, although only a small proportion of Idalion has been excavated. The plateau north of the Yialias, known as Ayios Sozomenos, has revealed many Late Cypriote remains; perhaps the settlement of that period is to be found in that area.

In any case, from the Cypro-Geometric period to the modern day, the city of Idalion shrank and grew along the south banks of the Yialias River, following the river northward when it shifted its course in that direction. In the late sixth century B.C. the city was so large that a fortification wall built to encircle its Lower City as well as its two acropoleis extended some six miles in circumference. Ohnefalsch-Richter noted the circuit of that wall a century ago (1893: pl. 3; cf. fig. 2 here). The need for the fortification may well have lain in the political upheavals taking place throughout the eastern Mediterranean. The huge fortification surrounding the citadel on the lower terrace of Ambelleri, the western acropolis, was dug in 4.00 m and was 11.00 m wide (Stager and Walker 1989: 31). Perhaps about 450 B.C. the monumental architecture within those fortifications was destroyed, and less substantial structures were erected in their place. Those structures were abandoned in turn around 300 B.C., as recent excavations by Hadjicosti of the Department of Antiquities of Cyprus have demonstrated (Hadjicosti 1993). During the turmoil suffered by the elite structures of the West Acropolis, the two houses and the industrial structures in the Lower City investigated by Stager and Walker in the 1970s (Stager and Walker 1989) and by Gaber in the 1980s and 1990s seem to have experienced continued occupation without interruption during the Classical and Hellenistic periods—from about the fifth through the second and first centuries B.C. (below).

Similarly, the east acropolis, Mouti tou Arvili, was the site of the Temenos of the Goddess of Idalion (Ohnefalsch-Richter 1893: 408–17) and of a Temenos dedicated to a male god identified with Resheph-Mekal in Phoenician and Apollo-Amyklos in Greek. In the last century, R. H. Lang excavated Archaic and Classical remains in the temenos of the god (Lang 1878a: 30–46). In 1992 and 1993 Gaber excavated Hellenistic and some early Roman-period remains in that temenos (Gaber and Morden 1992). Work there continues, but preliminary indications are that there was a continuous use of the cult site from the Archaic through the Hellenistic periods, with a major rebuild taking place only in the early Roman period (below).

In 1973, and again in 1992, remains of medieval houses were found between the western Lower City and the modern town, indicating that occupation continued there, probably without a break. Sometime in the Middle Ages the name was shortened to Dhali, as the village is known today. The migration of the Yialias River northward drew the town northward with it, leaving the ancient site exposed to the south of modern Dhali. Thus, instead of a *tell* formation, there is a kind of horizontal progression of occupation within the ancient city.

Idalion and the "Conquest–Collapse" Model.
Idalion is probably one of the best sites anywhere for testing the "conquest–collapse" model. The domestic architecture in the Lower City is not only well-preserved, but accessible. The Joint American Expedition to Idalion, working from 1971 through 1980, did extensive surface surveys, soil-core sampling, and archaeological soundings in the Lower City. They distinguished areas where domestic ar-

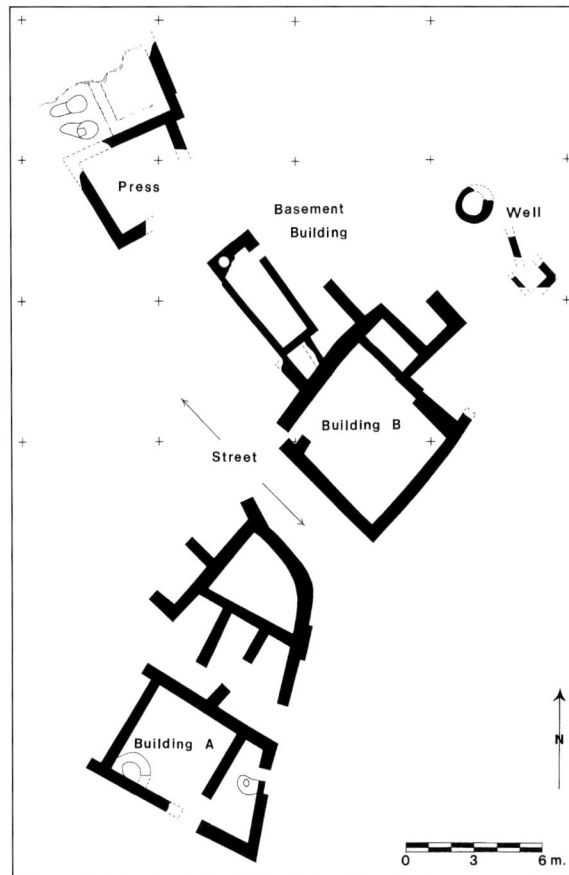

Fig. 3. Area B, Lower City block plan, 1992.

chitecture was to be found 10 cm below the modern surface. Between 1972 and 1977 they uncovered the complete floor plan of one house, together with the street running alongside it and fragments of its neighbors to the south, east, and north (Stager and Walker 1989; cf. fig. 3 here). The houses in question appear to be of a type known from medieval towns like Kakopetria and indeed from modern Cypriot villages. They were constructed of mudbrick over field stone socles, with beams in the ceilings. It appears quite likely that they consisted of more than one story, as there is evidence of animal quarters on the uneven earth floors of the ground floor rooms. In one case, a sort of basement room was dug into the virgin soil and pits underlying a house, and an olive-pressing operation was carried out there (Gaber 1992; figs. 4, 5 here). Here the living quarters must have been above. The lower levels of these houses are preserved throughout the Cypro-Archaic and Cypro-Classical periods (ca 675–300 B.C.). Toward the south,

Fig. 4. Area B, northern end of the "basement room," from the west.

Fig. 5. Area B, southern end of the "basement room," from the west.

Fig. 6. 1992 excavations in the Lower City of Idalion, Area B, looking south.

approaching the base of the western acropolis, the ground slopes upward into an almond grove, and at least one house was preserved as late as its Hellenistic layers. In the other cases on the lower ground to the north, however, the plow appears to have removed the later phases. Nonetheless, in the areas preserved the houses appear to have been built first in the late sixth century B.C. over refuse dumps of earlier houses somewhere nearby, and these sixth century houses continue without interruption well beyond the fifth century conquest of Idalion by Kition.

History of Excavation

Early Excavations. There has been a long line of excavators at Idalion, beginning in the last century. Some temples and thousands of tombs were uncovered and emptied by L. Palma di Cesnola in the 1860s (di Cesnola 1877). Then R. H. Lang, in the 1860s (Lang 1878a), cleared a temple dedicated to "Apollo Amyklos," according to Greek inscriptions found there. (The location of that temple has

caused a great deal of discussion in recent years; see below.) M. Ohnefalsch-Richter (1893) spent two years' concentrated effort at the turn of this century. The Swedish Cyprus Expedition under E. Gjerstad worked at Idalion between 1929 and 1931 (Gjerstad et al. 1935; 1948).

Previous American Excavations. The Joint American Expedition to Idalion excavated in a number of crucial areas in the 1970s. In addition to their wide-ranging site-catchment analysis studies, surface surveys, and many soundings on the site, the Joint American Expedition excavated in the central city (Stager and Walker 1989; fig. 2 here). There they discovered massive fortifications and monumental structures on a terrace of the West Acropolis and domestic structures in the Lower City.

These previous excavators uncovered only a tiny fraction of the numerous structures in the Lower City of Idalion, where investigation of an area of domestic architecture was begun in the 1970s (Walker 1974: 23–50; Walker and Gaber 1989: 66–82; fig. 6 here).

Here a sequence of occupation in domestic dwellings was uncovered that appears to reflect an expansion in this area of Idalion around the turn of the fifth century B.C. Before that time the central Lower City seems to have been an area of Archaic refuse and storage pits. Here matters remained until 1987 when the University of New Hampshire Expedition to Idalion fielded its exploratory season.

University of New Hampshire Expedition. During the 1987 summer season, the University of New Hampshire Expedition to Idalion, under the direction of P. Gaber, sank probe trenches in the monumental architecture of the Terrace of the West Acropolis and in the domestic architecture of the Lower City (Gaber 1992). Although two of the three probes sunk by that project were in the monumental architecture in Areas B and D (fig. 2), that area of the site has since been taken over by the Department of Antiquities of Cyprus, and it continues to be investigated by them under the direction of M. Hadjicosti. Both the UNH soundings and the Department of Antiquities excavations revealed massive destructions: one in the middle of the fifth century B.C. and one around 300 B.C.

In the Lower City, by contrast, while only one complete house had been uncovered through the 1987 season, the results of excavation there suggested a smooth, unbroken sequence of use and occupation extending from the beginning of the Cypro-Archaic period right down through the late Classical period. These findings formed the basis for the University of Arizona excavations in 1992.

University of Arizona Expedition. During July and August 1992 the University of Arizona Expedition to Idalion, under the direction of P. Gaber, with W. G. Dever, Associate Director, explored a significant portion of the Lower City architecture. Building on the work of the previous American expeditions, we continued digging in buildings originally found by previous projects in area B (figs. 2, 3, 6).

THE LOWER CITY; AREA B

Areas of Excavation

Building B. Building B (figs. 3, 7, 8) had been partially cleared by the Joint American Expedition, then sounded by the 1987 UNH project. Only the upper phase of the architecture had been planned, however, and neither the several subphases nor their dates were clear. Deeper excavation in the northern portion of Building B in our Areas Wα25 and Eα25, under field supervisor J. Hardin, revealed that all of the substantial house walls on plans published by previous excavations were dated not to the late sixth to late fifth centuries B.C., as had been suggested (Stager and Walker 1989: 66–72), but rather to the Hellenistic era, ca. second century B.C., with some first century B.C. pits possibly indicating a squatter occupation (fig. 7). Below these final phases were earlier walls on the same orientation but of different construction and alignment (figs. 7, 8). The lower phase of reused monumental masonry and floor levels dates to the fifth century B.C., with alterations suggesting a rebuild around 400 B.C., or early in the fourth century B.C. (figs. 8, 9). Further west in Building B, in our grid squares wβ26 and Wβ27, coins sealed in the wall fall in a subterranean burnt room (the same room sounded by the UNH team in 1987; below) confirm a date after 350 B.C. The subsequent use phase in those western squares yielded pottery of the third and second centuries B.C. Hence a continuous sequence of occupation can be documented, from the seventh century pits underlying Building B through the first century B.C. Nowhere else on Cyprus is such an uninterrupted stratigraphic sequence available for study.

Basement Building. In 1987 the UNH team laid a probe in Building B in a square that was designated Id WNW 9/20 according to the grid used by the Joint American Expedition in the 1970s under the direction of Stager and Walker. In a subterranean chamber, the perfectly preserved remains of a mudbrick wall on its side lay over the parallel charcoal remains of roof beams. Under the debris of a fire so hot that the insides of the mudbrick walls were fired hard, the UNH team found a fine floor dating to the Cypro-Classical I–II (Gaber 1992: 174–80; fig. 5 here). The excavators sectioned through the floor, revealing a series of Cypro-Archaic pits underneath, continuing the pattern of occupation noted by the previous Joint American Expedition (Stager and Walker 1989: 71–73). The sectioning of the floor left approximately one quarter of the floor undug, as well as perhaps one third of the northernmost end of the "basement room." It was here, therefore, that the University of Arizona team began excavations in 1992.

A new grid was laid out in accordance with the grid in use by the Department of Antiquities of Cyprus, in the excavations currently being carried out

Fig. 7. Area B, Building B, from the northwest.

Fig. 8. Area B, Building B; detail of earlier masonry (see fig. 7) at extreme eastern end of Building B, looking east.

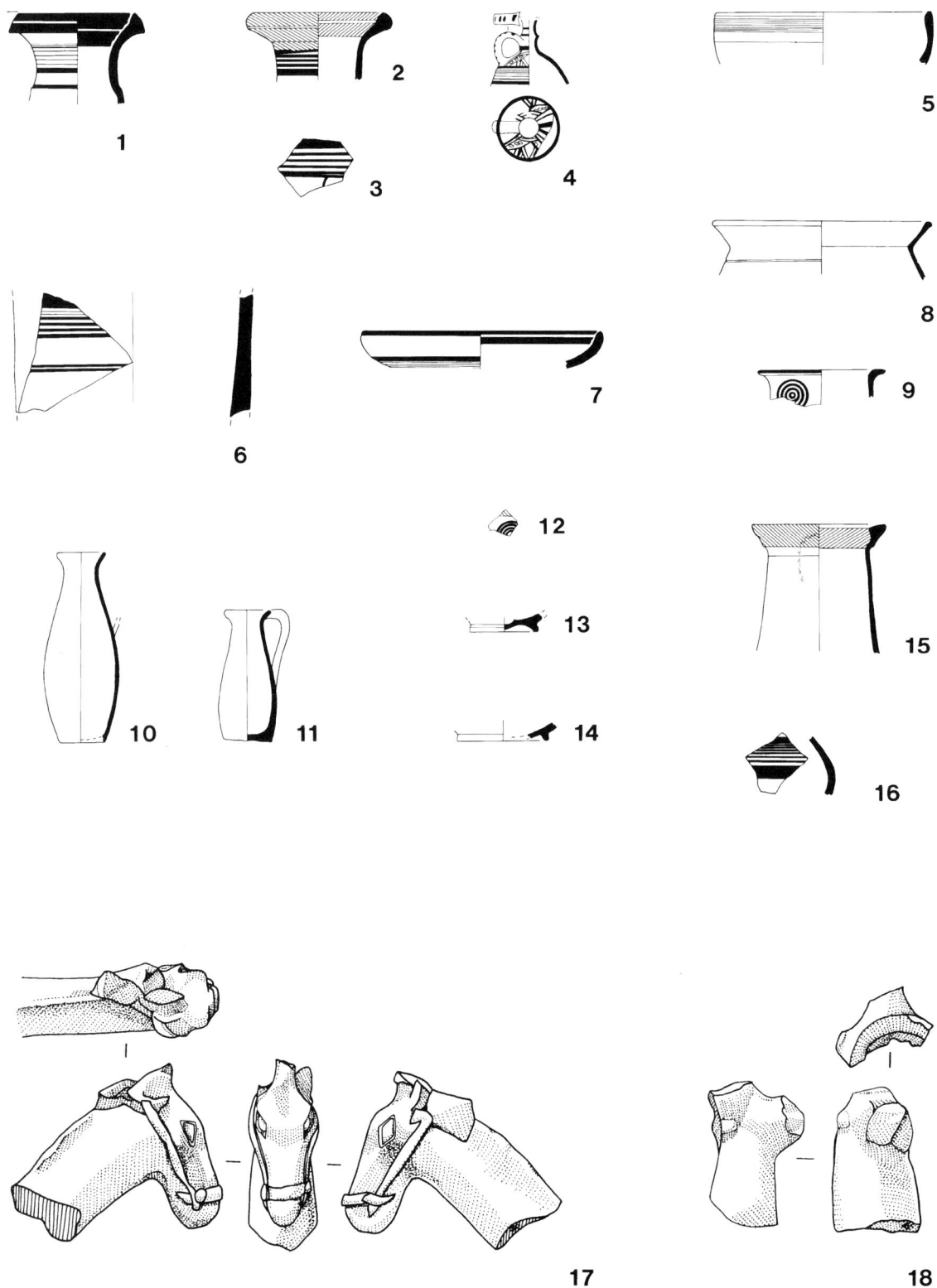

Fig. 9. Pottery from the Lower City, Area B, and figurines from the East Acropolis, Area T.

on Ambelliri under the direction of M. Hadjicosti. The Department of Antiquities' grid was extended northward, and the Lower City excavations were re-assigned square numbers accordingly. The "basement room" thus fell into grid square Wβ26 (fig. 10). The walls of the room were laid on virgin marl and were preserved in the east, west, and south to a height of 60–70 cm. They were built of roughly rectangular limestones with occasional blue pillow lavas inter-spersed. These dark stones are carried down from the Troodos foothills in great abundance by the Yialias River and were often incorporated into fieldstone walls. The walls were mortared with mud. An inter-esting phenomenon occurred in the eastern wall of the room. Built into the wall was a gap with a mud-brick sill or shelf—a kind of window, the sill of which was burnt, probably in the conflagration. This window, or gap, in the wall was mirrored by a similar gap in the western wall uncovered in 1987 by the UNH team (Gaber 1992). At the base of the walls a small portion of the floor associated with them was located.

In the northwest corner of the basement room the floor was evidenced by one flat-lying cobble at the same level as cobbles discovered by the UNH ex-cavations (figs. 4, 5). Also, immediately east of this cobble lay two large boulders used as leveling fill for the floor, and possibly as part of the surface itself.

The north wall of the basement room was discov-ered 60 cm from the center of the south balk. Its to-tal length was 2.35 m, its width 45–75 cm. Included as the northwest cornerstone of this wall is a stone with a nearly circular hole in it (fig. 10). This large limestone measures 1.1 m in length, 1 m in width, and 25 cm in height; the hole has a diameter of 45 cm. The stone may be a "well-head" in secondary use but contemporary with the rest of the architec-ture of the room. This northern wall of the room

is preserved to roughly the same level as the rest of the walls of the basement room (235.90 m) but is founded much higher on virgin soil (235.70 m).

Evidence of the room's destruction by fire after it had been in use for some time (as attested by surface buildup discovered by the UNH team) was copious. Burned architectural collapse including ash, charcoal, limestone and sandstone cobbles, and burned mud-brick filled the room from floor level to the preserved height of the architecture. The fire probably was caused by a home olive pressing operation, evidence of which was found in the pressing stone (fig. 11) and the many olive pits found in 1987 (Gaber 1992). It must have been during the fire that three large, gray mudbricks tumbled to the floor of the structure, blocking the 50 cm wide doorway in the north end of the eastern wall. This doorway falls in the east balk of Wβ26, and whether it led to another room or the exterior of the building will only be revealed when that balk is removed.

"Olive-Oil Processing Building." Immediately north of the basement room in Building B, the Uni-versity of Arizona team uncovered a cement and cobble floor surrounding a nearly 3 m^2 cement and pebble floor. East of that floor, two kidney-shaped vats were uncovered, some 1.25 cm deep, with a stone channel between them (figs. 12, 13). There was undoubtedly some liquid processing carried on in this area. The vats themselves are much smaller (± 0.75 m wide) than the similar installations at Styllarca near Paphos, where the vats are 2.5 m wide and occur in four pairs. That vast industrial area was undoubtedly devoted to olive oil production. While our vats are far smaller, they have the characteristic features of olive oil producing installations. They are paired, the first acting as a collecting vat, where the product of the olive pressing on the paved floor runs off. Since that product is 80% water, the 20%

Fig. 9. Details. 1. Cr131, EA26.012, PB52 Cypro-Archaic I Amphora rim; 2. Cr126, EA26.012, PB52 Cypro-Geometric III bichrome Amphora rim; 3. Cr148, EA26.013, PB46 Cypro-Archaic I bichrome body sherd; 4. Cr143, EA26.012, PB68 Cypro-Archaic I–II bichrome juglet; 5. Cr130, EA26.012, PB52 Cypro-Archaic II cup rim; 6. Cr157, EA26.005, PB19 Cypro-Archaic I bichrome body sherd; 7. Cr149, EA26.009, PB43 Cypro-Archaic I white painted bowl rim; 8. Cr497, Wβ25.007, PB52 Cypro-Classical II/Hellenistic I cooking pot rim; 9. Cr540, Wβ25.007, PB23 White Painted VII rim; 10. Cr4545, ETNW1.040, PB74 Plain white lekythos; 11. Cr98, WA25.008, PB31 Hellenistic red stirrup bottle; 12. Cr395, Wr26.002, PB17 Cypro-Archaic I bichrome body sherd; 13. Cr384, Wr26.002, PB9 Hellenistic I black wash-glaze bowl base; 14. Cr379, Wr26.002, PB6 Hellenistic I black wash-glaze bowl base; 15. Cr137, Wr26.012, PB16 Hellenistic I jug rim; 16. Cr416, Wr27.011, PB1 Cypro-Archaic I white painted body sherd; 17. Or261, ETNW2.039, PB131 Head and neck of hand-formed terracotta horse (bridle and trappings applied, eyes and ears are carved into surface, tips of ears are broken); 18. Or260, ETNW22.008, PB9 Upper left portion of terracotta torso (possible pendant at base of neck, left arm broken just below shoulder).

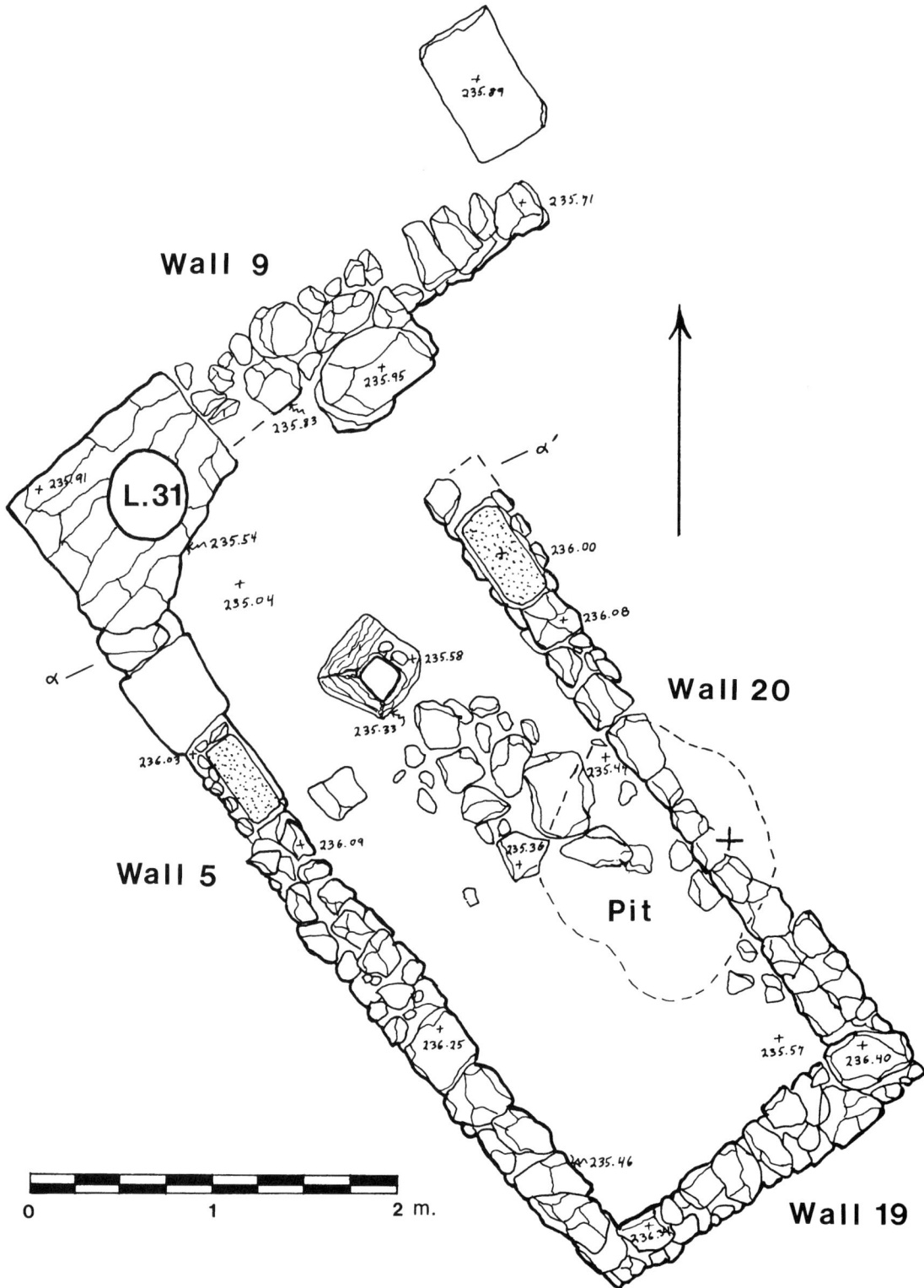

Fig. 10. Area B, plan of the "basement room."

Fig. 11. Area B, olive-pressing stone found in "basement room."

Fig. 12. Area B, possible olive-oil pressing bed and vats, looking south.

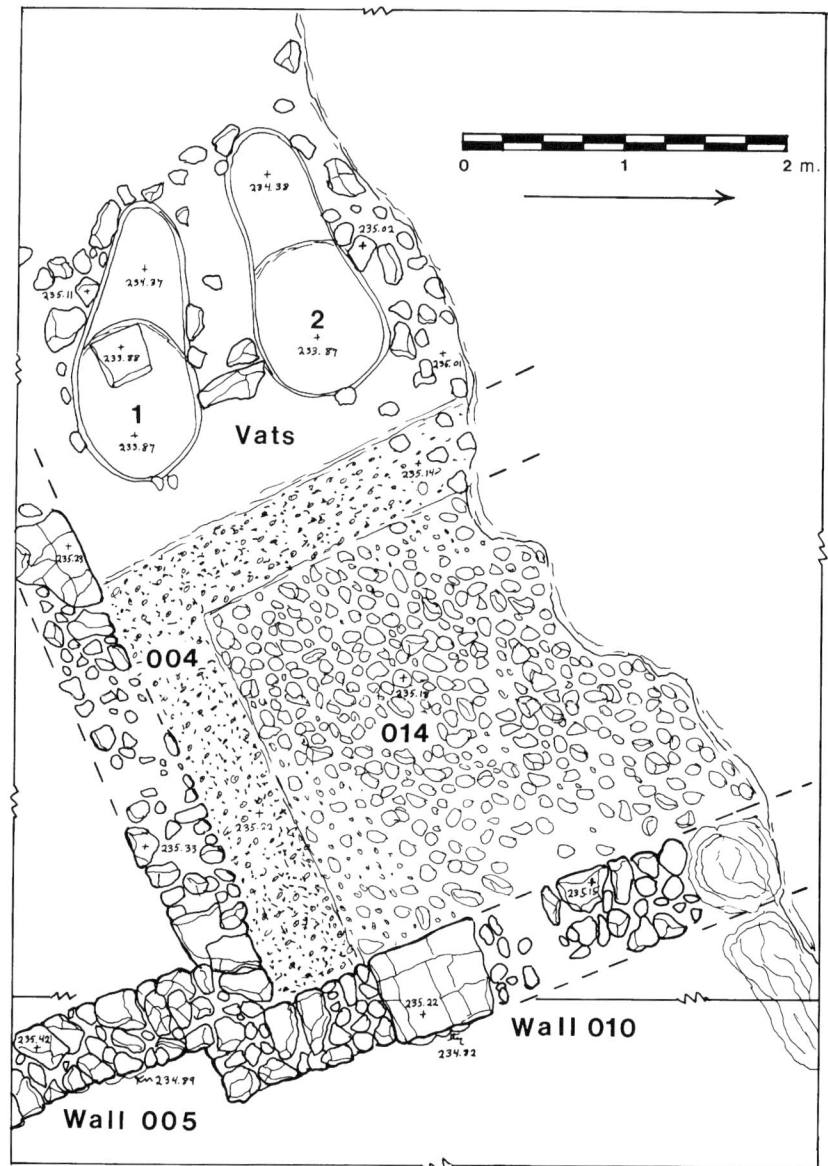

Fig. 13. Area B, plan of possible olive-oil pressing bed and vats.

oil rises to the top where a channel allows it to run off into the second, settling vat. The second tank has a typical round depression in the bottom; ours is smaller, but identical in every other way (Hadjisavvas 1992b: figs. 65, 87).

Immediately south of these possible oil installations is a street continuing the line of the street uncovered by the previous American excavators. As that thoroughfare continues along the western side of the olive oil processing installation, it apparently widens out into an open, paved area (fig. 3). That open area was uncovered during the last week of excavation in 1992.

"Horn-Working Area." East of Building B, the Arizona team made a careful backhoe cut on our east–west grid orientation. A square was opened investigating the westernmost structures exposed in that cut in grid square Eβ25. This trench revealed two walls and an apparent wellhead or cistern, Locus 6. This may indicate the courtyard or outer area of yet another building. Immediately north of the square containing wellhead Locus 6, a number of horn cores were found. S. Davis, the palaeoethnozoologist who was working at Khirokitia with the team from the Centre Nationale de Récherche Scientifique of France, informed us that in every case

in the eastern Mediterranean where he has found horn cores there has been a horn-working area. Also in the area of square Eα26 and Eβ26 were found a number of heavy earthenware trays. If Davis's suggestion is correct, these may be associated with the horn-working process. Further investigation may answer such questions.

If indeed we do have a horn-working area at Idalion, that suggests yet another industry in the domestic quarter. It will be of great interest in the future to attempt to discover whether these industries are purely for local use, or whether they produced enough volume to leave surplus for trade.

Questions Raised by the Lower City Structures. In the six weeks of digging, our knowledge of the extent of the domestic architecture of ancient Idalion was vastly expanded, both in time and space. It became clear that the domestic architecture extends the full length of the University of Arizona permit area (below). In addition, the houses and courtyards that were excavated during the 1992 season extended the known dates of continuous occupation of the Lower City down through the third and second centuries B.C. and into the first century B.C.

The partial exposure of three "houses" in the Lower City has already raised several questions about the "domestic" quarter of ancient Idalion. (1) Although we find large quantities of cooking pots and plain wares in these structures, is there evidence of actual habitation available, or is it possible that we are investigating a local industrial area? (2) Conversely, is the liquid processing area (whether it turns out to be oil, wine, or something else) associated with a dwelling, or is this some sort of small-scale industrial production area? The same question would apply to the possible horn-processing area to the east. (3) What is the function, in terms of urban planning and use patterns, of the open, paved area to the West of the vats in W$_\gamma$27? None of these questions of urban use can be answered without greater exposure of the Lower City structures and installations.

"THE ADONIS TEMENOS:" AREA T

History of Investigation

The Controversy. The sacred site discovered by Lang was conscientiously described along with its finds in a number of publications (Lang 1878a, 1878b; 1905). Unfortunately, in none of those articles did he locate the sanctuary on a map of Dhali or on a plan of

the site. Thus it was that in 1893 when Ohnefalsch-Richter published his map of Idalion (1893: pl. 3), it was assumed that his placement of "Lang's Temple" as he termed it, was correct (see, e.g., Masson 1961: pl. 5).

Then, in the 1970s, the Joint American Expedition under Stager and Walker undertook excavation of the location designated by Ohnefalsch-Richter. They found a previously undisturbed bath complex, apparently of a Roman villa (Stager and Walker 1974: 77). Clearly Lang had not dug there. In subsequent years, they dug in various spots in the vicinity looking for "Lang's Temple" (fig. 2, Areas E, F). Gradually it became clear that the location of Lang's excavations had been lost sometime between the visit of Colonna Ceccaldi, who reports seeing the site (1882), and 1898 when Ohnefalsch-Richter published the erroneous location.

There remained many who felt, until 1993, that Ohnefalsch-Richter must have been correct, and that the Americans had simply missed finding the temple complex by a few meters (Masson 1961; Senff 1993). After all, Lang's verbal description is clear enough: "Taking the road to Limpia from the present village of Dali, we are led in a southerly direction, and at the distance of about half a mile we come to the base of two hills, between which the road defiles [cf. plan, fig. 2]. Near us on our left, as we reach this point, is the temple my men discovered" (1878a: 32).

Location of the "Temple." During the summer of 1992, we noticed an odd-looking terrace wall about halfway up the East Acropolis. The next day field supervisor M. Morden and foreman G. Demosthenous returned to that terrace wall, where they discovered the steps leading down to the north, indicated on Lang's 1878 plan (figs. 14, 15).

To verify that we had actually located Lang's "temple," we converted the measurements of his plan (fig. 14) into metrics. We then developed on paper a large field on a 6.00 m grid. We experimented with this grid, first by overlaying it on an enlarged contour plan (fig. 2 here), then by doing the same with Lang's plan (fig. 14 here). Finally, we triangulated from the fixed points of the now visible steps, calculating how best to lay the field so that the walls of Lang's building "E" (fig. 14)—if it was still preserved—would fall within our squares. Within two days, we came upon the northeast corner of that building (fig. 16), as well as indications of the limits of Lang's trenches. Subsequently this became Area T, and by 1993 the grid was expanded to eleven 5.00 × 5.00 m squares (fig. 2).

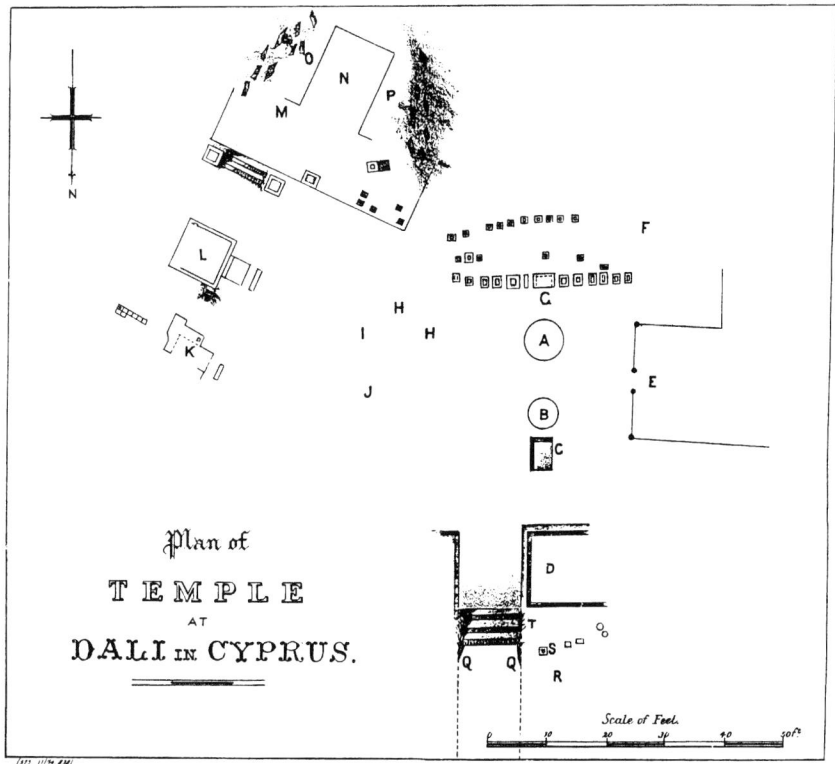

Fig. 14. Plan of the "Apollo Temple" (Adonis temenos here) published by Lang (1878a) of the structures he excavated.

Fig. 15. Terrace wall on the East Acropolis (Area T) incorporating the temenos steps.

Fig. 16. Area T, northeast corner of Lang's "Building E," looking east.

The "Temple" Site. The reason the location of the sacred complex had remained elusive became clear as soon as we found it. First, there was Ohnefalsch-Richter's plan indicating clearly "Lang's Temple" at our Area G (fig. 2). It was natural for twentieth-century archaeologists to take him at his word.

Second, once the real site was located at Area T (fig. 2), it became obvious that Ohnefalsch-Richter had marked his plan according to Lang's verbal description (above), not from any first-hand knowledge of his own. We can say at last that, in referring to the only known road from Dhali heading south to Lymbia, when he said, "Near us on our left . . . ," Lang meant some 150 m east, rather than the 10–20 m estimated by Ohnefalsch-Richter.

The actual site of the sanctuary reveals something of the nature of the ancient cult and its place in the life of the ancient city. From the domestic and industrial quarters in the Lower City, the bowl in the hillside of the East Acropolis where the sanctuary lies rises dramatically against the sky (fig. 17). Its southern perimeter wall lies a scant 10–15 m from the northern perimeter wall of the sanctuary dedicated to the Great Mother designated the "Aphrodite Temple" on Ohnefalsch-Richter's plans (1893: pl. 3), our Area "G" (fig. 2).

Given the fact that the crown of the east acropolis was devoted to the worship of the goddess and the shoulder of the hill below was devoted to the worship of the male deity of the sanctuary, it may be suggested that she was the primary deity and he the secondary. This remains in the realm of speculation, however, without more tangible evidence (below). In any case, both sacred precincts tower majestically over the secular complexes, not only of the Lower City, but over the monumental administrative complex located on the terrace of the west acropolis, Ambelliri. Indeed, two thirds of the east acropolis is devoted to the sanctuaries of these two deities, and only below the

Fig. 17. View of the east acropolis from the lower city (Area B).

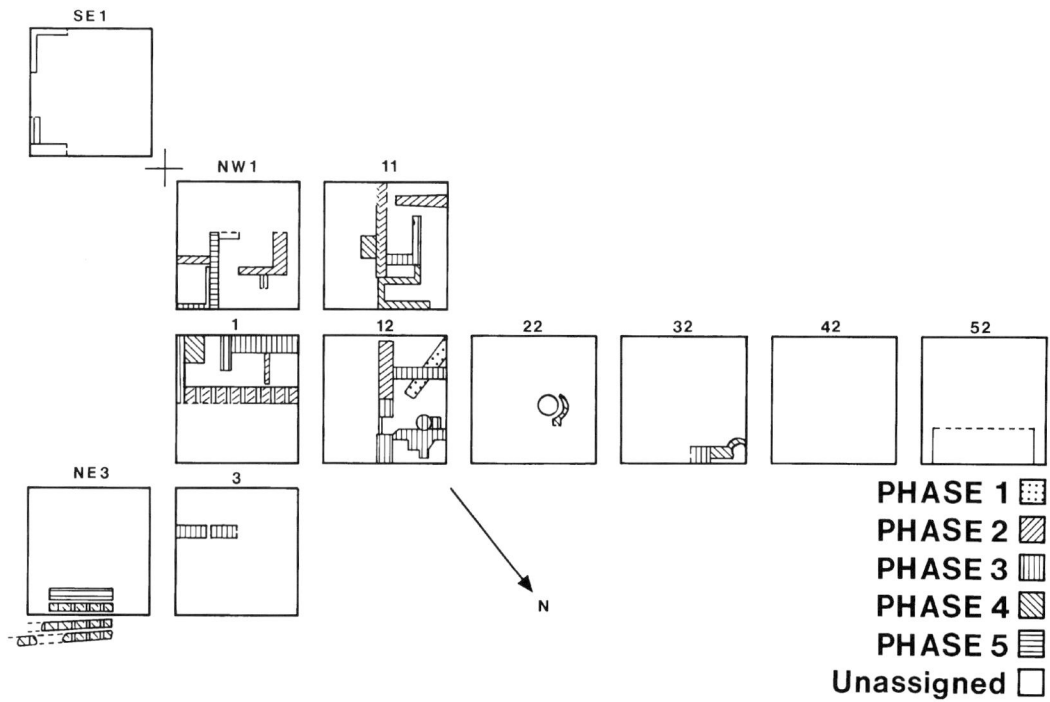

Fig. 18. Plan showing architectural phases in the Temple Field, Area T, as of 1993.

Fig. 19. Area T, Square ET NW 11 looking east, showing olive-pressing stone and square installation.

temenos of the god (Area F; fig. 2) are there monumental structures not part of the temenos complex (Stager, Walker, and Wright 1974: 63–75).

1992 Excavations

Having assured ourselves that the structures we had found were indeed part of "Lang's Temple," we immediately set about excavation to the west of Building "E" on his plans, to explore material possibly undisturbed by Lang (fig. 18). It was serendipitous that the undisturbed portions of that temple complex dated to precisely the same Late Hellenistic and Early Roman periods attested in the dwellings of the Lower City.

Phasing. During the final two weeks of the 1992 excavation season, the University of Arizona team uncovered several small installations within the sacred precinct dating to the second and first centu-ries B.C. In two grid squares, NW 11 and NW 12, we located undisturbed deposits including a succession of six floor levels and some small installations that may be cultic (figs. 19, 20). Sealed between the floors were sherds from vessels of types that are usually assumed to be domestic, including cooking pots and plain ware cups, plates, and bowls. However, there were also two complete lamps of second to first century date (fig. 21), as well as a high concentration of fragments of luxury wares that must have been hundreds of years old when they were deposited in their find spots. One of the sherds was a fragment of an Attic Black Glaze vessel and one was a Cypriot bichrome jug; both probably were manufactured in the fifth century B.C. The presence of these older luxury wares indicates that somewhere in the vicinity older use areas exist, certainly going back at least to the fifth century B.C. Other objects of high-quality craftsmanship, such as a fragment of a basalt bowl and a terracotta bull protome,

Fig. 20. Area T, Square ET NW 12 looking west, showing earliest architecture on a different orientation below a series of six floors.

Fig. 21. Area T, Hellenistic lamps from floors in ET NW 11 and 12.

were built into the walls of this upper phase of the structures in these squares.

Although the complete phasing of these structures would only become clear in 1993, it was already evident that an earlier phase of the architecture in Squares NW 11 and NW 12 had been cut into the bedrock on a different orientation at an earlier date (fig. 20, Phase 1 of Square NW 12 in fig. 18). The perpendicular Phase 2 wall, Locus 6, appears to be a late curtain-wall dividing the northern chamber in Grid Square NW 12 from the "inner" chamber, much of which falls in NW 11. There are only two floors and their associated build-up in this "inner," southern room, while the six floors mentioned above lie north of curtain-wall Locus 6. It would appear, then, that the room to the north of wall Locus 6 saw more traffic than the room to the south, although they are apparently contemporary (Gaber and Morden 1992: 22). The pottery of the successive floors appears as numbers 4–13 in fig. 22.

The room south of wall Locus 6 lies in Square NW 11. This room had features unlike any others known from elsewhere on the site. The south balk of the probe in NW 11 cuts across what at first appeared to be a roughly built bin (fig. 19). On cleaning, however, it became apparent that it was a well-built, rectangular structure, the walls of which are 50–75 cm wide and preserved to a height of 50–65 cm. The portion of the installation that falls within our trench has an interior width of 75 cm. The function of the structure is still unclear, but immediately outside it, against its northern wall, were five paving stones surrounding an empty space in the floor. Immediately north of these stones, on the later of the two floors in the room, stood a votive column (fig. 23). The easternmost paver has a spiral groove on its upper surface, ending in an indentation down the western face of the stone, which faces the empty space (fig. 19). O. Borowski of Emory University, an expert on Levantine agricultural practices during the Persian period, identified this stone as an oil-extracting stone (cf. Hadjisavvas 1992a: pl. 1), where the olives were cracked and placed on the incised stones so that the purest oil would run out slowly, of its own accord, usually into a vessel placed below the runoff channel. Such oil extraction was common in Levantine temples of the first millennium B.C. such as those at Dan, Ta^{c}anach, Tell el-Far^{c}ah, and other sites in Palestine (e.g., Heltzer and Eitam 1987), as well as in Cyprus (Hadjisavvas 1988: fig. 2; 1991: 7–73; 1992: 233–49).

1993 Excavations

In 1993 the entire focus of the Expedition was on the East Acropolis. By the end of the six-week season there, it was clear that a number of long-held ideas about the so-called "Temple of Apollo" discovered by Lang would have to be revised.

The Temenos. First, the sacred site was not a temple *per se*. It gained a reputation among the villagers as the "theater" of ancient Idalion because it is situated in a bowl-like depression in the side of the east acropolis (fig. 17). Not long after the beginning of the 1993 season we realized that the entire six-acre bowl in the hillside was ringed by a substantial peribolos wall. By sectioning through the wall and laying a series of modified "gaspipe" probe trenches from the structures to that wall (fig. 18, Square NW 52; cf. fig. 2), we demonstrated that the entire area encircled by the wall is probably a single temenos. It was probably an outdoor sanctuary rather than a temple structure.

In support of this conclusion, in Grid Square NW 22, we found a uniformly round pit cut into the bedrock, 78 cm deep and 40 cm across. Along the northwest rim of the pit, a row of stones was laid in a shape resembling the top of a question mark (fig. 18). When we found a similar row of stones in NW 32, we began to suspect that they may have been tree pits, somewhat similar to those found in the sanctuary dedicated to Apollo Hylates at Kourion (Soren 1984: 289–91; 1987: 35–36). The most common type of terracotta figurine we found in the 1993 season were horse figures (fig. 9). Terracotta horses, riders, and chariots are also common at Kourion (e.g., Young and Young 1955). It may be that there is a connection between the cults at Kourion and those at Idalion, although such ideas will remain in the realm of speculation for some time.

A feature unlike any published thus far is the great number of sherds with holes in them, indicating that they were pierced before firing (fig. 21: 32–34). Perhaps there was a common type of vessel (almost all such sherds are plain white ware) designed to be hung—perhaps from trees. In any case, it seems reasonable to suggest now that instead of the "Lang's Temple" of archaeological tradition, what we have found is an outdoor temenos in which trees may have played an important part, perhaps a sacred grove like the one found in Kourion (Soren 1987: 35–40). The main business of worship would have taken place

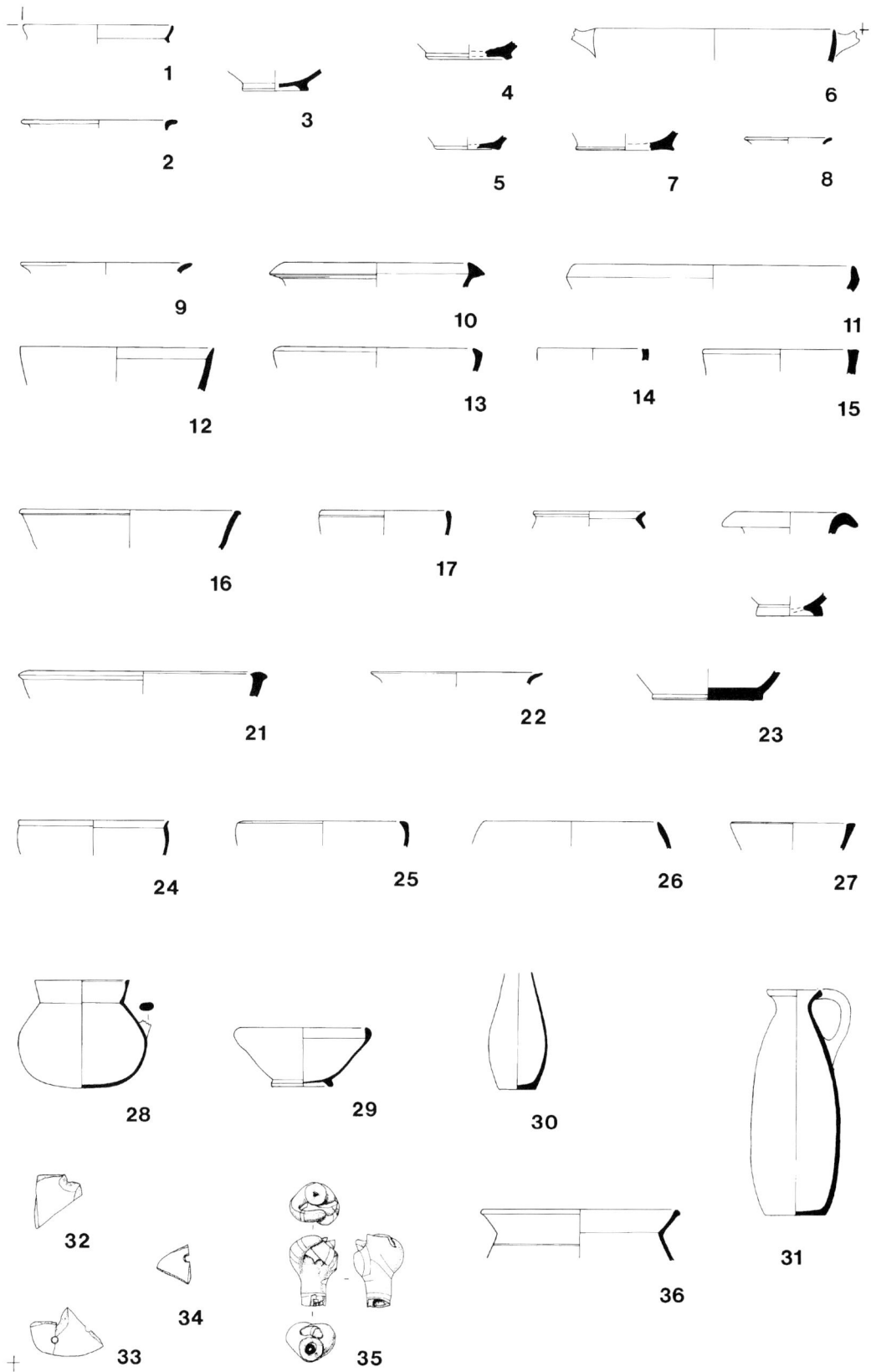

Fig. 22. Pottery and figurine from the east acropolis excavations, Area T.

outdoors, in what Lang described as a court, and the altars would have been open to the air (fig. 24). The buildings were undoubtedly utilitarian places, where storage, preparation, and other functions having to do with materials used in the ceremonies took place. Some of them, such as the one where the oven was found (below), probably were enclosures open to the sky. The entire complex must have been eerily impressive, with the green of the trees rising abruptly out of the stark white of the limestone hillside. The hillside itself was carefully shaped, as we discovered, by a series of terrace-like cuttings beside various installations. The temenos, therefore, was really the entire shoulder of the hill, at least by the third to first century B.C.

Phasing. As the 1993 season progressed, we discerned a complicated sequence of phasing (fig. 18). The area in which we were excavating was undoubtedly among the latest used in the temenos, judging by the artifacts and pottery published by Lang (1878a; 1878b) and Reyes (1994: pl. 11). The majority of our pottery and finds date to the Hellenistic period of the third to first century B.C., with some Roman sherds beginning to appear in the latest levels (fig. 20). As we expanded our excavated area, we saw that the walls drawn together as Lang's "Building E" (fig. 14) were, in reality, walls of separate structures, and in some cases of considerably different dates. For instance, the southernmost wall of that "building" on Lang's plan lies 1.25 m below the eastern and northern walls he includes. These structures lie in our Grid Squares NW 2 (the eastern and northern walls) and NW 1 (the southern, north–south wall; fig. 18).

Fig. 23. Area T, votive column associated with oil-extraction installation in ET NW 11.

In fact, the walls Lang included on his plan actually belong to at least two separate structures and at least three separate phases of construction.

The picture that emerges is one of small structures within an immense, open area. The installations appear to have been largely utilitarian in nature. The

Fig. 22. Details. 1. Cr700, ETNW12.017, PB46 Cypro-Classical I cooking pot rim; 2. Cr701, ETNW12.017, PB46 Cypro-Classical II cooking pot rim; 3. Cr753, ETNW12.017, PB45 Hellenistic wash-glaze base; 4. Cr811, ETNW12.021, PB47 coarse ware base; 5. Cr808, ETNW12.021, PB47 plain white base; 6. Cr815, ETNW12.021, PB47 Hellenistic wash-glaze handle; 7. Cr807, ETNW12.021, PB47 plain white base; 8. Cr813, ETNW12.021, PB47 cooking pot rim; 9. Cr803, ETNW12.022, PB50 plain white rim; 10. Cr800, ETNW12.022, PB50 Cypro-Classical II plain white rim; 11. Cr802, ETNW12.022, PB50 Cypro-Classical II/Hellenistic I plain white rim; 12. Cr736, ETNW12.022, PB48 plain white rim; 13. Cr737, ETNw12.022, PB48 Hellenistic I plain white rim; 14. Cr794, ETNW12.022, PB48 cooking pot rim; 15. Cr801, ETNW12.022, PB50 Cypro-Classical I plain white rim; 16. Cr766, ETNW1q2.024, PB53 Hellenistic wash-glaze rim; 17. Cr767, ETNW12.024, PB53 Hellenistic wash-glaze rim; 18. Cr765, ETNW12.024, PB53 cooking pot rim; 19. Cr760, ETNW12.024, PB53 Cypro-Classical II plain white rim; 20. Cr758, ETNW12.024, PB53 plain white base; 21. Cr777, ETNW12.020, PB49 Cypro-Classical II plain white rim; 22. Cr778, ETNW12.020, PB49 Cypro-Classical I–II plain white rim; 23. Cr774, ETNW12.020, PB51 plain white base; 24. Cr718, ETNW12.025, PB56 Hellenistic wash-glaze rim; 25. Cr755, ETNW12.025, PB57b Hellenistic I plain white rim; 26. Cr754, ETNW12.025, PB57b plain white rim; 27. Cr716, ETNW12.025, PB56 cooking pot rim; 28. Or273, ETNW1.040, PB74 cooking pot; 29. Or253, ETNW1.040, PB74 coarse ware bowl; 30. Or303, ETNW1.040, PB74 Hellenistic wash-glaze juglet; 31. Cr94, WA25.008, PB31 Cypro-Classical II plain white juglet; 32. Cr559, ETNW12.004, PB28 pierced plain white body sherd; 33. Cr558, ETNW12.004, PB28 pierced plain white body sherd; 34. Cr549, ETNW12.004, PB9 pierced plain white body sherd; 35. Or255, ETNW3.021, PB50 terracotta figurine, arms holding bird to chest, head and lower body missing; 36. Cr497, Wβ25.007, PB52 Cypro-Classical II/Hellenistic I cooking pot rim.

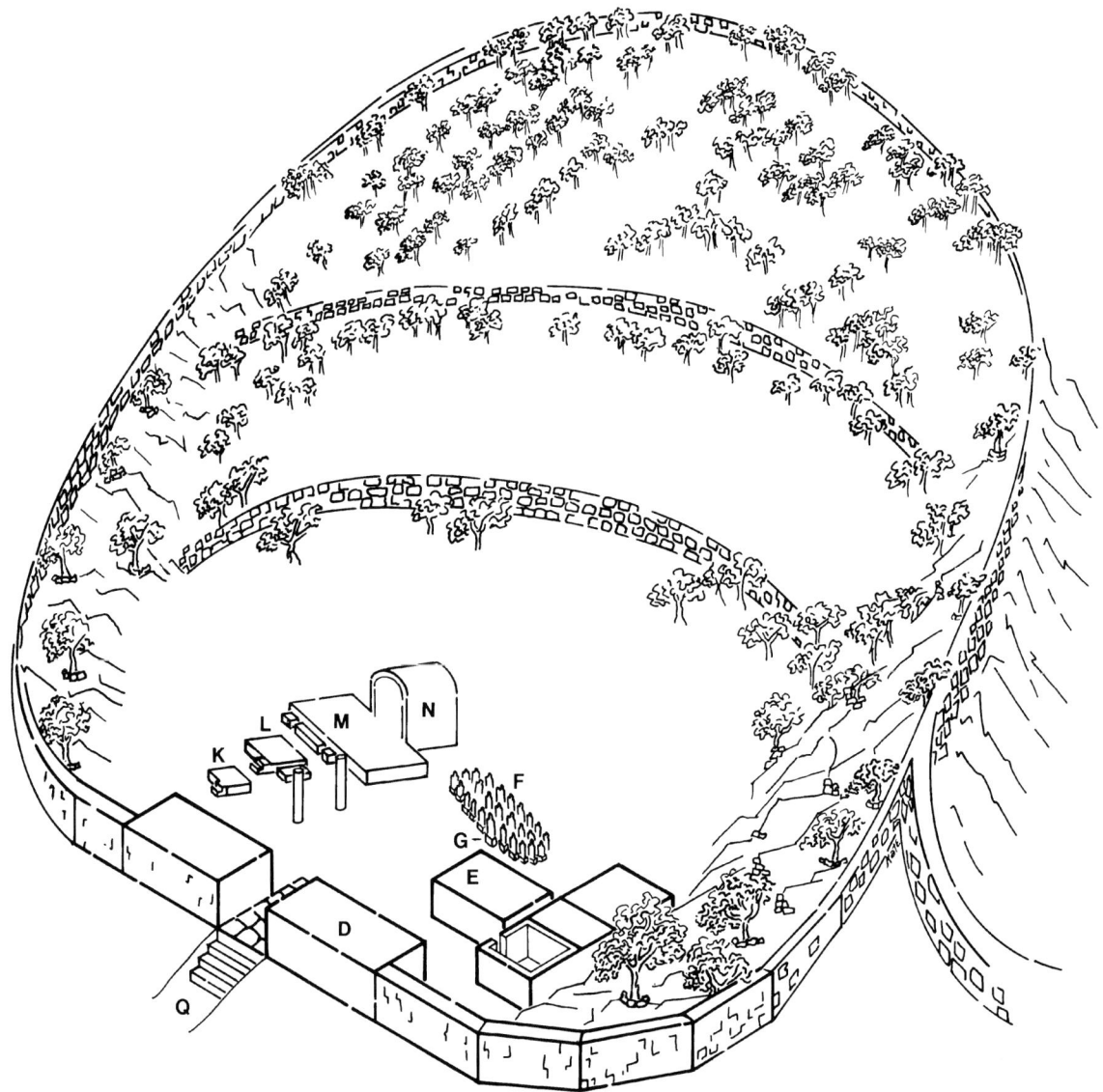

Fig. 24. Area T, reconstruction drawing of the "Adonis Temenos"; Kate MacKay.

small chamber with the olive-oil extracting stone located in 1992 was typical of the sorts of installations we uncovered in 1993. In Square NW 12, a *tabun*, or oven, was placed into a cut in bedrock and used during phases 2 and 3 of the architecture (figs. 18, 25). The soil around the oven was heavily laced with ash, and a number of deposits of a sulfurous-looking yellow soil appeared among the ashes. Samples were taken (below).

In Grid Square NW 1, in layers belonging to Phases 3 and 4 of the architecture, a deposit of pestles

and grinding stones, as well as carved stones of unknown purpose and small pottery vessels, was found associated with (and in one case encrusted by) similar yellow chemical deposits (fig. 26). Samples of these were taken to the Copper Institute of the University of Arizona for analysis.

Deity of the Temenos.   The working hypothesis with which we submitted the samples for testing was based on the suggestion that if the samples yielded copper sulfide, they might give a clue to the nature of the deity worshipped in the temenos, since copper sulfide was used in treating eye ailments. This suggestion caused great excitement, since the inscriptions found by Lang referred to the god as "Apollo Amyklos" in Greek, and Resheph-Mekal in Phoenician (Lang 1905: 629). Apollo was the Greek god of medicine, as Reshef was the Phoenician god of pestilence and healing. If we could find some evidence of medicines being produced within the sacred precinct we might have an indication that one aspect of the Cypriot deity worshipped there had to do with health or healing.

Among the first test results, only one sample, from the soils near the *tabun* installation, yielded any copper sulfide. The other compounds present included potassium iron sulfate, potassium iron sulfate hydroxide, copper iron sulfide, calcium carbonate, and jarosite. The uses, if any, of those compounds are unknown thus far; but all are consistent with the processing of copper ores. In terms of our hypothesis that the presence of copper sulfide might indicate some medicinal production within the sacred precinct, the results thus far are inconclusive. However, further tests were scheduled for the spring of 1994, and further samples would be taken in future excavation seasons.

The identification of the deity of the temenos on the east acropolis continues to be the subject of much discussion. We have suggested elsewhere that he might be the consort of the Great Mother (Gaber and Morden 1992: 25; Gaber 1994). Just as she is referred to in Cypriot inscriptions as *Wanasa*, "The Queen [of Heaven]," or "the Lady," so might her consort be referred to as "the Lord." Were this title to be translated into Phoenician, it might be rendered as "Adon." Then, just as Mekal in Phoenician comes

Fig. 25. Area T, oven installation, apparently for copper processing, in ET NW 121 looking south.

Fig. 26. Area T, small grinders, pounders, and vessels found in ET NW 1, apparently used in copper processing.

to be rendered "Amyklos" in Greek, so might Phoenician "Adon" come to be rendered as "Adonis" in Greek. Certainly the story of Venus and Adonis was sometimes set at Idalion, at least by Roman times (e.g., Propertius: II, xiii.51).

As for the aspects of the deity of our temenos that caused the Phoenicians and Greeks to liken him to Mekal, these still remain a mystery. Perhaps future seasons will provide evidence to answer that question.

CONCLUSION

The preliminary conclusion to be drawn from the excavations at Idalion, Cyprus, point to a demonstration of the principle of "near-decomposability" (Simon 1965). Clearly, in the face of violent conquest first in 450 B.C., and then again around 300 B.C., the monumental structures in the elite area of the western acropolis, Ambelliri, were destroyed. The Lower City domestic and industrial areas, however, show not only continuity but expansion in some cases, as in the northwest quadrant of Building B, the olive-oil processing area. The cult center on the eastern acropolis, Mouti tou Arvili, continued in use with modifications and rebuilding of structures down into the Roman period (first century B.C.–first century A.D.). It was only during the Roman period that Idalion began to shrink as a city and, centuries later, to dwindle into a village.

Thus conquest did not lead to collapse of any sort. Indeed, since the conquests in question were almost certainly economically motivated, aimed at capturing Idalion's control of its copper sources in the Troodos foothills, the conquerors had no intention of killing the goose that laid the golden egg. The working folk of ancient Idalion apparently were left alone to continue working, that is, to continue producing the economic prize sought by the conquerors.

The eventual decline of the city of Idalion under the Roman and Byzantine overlords also may be attributed to the vagaries of the copper industry. The Romans introduced a new, high-temperature, one-step process of smelting copper, so that the intermediate step of secondary smelting was eliminated. Idalion, therefore, may have been immediately diminished in importance, although a first century B.C. Roman villa with a bath complex excavated by the Joint American Expedition (Stager and Walker 1974: 77) seems to indicate the presence of an elite on the site in some capacity. In addition, the Roman smelting process required great quantities of wood for the smelting fires. The resulting deforestation of the island may also have contributed to the decline of some urban centers, including Idalion.

Whatever the direct causes of the decline of urban Idalion may have been, they certainly took centuries to take effect and did not follow directly on the conquest in either 450 B.C. or 300 B.C. The daily life of the citizens of the ancient city were for the most part unchanged by the cataclismic events of war and conquest that cost the lives of soldiers (and perhaps of rulers) and destroyed monumental structures time and again. Instead, the metamorphosis of the powerful, wealthy, populous city of ancient Idalion into the sleepy dairy and farming village of medieval and modern Dhali provides a textbook example of *la longue durée* described by Braudel and the *annales* school of historians.

ACKNOWLEDGMENTS

Since 1987 the current Idalion Expedition has had much help and support. In particular, the Department of Antiquities of the Republic of Cyprus, then under the direction of V. Karageorghis, and now under the direction of D. Christou, has been unfailingly gracious and helpful. The staff of the Cyprus Museum in Nicosia must also be mentioned in this regard. The 1987, 1992, and 1993 seasons could not have been fielded without the support of the Cyprus American Archaeological Research Institute and its director, S. Swiny. The town council of Dhali, Cyprus, has been a mainstay of our work. There have been a number of faithful donors to the fieldwork at Idalion who must be mentioned. Mr. and Mrs. Joseph Radov, Mr. Martin Gaber, Dr. Susan Lazar, the Joukowsky Foundation, Mr. Nicholas Kronwall, Ms. Charlotte Devers, and Ms. Gladys Callahan, as well as anonymous donors have given major support.

We are grateful to these, as well as many others who have helped by donating their services and time. Although these are too numerous to name individually, Ms. Sylvie Hartmann-Kaimakliotis and Mr. Manthos Mavromatis have consistently pitched in, and must be mentioned here. Without the efforts of Mr. George Demosthenous neither the current project nor the previous American Expedition could have carried out our work. The pottery drawings were the work of Jane Ravenhurst and William Dever. The architectural reconstruction of the Temple Field is the work of Kate MacKay. The photographs were done by William Dever, Charalambos Tilliros, and Pamela Gaber, and the architectural drawings used here were the work of William Dever and Pamela Gaber. Our thanks go to all those who have aided our efforts at Idalion.

NOTES

[1] William Childs, Nancy Serwint, personal communication. Sanctuary sites lie in surrounding agricultural land.

[2] M. Hadjicosti, personal communication.

[3] It may be significant that in the Hebrew Bible the term "asherah"—both the name of the Canaanite–Hebrew Mother Goddess, and the designation of some sort of tree image connected with her—is regularly rendered in the Septuagint by ἄλγος, "grove," followed by the Vulgate, with *lucus*, "wood," or *nemus*, "grove." The unanimous testimony of the ancient versions, supplemented by the tradition of the Mishnah, is that in Iron Age Palestine the cult of Asherah and her consort was often celebrated in open-air sanctuaries among groves of trees regarded as sacred. Furthermore, Asherah's consort, at least in the later biblical tradition, was Ba[c]al, or "the Lord," the Semitic equivalent of Phoenician-Greek Adonis.

[4] This suggestion was made by S. Swiny, director of the Cyprus American Archaeological Research Institute.

REFERENCES

Aurenche, O.
　1977　*La maison orientale. L'architecture du proche orient des origines au milieu du quatrieme millénaire. Dictionaire illustré multilingue de l'architecture du proche orient ancien.* Paris: de Boccard.

Bikai, P. M.
　1990　The Phoenicians: Rich and Glorious Traders of the Levant. *Archaeology* 43/2: 22–30.

Bintliff, J., ed.
　1991　*The* Annales *School and Archaeology.* Leicester: Leicester University.

Braemer, F.
　1982　*L'architecture domestique du Levant a l' age du fer.* Paris: Recherches sur les civilisations.

Buchholz, H. G.
　1990　Antike Personen in Tamassos. Pp. 55ff. in *Echo*, J. B. Trentini Festschrift.

di Cesnola, L. P.
　1877　*Cyprus: Its Ancient Cities, Tombs, and Temples.* London: John Murray.

Colonna-Ceccaldi, G.
　1882　*Monuments antiques de Chypre.* Paris: Librairies academique, Didier et Cie.

Daszewsky, W. A.
　1992　Nea Paphos 1991. *Report of the Department of Antiquities of Cyprus* 1992: 215–54.

Dever, W. G.
　1985　Syro-Palestinian and Biblical Archaeology. Pp. 31–74 in *The Hebrew Bible and Its Modern Interpreters*, eds. G. A. Knight and G. M. Tucker. Philadelphia: Fortress.
　1988　Impact of the "New Archaeology." Pp. 337–52 in *Benchmarks in Time and Culture: Introduction to Palestinian Archaeology*, eds. J. F. Drinkard, Jr., G. L. Mattingly, and J. M. Miller. Atlanta: Scholars.

Dever, W. G., and Cohen, R.
　1981　Preliminary Report of the Third and Final Season of the "Central Negev Highlands Project." *Bulletin of the American Schools of Oriental Research* 243: 5–77.

Dever, W. G., and Lance, H. D., eds.
　1978　*A Manual of Field Excavation. Handbook for Field Archaeologists.* Jerusalem: Hebrew Union College.

Eitam, D.
　1987　Olive Oil Production During the Biblical Period. Pp. 16–36 in *Olive Oil in Antiquity*, eds. M. Heltzer and D. Eitam. Haifa: Ministry of Education.

Gaber, P.
　1992　The University of New Hampshire Expedition to Idalion: the 1987 Season. *Report of the Department of Antiquities of Cyprus* 1992: 167–80.
　1994　In Search of Adonis. Pp. 161–65 in *Proceedings of the Symposium, The Sculpture of Ancient Cyprus*, Brussels, May, 1993. Brussels: University of Belgium.

Gaber, P., and Morden, M.
　1992　University of Arizona Expedition to Idalion, Cyprus 1992. Pp. 21–30 in *Centre d'études chypriotes: Cahiers 18*, no. 2. Paris: Editions Diffusion.

Gjerstad, E., et al.
　1935　*The Swedish Cyprus Expedition*, Vol. II. Stockholm: Pettersons.
　1948　*The Swedish Cyprus Expedition*, Vol. IV, Part 2. Stockholm: Pettersons.

Hadjisavvas, S.
　1988　Olive Oil Production in Ancient Cyprus. *Report of the Department of Antiquities of Cyprus* 1988: 111–20.
　1992a　Olive Oil Production and Divine Protection. Pp. 129–42 in *Acta Cypria: Acts of an International Congress on Cypriote Archaeology held in Göteborg on 22–24 August 1991*, ed. P. Åstrom. Partille, Sweden: Åstroms.
　1992b　*Olive Oil Processing in Cyprus from the Bronze Age to the Byzantine Period. Studies in*

Mediterranean Archaeology XCIX. Göteborg: Åstroms.

Helzer, M., and Eitam, D.
1987   *Olive Oil in Antiquity: Israel and Neighbouring Countries from Neolithic to Early Arab Period.* Jerusalem: Ministry of Education and Culture.

Hohlfelder, R. L.
1992   The Paphos Ancient Harbor Explorations 1992. *Report of the Department of Antiquities of Cyprus* 1992: 235–56.

Karageorghis, V., ed.
1985   *Archaeology in Cyprus 1960–1985.* Nicosia: Leventis Foundation.
1986   *Acts of the International Archaeological Symposium: Cyprus Between the Orient and the Occident.* Nicosia: Zavallis.

Knapp, A. B. ed.
1992   *Annales. Archaeology and Ethnohistory.* Cambridge: Cambridge University.

Lang, R. H.
1871   On Coins Discovered During Recent Excavations in the Island of Cyprus. *The Numismatic Chronicle and Journal of the Numismatic Society* 1871: 1–18.
1878a   Narrative of Excavations in a Temple at Dali (Idalium) in Cyprus. *Transactions of the Royal Society of Literature*, 2nd Ser. XI: 30–71.
1878b   On the Discovery of Some Cypriote Inscriptions. *Transactions of the Royal Society of Biblical Archaeology* I, 18: 116–29.
1905   Reminiscences—Archaeological Researches in Cyprus. *Blackwood's Edinburgh Magazine*, Vol. 177, No. 1075: 622–39.

Lund, J.
1986   *Sukas VIII. The Habitation Quarters.* Publications of the Carlsberg Foundation Expedition to Phoenicia 10. Copenhagen: Royal Danish Academy of Sciences and Letters.

Maier, F. G.
1966   *Alt-Paphos auf Cypern: Ausgrabungen zur Geschichte von Stadt und Heiligtum.* Mainz: von Zabern.

Maier, F. G.
1985   Factoids in Ancient History: The Case of Fifth-Century Cyprus. *Journal of Hellenic Studies* 105: 32–39.

Marvin, M.
1974   The History of Idalion. Pp. 22–28 in *Excavations at Idalion: 1971–1972*, eds. L. Stager, A. Walker, and G. E. Wright. Cambridge: American Schools of Oriental Research.

Masson, O.
1961   *Les inscriptions Chypriote syllabiques.* Athens: École française d'Athenes.

Ohnefalsch-Richter, M.
1893   *Kypros, the Bible and Homer.* London: Asher.

Petit, T.
1989   Un Depot de Fondation au "Palais" d'Amathonte. *Bulletin des Correspondences Helleniques* 113: 135–48.

Pritchard, J. B.
1975   *Sarepta. A Preliminary Report on the Iron Age.* Philadelphia: University of Pennsylvania.

Reyes, A. T.
1994   *Archaic Cyprus: A Study of the Textual and Archaeological Evidence.* Oxford: Clarendon.

Senff, R.
1993   *Das Apollosheiligtum von "Idalion": Studies in Mediterranean Archaeology* 94. Jonsered: Paul Åstroms.

Simon, H.
1965   The Architecture of Complexity. *General Systems* 10: 63–76.

Soren, D.
1984   The Mysterious Rock-Cut Channels of Kourion. *Report of the Department of Antiquities of Cyprus* 1984: 285–93.

Soren, D., ed.
1987   *The Sanctuary of Apollo Hylates at Kourion, Cyprus.* Tucson: University of Arizona.

Stager, L., and Walker, A.
1989   *American Expedition to Idalion Cyprus 1973–1980.* Chicago: Oriental Institute.

Stager, L.; Walker, A.; and Wright, G. E.
1974   *First Preliminary Report of the Joint American Expedition to Idalion, Cyprus, 1971–1972.* Cambridge, MA: American Schools of Oriental Research.

Stern, E.
1993   Tel Dor, 1992: Preliminary Report. *Israel Exploration Journal* 43: 126–50.

Tainter, J. A.
1989   *The Collapse of Complex Societies.* Cambridge: Cambridge University.

Tatton-Brown, V., ed.
1989   *Cyprus and the East Mediterranean in the Iron Age.* London: British Museum.

Walker, A.
1974   Cypro-Archaic and Cypro-Geometric Periods in the Lower City. Pp. 42–49 in *First Preliminary Report of the Joint American Expedition to Idalion, Cyprus, 1971–1972*, eds. L. Stager, A. Walker, and G. E. Wright. Cambridge, MA: American Schools of Oriental Research.

Walker, A., and Gaber, P.
1989   Excavations at Idalion 1973–1980: West Lower City Domestic Precinct, Pp. 66–83 in *American Expedition to Idalion, Cyprus 1973–1980*, eds. L. Stager and A. Walker. Chicago: The Oriental Institute.

Woolley, C. L.
1938   Excavations at Al Mina, Sueidid, I–II. *Journal of Hellenic Studies* 57: 1–30, 133–70.

Yoffee, N., and Cowgill, G.
1989   *The Collapse of Ancient States and Civilizations*. Tucson: University of Arizona.

Yon, M., and Sznycer, M.
1992   A Phoenician Victory Trophy at Kition. *Report of the Department of Antiquities of Cyprus* 1992: 157–65.

Young, J., and Young, S.
1955   *Terra Cotta Figurines from Kourion in Cyprus*. Philadelphia: University Museum, University of Pennsylvania.

Early Town Development and Water Management in the Jordan Valley: Investigations at Tell el-Handaquq North

Jonathan B. Mabry

Center for Desert Archaeology
3975 North Tucson Blvd.
Tucson, Arizona 85716

with contributions by

Marcia L. Donaldson
Katherine Gruspier
Grant Mullen

Gaetano Palumbo
Michael N. Rawlings
Marcus A. Woodburn

Field investigations at Tell el-Handaquq North in the east-central Jordan Valley in 1987–88 identified the remains of a large, protohistoric walled town occupied from the early fourth to mid–third millennium B.C. During an architectural survey, visible fortifications, house walls, water control features, and tomb fields were recorded over an area of 25 to 30 hectares. Surface and buried artifacts and features indicate initial occupation during the Late Chalcolithic period. The enclosing defensive wall and stratified Early Bronze I and II architecture and cultural deposits were recorded in a long bulldozer cut through the site. A test excavation on another part of the site revealed multiple phases of domestic architecture, and recovered stratified sequences of pottery, stone tools, and subsistence remains dating from the late Early Bronze I to the mid–Early Bronze II periods. Botanical remains include crops and crop varieties that imply either irrigation or higher rainfall than today. One of the six accelerator radiocarbon dates obtained indicates that the settlement fortifications were built before 3000 B.C. The other radiocarbon dates range in age from the Late Chalcolithic-Early Bronze I transition to the Early Bronze IV period. On the basis of these data, the site is an important example of early town development and community–based water control in the Jordan Valley, related to other known protohistoric towns with water control systems in the southern Levant.

The results of fieldwork conducted at Tell el-Handaquq North in the east-central Jordan Valley (Palestine Grid Coordinates 206.5, 189.8; fig. 1 here) between November 1987 and March 1988 were previously summarized in a preliminary report (Mabry 1989). Those investigations identified the remains of a 25–30 ha protohistoric settlement with fortifications, water control features, and tomb fields, occupied from the early fourth to the mid-third millennium B.C. (fig. 2). The current article

is the final report; it includes analyses of the ceramic assemblage, subsistence remains, and radiocarbon samples, and presents a discussion of the significance of a stamp seal impression and a possible stamp seal. A stratified sequence of late EB I to mid–EB II pottery is type-seriated and cross-dated with other excavated ceramic assemblages in the region. The botanical evidence includes crops and crop varieties that imply either higher rainfall or irrigation during site occupation, and the earliest recovered remains of

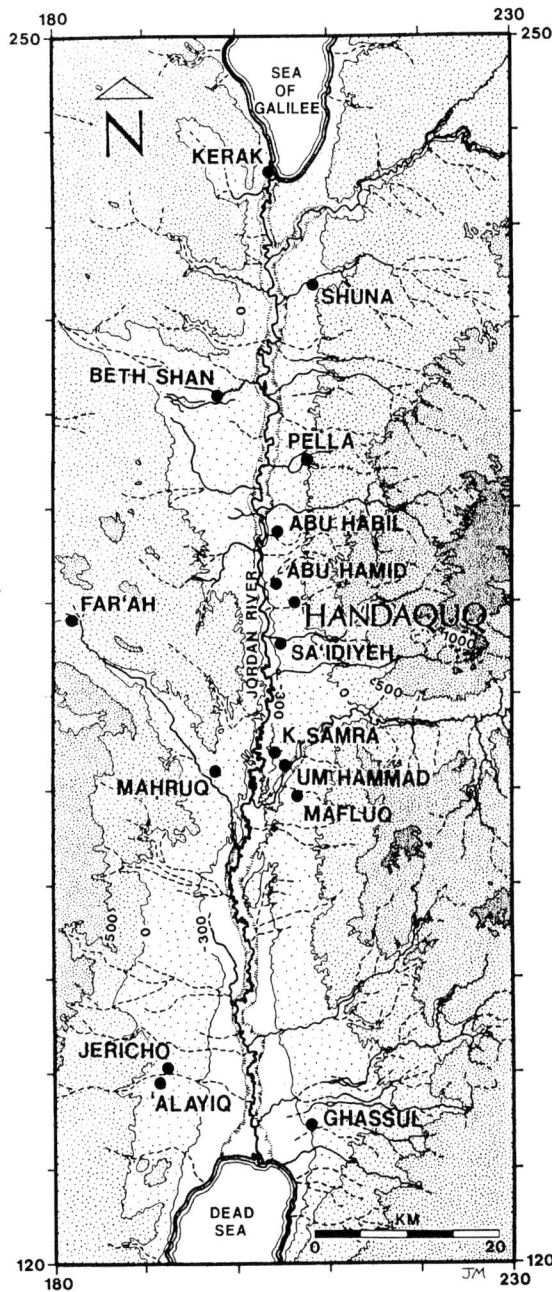

Fig. 1. Location of Tell el-Handaquq and related excavated sequences in the Jordan Valley.

Setting

The site is near the eastern escarpment of the Jordan Valley (the central Jordan Rift between Lake Tiberias and the Dead Sea), on a group of three hills that overlook its narrowest part. This 5-km-wide part of the valley is presently the boundary between arid and semiarid climates, receiving an average of about 225 mm of rainfall annually. Cultural deposits on the western part of the site have accumulated upon a steep natural hill that is an erosional remnant of Pleistocene limestone conglomerates and travertines. A gravel ridge—a stranded beach of the "Lisan Lake" that filled most the Jordan Rift during the late Pleistocene—extends northward from this hill along the −180 m elevation contour (the maximum level reached by the lake). Exposed alluvial deposits indicate that from the early to mid-Holocene the Wadi es-Sarar flowed nearer to the surface than it does today. During this cycle of aggradation a shallow, shifting channel regularly deposited silt and gravel to form an alluvial fan up to 1 km wide and 4 m thick. This aggradation was interrupted sometime during the mid-Holocene, and the wadi began to cut downward into the alluvial fan. Today the wadi flows only during the winter rainy season, on its new bed 2 to 4 m below the fan surface.

Previous Surface Explorations

The site was first explored by western scholars in the early twentieth century. F.-M. Abel (1911: 416), a French Jesuit priest and biblical geographer, was the first to describe the ruins of Tell el-Handaquq, though he remarked mostly on its elevated position and the surrounding fertile reddish soil. The classicist and art historian C. Steuernagel (1925: 349–50) also reported the location of the ruins of "Tell el-Handakuk" on the Wadi Sofara (the upstream reach of Wadi es-Sarar), which he described as a "rather large settlement" with fortification walls and an "artificial rock basin." Archaeologist A. Mallon (Mallon, Koeppel, and Neuville 1934: 156) subsequently described the visible architecture and surface artifacts at a tell he found on the south bank of the Wadi Zarqa, which local villagers also called "Handaquq." Glueck (1951: 285–88), confused these two sites when he briefly visited the more northern one described here; he apparently did not find the identically named southern site during his extensive surveys of Jordan in the 1940s. North (1961: 50; fig. 19) did not correct

bread-wheat in the Jordan Valley—directly radiocarbon dated. Another radiocarbon date indicates that the settlement fortifications were constructed prior to 3000 B.C., the beginning of EB II, when walls were built around a number of southern Levantine towns.

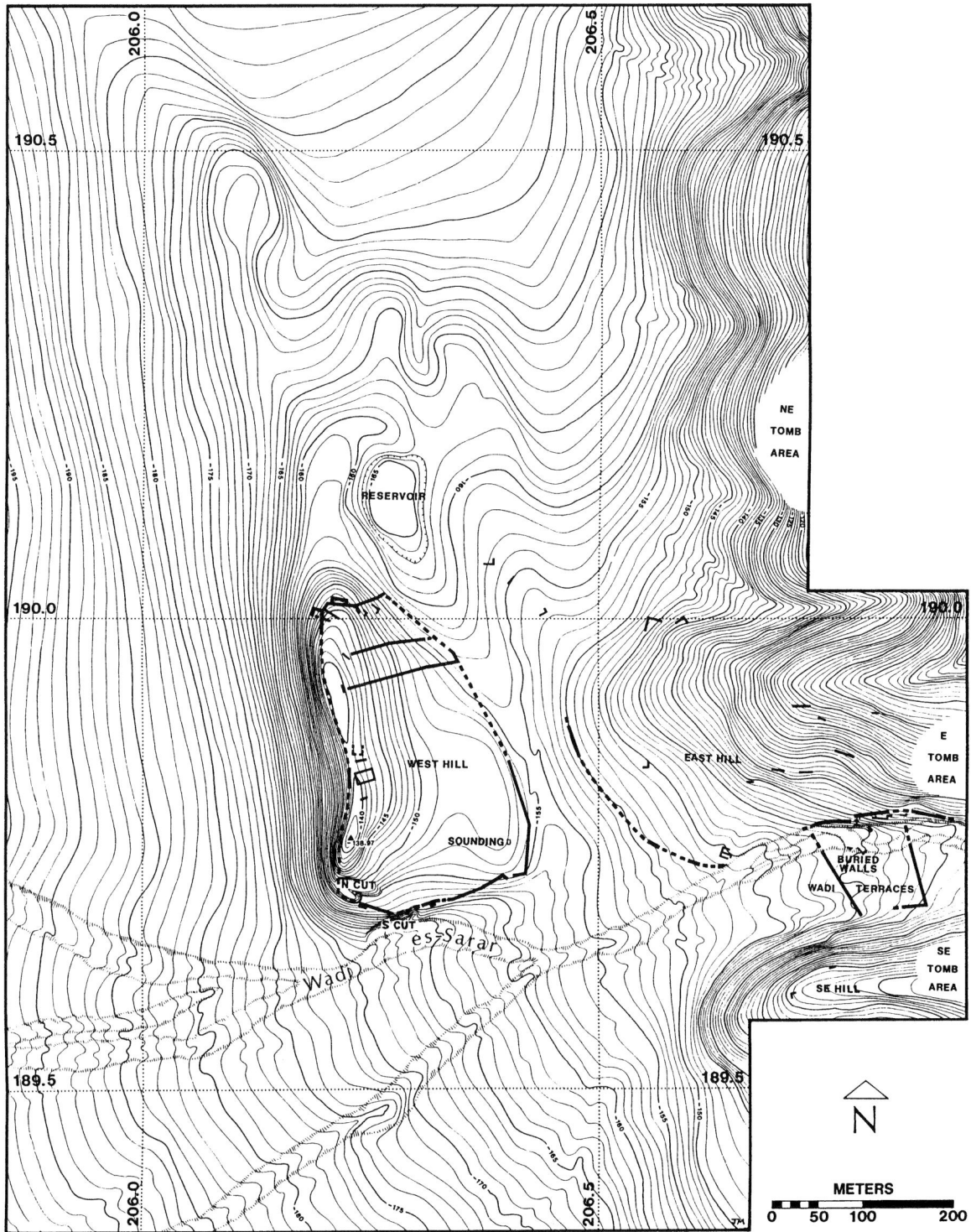

Fig. 2. Topography and visible architecture of Tel el-Handaquq North.

this mixup in his uncritical compilation of early fourth millennium B.C. sites reported in Palestine and Jordan.

Glueck noticed numerous traces of stone walls and "Middle" and "Late Chalcolithic" (equivalent to Late Chalcolithic and Early Bronze I in current terminology) pottery sherds, but he did not recognize the water-control features or the substantial defensive walls that Steuernagel traced around much of the site. Ibrahim, Sauer, and Yassine (1976: 51; fig. 16) found flint tools and pottery sherds from the Late Chalcolithic, EB I, and EB II–III periods, but they also made no remark about the fortification system in the report of their 1975 visit. During a survey of prehistoric cave sites in the eastern Jordan Valley during 1985, Muheisen (1988: Site 35) found numerous tombs carved into the limestone cliffs east of the ancient settlement.

Goals and Methods

The goals of the field investigations were fourfold: to identify the boundaries of the site and the history of settlement occupation; to define the plan of the settlement and the locations of structural remains representing habitation, defense, and water-control functions; to record the stratigraphy of cultural deposits; and to recover, from stratified contexts, samples of chronologically diagnostic artifacts, organic materials for radiocarbon dating, and remains of subsistence resources. To achieve these four goals, fieldwork included systematic surface collection of chronologically diagnostic artifacts, mapping of the site's topography and visible architecture,

profiling and recording of exposed cultural deposits, and excavation of a test trench where the deepest cultural deposits are likely to be preserved. The specific methods used for these tasks are described at the beginning of each of the following sections. The illustrated artifacts are described in the figure captions.

HISTORY OF OCCUPATION REPRESENTED BY SURFACE ARTIFACTS

Chronologically diagnostic ceramic and lithic artifacts were collected from the surface of the site during a systematic survey, with an average space of 10 m between passes. Pre-Early Bronze Age strata were not reached in the 1988 sounding and were not evident in the South Cut (below), but "Late Chalcolithic" sherds and flint tools (fig. 3) were found over much of the site's surface, indicating that a settlement was established at Tell el-Handaquq by at least the early fourth millennium B.C. Late Chalcolithic artifacts were also found in association with two partially exposed masonry structures buried by more than 1 m of alluvium in the south bank of the wadi (figs. 2; 3:1,5,10). A fragment of wood charcoal collected from the alluvium trapped behind a masonry channel-bottom dam near these structures (see discussion of water management features below) yielded a mid-fourth millennium B.C. radiocarbon date (below), which supports the artifact-based dating of the structures, as well as the dating of the initial occupation of the settlement to the Late Chalcolithic period.

Several typical pottery forms from this early stage of occupation were represented by sherds,

---

Fig. 3. Early fourth millennium B.C. (Late Chalcolithic) ceramic and chipped stone artifacts.

Location	Description
1. Wadi terrace	Everted jar rim, low-fired, very pale brown 10YR8/4 ware, very coarse grit temper, wet-smoothed.
2. Surface	Everted jar rim, medium-fired, pink 5YR7/4 ware, coarse grit temper, wet-smoothed.
3. Surface	Thickened jar rim, low-fired, very pale brown 10YR8/3 ware, very coarse grit temper.
4. Surface	Thickened jar rim, low-fired, very pale brown 10YR8/3 ware, very coarse grit temper.
5. Wadi terrace	Medium-fired, reddish-yellow 5YR7/6 ware, coarse grit and grog temper, raised and indented band of decoration, red 10R4/6 trickle paint exterior.
6. Surface	Low-fired, gray 5YR6/1 ware, coarse grit temper, raised and indented band of decoration, red 10R4/2 trickle paint exterior.
7. Surface	Low-fired, pink 7.5YR8/4 ware, very coarse grit temper, raised and indented band of decoration, red 10R4/6 trickle paint exterior.
8. Surface	Chisel with trapezoidal cross-section and ground distal end.
9. Surface	Chisel/scraper with trapezoidal cross-section and abruptly retouched distal end.
10. Wadi terrace	Bladelet backed with steep unifacial retouch.
11. Surface	Tabular flint fan scraper with remaining cortex and unifacially retouched edge.
12. Surface	Tabular flint fan scraper with remaining cortex and bifacially retouched edge.

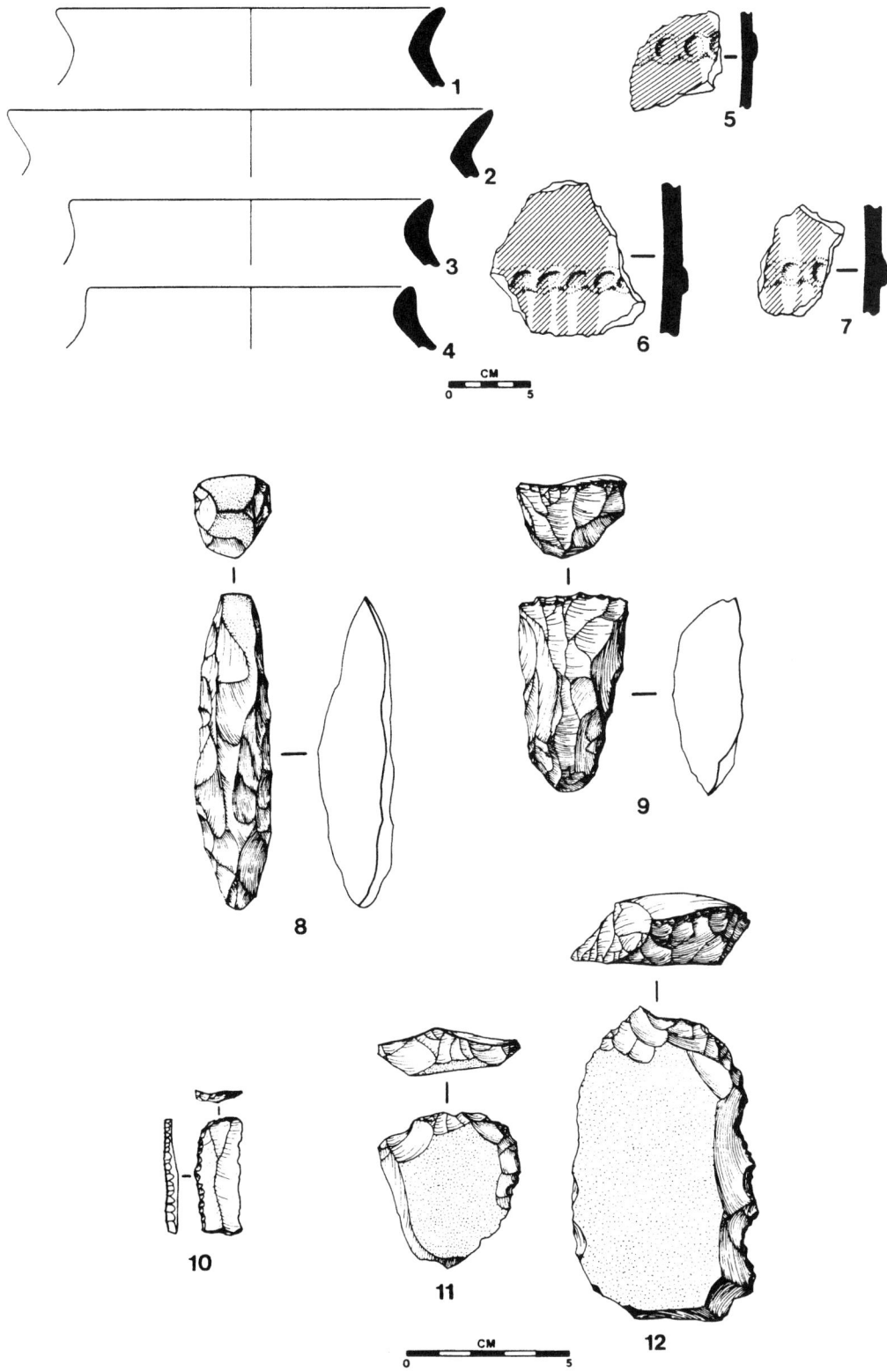

Fig. 3. Early fourth millennium B.C. (Late Chalcolithic) ceramic and chipped stone artifacts.

including low-fired, everted- and thickened-rim jars with coarse grit temper ("coarse wares"; fig. 3:1–4) and body sherds of a similar ware decorated with raised, indented bands and red trickle paint (fig. 3:5–7). Chipped stone tools from this period included chisels (fig. 3:8,9), backed bladelets (fig. 3:10), and fan scrapers on tabular flint (fig. 3:11,12). This ceramic and lithic assemblage is clearly similar to those found on the surface at Subeirra (Mabry and Palumbo 1988: figs. 3–6) and in excavations at other nearby early fourth millennium B.C. sites: the Pella tell (Smith 1973: pl. 34) and Area XIV (McNicoll, Smith, and Hennessy 1982: 31–34; Hanbury-Tenison 1986, figs. 24–26), Abu Hamid (Dollfus and Kafafi 1986a; 1986b; 1987), Abu Habil (de Contenson 1960a; Mabry and Palumbo 1988; Leonard 1992), and Saᶜidiyeh el-Tahta (de Contenson 1960a).

Shallow plowing has disturbed the surface distribution of artifacts over much of the site, but "Early Bronze I" sherds (fig. 4) are the most common on the surface, perhaps reflecting rapid growth of the settlement during the mid- to late fourth millennium B.C. Holemouth jars with incised decoration and trickle paint (fig. 4:1), rolled rim jars with incisions, and unpainted holemouth jars with pushed-up lug handles and incised decoration (fig. 4:2) were represented by surface sherds. These pottery types have been found together in stratified EB IA (Stage 2) deposits at nearby Tell Um Hammad (Helms 1984: fig. 12; 1986: fig. 16), at Tell esh-Shuna North (de Contenson 1960a; 1960b; Gustavson-Gaube 1985; 1986; Leonard 1992), and at Jericho (Kenyon 1952: fig. 5:3).

Sherds of incised ware, referred to as "Jawa type" by Hanbury-Tenison (1986: 123–25), are also common on the site surface. This distinctive ceramic type was first found at the fourth millennium B.C. fortified settlement at Jawa, on the southeast flank of the Jebel Druze in the interior basalt desert of Jordan (Helms 1975; 1976a; 1977; 1981; 1991). This type includes holemouth and flared-rim jars with pushed-up lugs or "axe-blade" ledge handles, incised decoration, and occasional paint. In a test excavation at Jelmet esh-Shariyeh (Wadi Yabis Survey, Site 120) in the eastern foothills of the central Jordan Valley, this ware was found in the same stratum with trickle-painted coarse ware, red-slipped ware, and stripe-painted ware, which overlay a stratum with dark burnished ware (Palumbo, Mabry, and Kuijt 1990: 109).

In addition to the stratified contexts listed, incised ware sherds have been found in the Jordan Valley on the surface at Pella (Hanbury-Tenison 1986: 124), Kataret es-Samra (Leonard 1983: fig. 9:7–8), and at Tell el-Hammam South. They have also been found on the surface at sites in the lower (Gordon and Villiers 1983) and upper Wadi Zerqa (Glueck 1951: pl. 163:9; Hanbury-Tenison 1986), and in Early Bronze Age strata at Tell el-ᵓUmeiri on the Jordan Plateau near Amman (L. Herr, personal communication 1990). The presence of this distinctive mid- to late fourth millennium B.C. (EB IA) ceramic ware therefore links Tell el-Handaquq with these other valley sites, with sites on the eastern plateau, and with the fortified settlements on the edge of the interior desert that are based on conservation of runoff.

Fig. 4. Late fourth millennium B.C. (EB I) ceramic artifacts.

Location	Description
1. Surface	Holemouth jar rim, medium-fired, very pale brown 10YR8/4 ware, fine grit temper, incisions around rim.
2. Surface	Holemouth jar rim, medium-fired, pink 7.5YR7/4 ware, coarse grit temper, incisions around rim, pushed-up lug handles below rim.
3. Surface	Rolled jar rim, low-fired, pink 7.5YR7/4 ware, coarse grit temper, incisions below rim, wet-smoothed.
4. Surface	Rolled jar rim, low-fired, pinkish-white 7.5YR8/2 ware, coarse grit and grog temper, incisions around top of rim, red 10R5/6 slip exterior.
5. Surface	Inverted bowl rim, medium-fired, reddish-yellow 5YR6/6 ware indented decoration around carination.
6. Surface	Straight bowl rim, low-fired, pink 5YR7/4 ware, coarse grit temper, indented decoration below rim, wiped exterior.
7. Surface	Everted jar rim, medium-fired, light red 2.5YR6/6 ware, dark gray 2.5YRN4/ core, coarse grit temper, raised decoration below rim.
8. Surface	Plain ledge handle, low-fired, pink 7.5YR8/4 ware, medium grit temper, red 2.5YR5/6 slip exterior.
9. Surface	Plain ledge handle, low-fired, pink 7.5YR8/4 ware, medium grit temper.
10. Surface	Plain ledge handle, low-fired, very pale brown 10YR8/3 ware, fine grit temper, reddish brown 2.5YR5/4 slip exterior.
11. Surface	Plain ledge handle, medium-fired, pink 7.5YR8/4 ware, coarse grit temper.

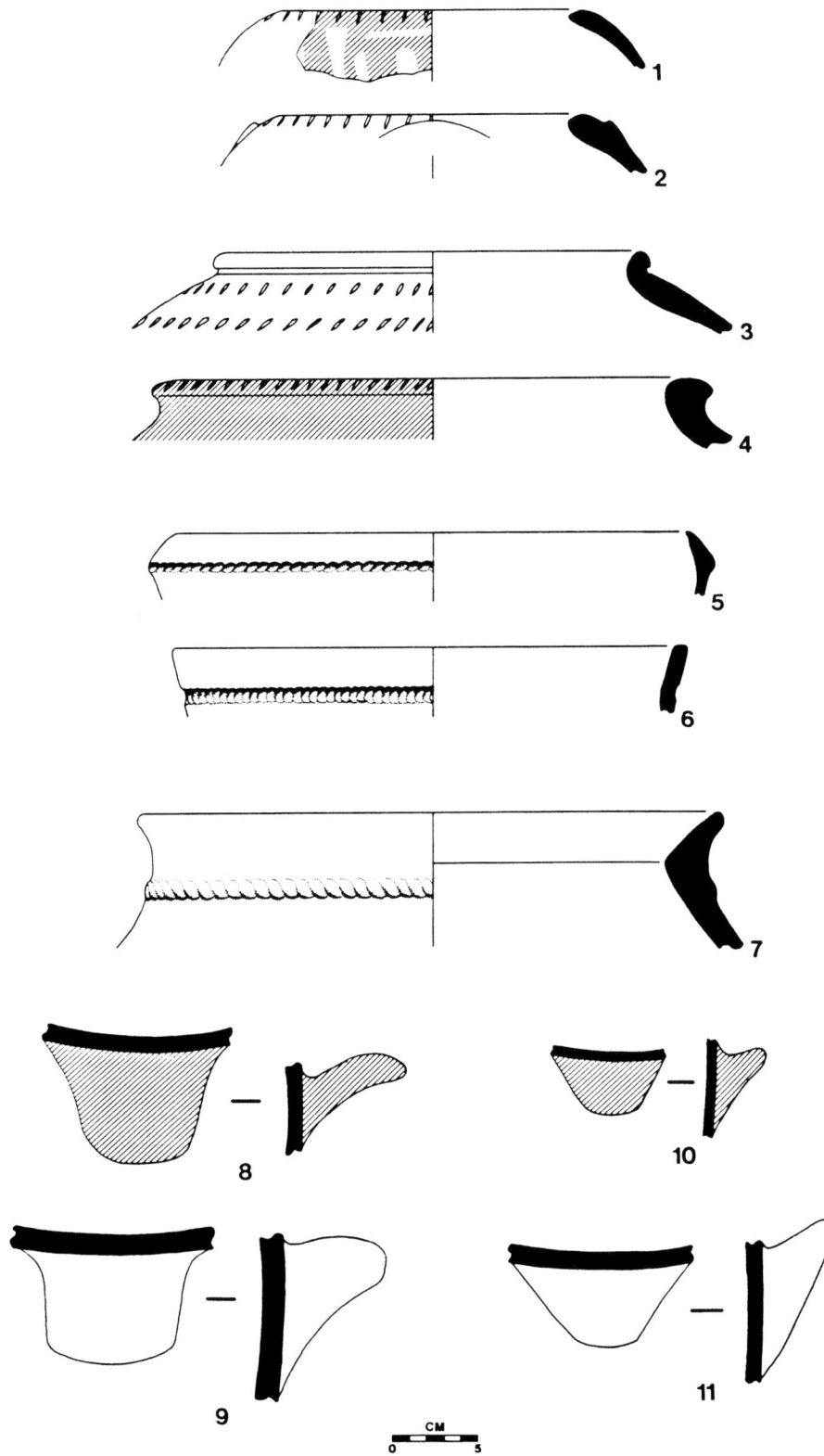

Fig. 4. Late fourth millennium B.C. (EB I) ceramic artifacts.

Inverted- and straight-rim bowls with indented decoration (fig. 4:5, 6), common on the surface of Tell el-Handaquq, were included in an excavated assemblage from Tulul Abu el-ᶜAlayiq, near Jericho (Pritchard 1958: pl. 27:7). Reddish "Proto-Urban D" ware (or "Um Hammad" ware) with bands of raised decoration (fig. 4:7) is also common on the surface. This ware has been found stratified in EB IB (Stage 3) strata at Tell Um Hammad (Helms 1984: fig. 15), and in Stratum XVI at Beth Shan (Fitzgerald 1935: pl. 1:3). It represents a long pottery tradition, however, that lasted from the early to late fourth millennium B.C. in northern Palestine and Jordan (cf. Glueck 1945: 10; 1951: 318–29; de Miroschedji 1971; Hanbury-Tenison 1986: 127–29). Typical EB I plain ledge handles, some with a thin red slip or wash, were also found over much of the site (fig. 4:8–11).

Early Bronze II sherds are second in frequency on the surface. A handful of EB IV sherds, including high-fired, cream-slipped "combed ware," and folded "envelope" ledge handles (fig. 5:1–4) are the latest found on the site, except for a small number of Byzantine sherds. These patterns in the surface artifact assemblage indicate contraction and eventual abandonment of the settlement during the mid-third millennium B.C., before the beginning of the EB III.

Except for brief encampments during the late third millennium B.C. (EB IV), Tell el-Handaquq was never occupied again. The masonry ruins of the protohistoric town are therefore not obscured by later occupations; the foundations of some of the fortifications, internal divisions, public architecture, houses, and water-control features can be traced on the surface.

TOPOGRAPHICAL-ARCHITECTURAL SURVEY

Jonathan B. Mabry, Michael N. Rawlings, and Marcus A. Woodburn

A detailed survey of the topography and visible architectural remains at the site was conducted during several visits between November 1987 and March 1988. Using an electronic theodolite/distance measurer (EDM), the survey team mapped an area of about 1 km² at 1-m contour intervals (fig. 2). Traces of prehistoric masonry structures were recorded over an area of 25–30 ha, mainly on two opposing western and eastern hills. Some visible segments of the western defensive enclosure and its towers are preserved up to three courses above the present ground surface.

Fig. 5. Late third millennium B.C. (Early Bronze Age IV) ceramic artifacts; ceramic and lithic artifacts from burial 021, Sounding Stratum 2; and ceramic artifacts from Tomb NE.1.

Location	Description
1–2. Surface	Flared jar rim and flat base (same vessel), very high-fired ("metallic ware"), reddish-yellow 5YR7/6 ware, gray 10YR6/1 core, fine sand temper, white 10YR8/2 slip exterior and rim interior, raised decoration below neck, combed decoration on lower body.
3. Surface	Folded "envelope" ledge handle, high fired, gray 10YR5/1 ware, fine sand temper.
4. Surface	Folded "envelope" ledge handle, high-fired, reddish-yellow 5YR7/6 ware, fine sand temper.
5. Sounding, Stratum 2, Burial 021	Plain bowl (lamp) rim, high-fired, pink 5YR7/4 ware, uncertain temper, horizontally burnished red 10R4/6 slip interior and exterior, soot on rim.
6. Sounding, Stratum 2, Burial 021	Everted jar rim, high-fired, pale red 10R6/4 ware, medium grit temper, burnished self-slip exterior and rim interior.
7. Sounding, Stratum 2, Burial 021	Ground and drilled basalt ring fragment.
8. Tomb NE.1	Carinated bowl rim, medium-fired, reddish-yellow 5YR7/6 ware, no temper, burnished dark red 10R3/6 slip interior and exterior.
9. Tomb NE.1	Folded jar rim, medium-fired, very pale brown 10YR7/3 ware, fine grit temper, weak red 10R5/4 slip exterior and rim interior.
10. Tomb NE.1	Cup (with loop handle?), medium-fired, pink 5YR7/4 ware, no temper, red 10R4/4 "line-painted" stripes exterior.
11. Tomb NE.1	Inverted platter-bowl rim, low-fired, very pale brown 10YR7/3 ware, medium grit temper, burnished weak red 10R4/3 slip interior and above carination exterior, burnished reddish brown 5YR5/4 slip below carination exterior.

The Fortified Settlement

Connecting to enclose the western hill are long sections of a boulder-constructed, 3-m-wide defensive wall with regularly spaced rectangular towers on the northern and southern sections, and possibly a bent-entry gate near the southeast corner. This type of fortification system protected many late fourth to mid-third millennium B.C. towns in the southern Levant (Helms 1976b). Within the western enclosure

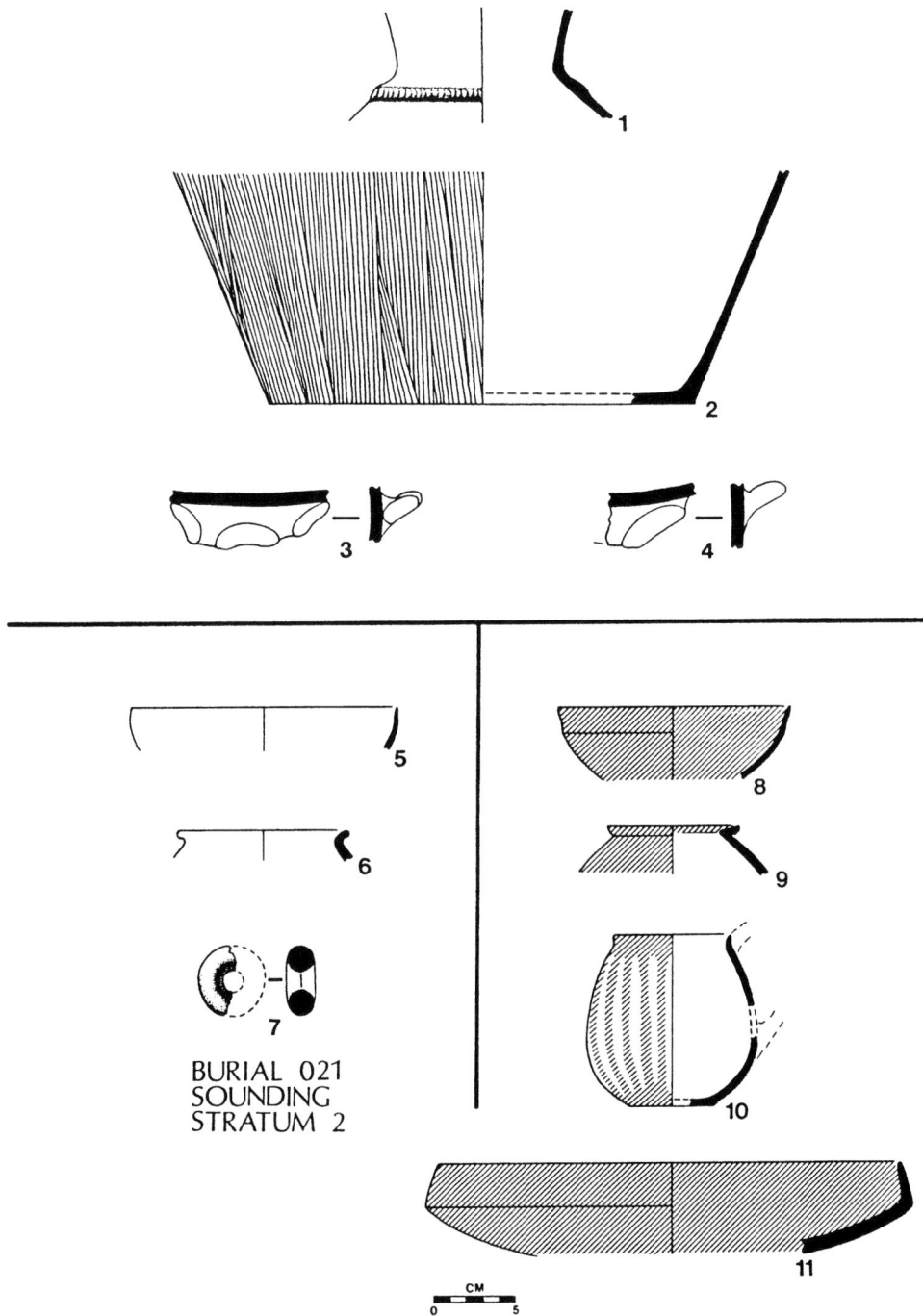

Fig. 5. Late third millennium B.C. (Early Bronze Age IV) ceramic artifacts; ceramic and lithic artifacts from burial 021, Sounding Stratum 2; and ceramic artifacts from Tomb NE.1.

are the foundations of at least three large masonry buildings (possibly for "public" functions) in a shallow saddle between the two high points of the steep western summit, and walls and corners of rectangular masonry houses on the northern slope. A flat lower mound in the southeast is the area with the deepest cultural deposits. Two parallel walls ascend from the northeastern section of this enclosure to the northern summit of the western hill, thereby dividing this part of the settlement into separate precincts within the town wall.

Shorter sections of a second massive, boulder-constructed wall appear to connect to skirt the base of (and probably enclose) the eastern hill and an area on the north bank of the wadi. Stone foundations of rectangular buildings and slope-retaining walls are visible over much of the eastern hill, and are exposed in the eroded north bank of the wadi immediately below this defensive wall. As described above, masonry house walls and corners are also found in the opposite bank of the wadi, buried by more than 1 m of alluvial silt and gravel. Traces of at least two masonry structures (one perhaps a watchtower) are also visible on the summit of the steep southeastern hill on the south side of the wadi, directly opposite the eastern hill.

Water Management Features

The topographical-architectural survey also identified several features designed for capture and storage of local slope runoff and wadi floods. It is likely, in my opinion, that these were contemporary with the protohistoric settlement because of their clear incorporation into the town plan and the absence of any evidence for a historic occupation at the site (fig. 2).

Two boulder-constructed dams, originally about 100 m long, span the width of the low terrace of Wadi es-Sarar, opposite the visible structures on the northern bank. Their foundations are above the buried structures exposed in the southern bank, indicating that the dams were constructed after abandonment of the buildings. Alluvial silts and gravels have accumulated up to their tops, forming a series of stepped terraces. As briefly noted (above; discussed in more detail below), charcoal collected from alluvial silt trapped behind the lower of the two dams (and stratigraphically higher than the buried structures) yielded a mid-fourth millennium B.C. radiocarbon date, indicating that they were built before the end of the Late Chalcolithic period. Like similar systems used historically and today in Palestine and Jordan, these an-

cient dams captured the silt carried by winter floods. The stepped arrangement of terraces also slowed the flood water long enough to saturate fields planted on the silt trapped behind the dams. Both of these dams were breached during a valley-wide cycle of wadi incision in the mid-Holocene (Mabry 1992).

A large basin, about 1.5 ha in area and 3 m deep, was also found in the northwest part of the site. Elders in the neighboring villages recall that, until early in this century, this basin was partially filled by winter runoff from the surrounding slopes and used to water livestock and irrigate fields below. It was still in use as a water supply for travelers to Mecca during the time of Steuernagel's visit (1925: 349–50). It is likely that during protohistoric times, when the wadi was flowing nearer the surface, wadi floods also were diverted through the shallow gully that separates the fortified western and eastern hills to fill the basin completely. A shallow core sample taken from the center of the basin revealed that at least 1.5 m of dark, silty clay forms a virtually impermeable lining on the bottom. This basin is under cultivation today, but its clay lining still causes it to remain swampy for several months after the last winter rains.

The thick accumulation of silty clay sediments also indicates that the basin was substantially deeper in antiquity. The core sample shows that the original depth was at least 4.5 m, such that the volume has declined from at least 67,500 m^3 to the present 45,000 m^3. On the basis of ethnographic data, Helms (1981: 189; 1982: 106) has calculated that the estimated 3,000 to 5,000 people and their livestock at contemporaneous Jawa required about 1800 m^3 of water per month, or 21,600 m^3 per year. If similar figures are used, it may be calculated that only one-third of the total volume of the single reservoir at Tell el-Handaquq could have supplied a population of 5,000 and their livestock through the dry summer, with a surplus of about two-thirds left for irrigation of fields below, even after evaporation loss. The bottom of the reservoir was not found, however, and it may have had an even greater volume originally.

The presence of water management features may imply drier climatic conditions than today, requiring water conservation during the occupation of the settlement. However, the capacity of this flood storage system is efficiently suited to current hydrological conditions. The reservoir originally could hold at least 90 percent of Wadi es-Sarar's present estimated total annual flood flow of 75,000 million m^3, which is 22 percent of the total combined surface and groundwater flow of 340,000 m^3 from a catchment of 13 km^2

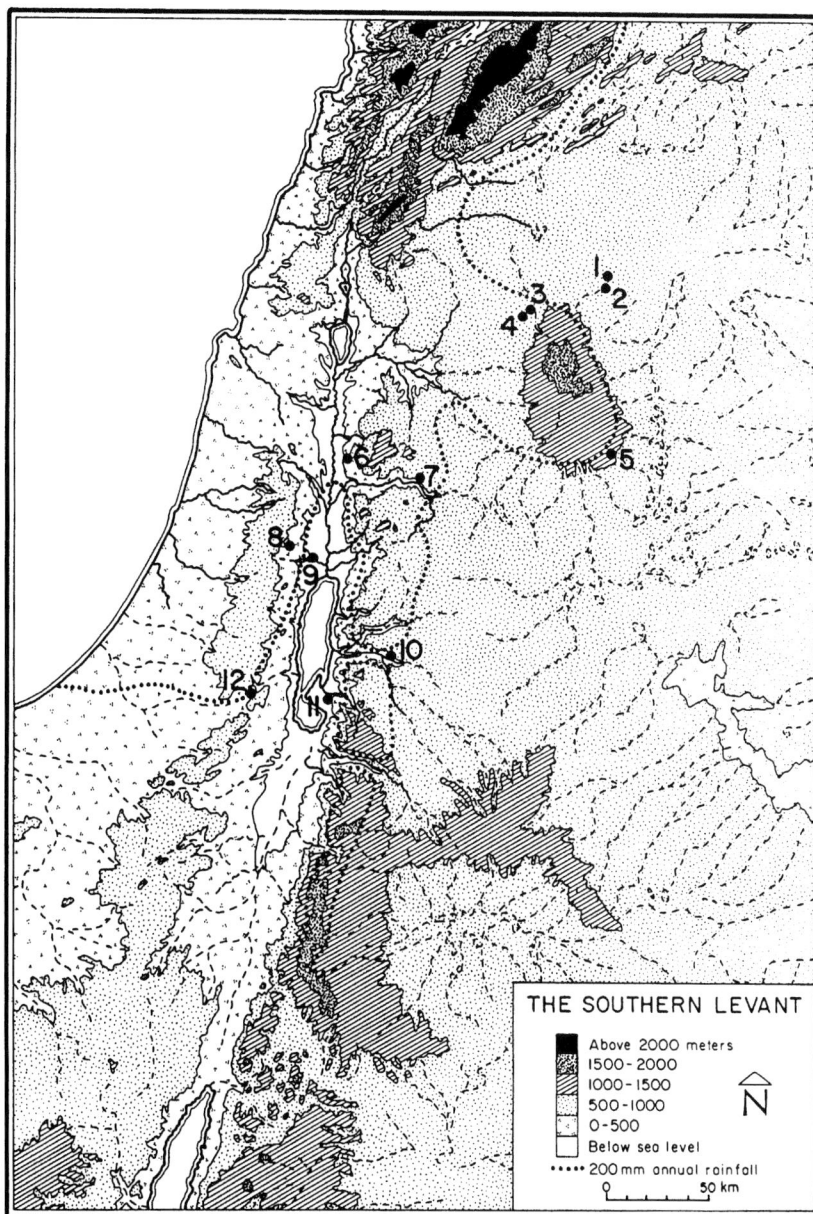

Fig. 6. Locations of protohistoric settlements in the southern Levant with runoff conservation systems. 1. Khirbet el-Umbashi; 2. Hebariyeh; 3. El-Laboueh; 4. Majedal; 5. Jawa; 6. Tell el-Handaquq; 7. Jebel Mutawwaq; 8. ᶜAi 9. Jericho; 10. Lehun; 11. Bab edh-Dhraᶜ; 12. Arad.

(National Water Master Plan 1977). Historically, local slope runoff from an area of only ca. 5 ha partially filled the reservoir every year. Excavation will be necessary to determine the original depth, and whether this is a natural basin or an artificial reservoir created by construction of a dam at its northern end.

Protohistoric runoff conservation at Tell el-Handaquq was not a unique development in the southern Levant (fig. 6). The reservoir at this site is similar in size and design to the extramural reservoirs found in association with the contemporaneous fortified

settlement at Jawa, on the southeastern flank of the Jebel Druze in northern Jordan (Helms 1975; 1976a; 1977; 1981). Archaeological explorations in southern Syria have also shown that systems for diversion and storage of runoff supported a network of fortified protohistoric towns in this interior basalt desert. Smaller reservoirs and canals have been found at Khirbet el-Umbashi and Hébariyeh (Dubretet and Dunand 1954; Braemer 1988: 132), and el-Laboueh (al-Maqdissi 1984), possibly fortified settlements on the northern flanks of the Jebel Druze with ceramic types related to Palestinian pottery traditions, including late EB I and EB IV wares (S. Helms, personal communication 1992).

The location of some reservoirs inside defensive enclosures indicates that protection of stored runoff was critical for the survival of those towns. Intramural reservoirs also have been found at contemporaneous fortified town sites at ᶜAi (et-Tell) in the hills near Jerusalem (Callaway 1978) and at Arad in the northern Negev Desert (Amiran 1978). Helms (1982) has hypothesized similar intramural reservoirs for the Early Bronze Age towns at Jericho and at Bab edh-Dhraᶜ and other Early Bronze Age town sites southeast of the Dead Sea. Another has been recognized at Lehun (K. Yassine, personal communication 1989), an Early Bronze Age town on the edge of the Jordan Plateau above the Dead Sea. Large intramural cisterns were found carved into the bedrock at Tell el-Maqlub in the Wadi Yabis (Mabry and Palumbo 1988: Site 43), and at Jebel Mutawwaq in the upper Wadi Zerqa (Hanbury-Tenison 1986: 75), both fortified Early Bronze Age settlements in the hills of northern Jordan. In the Jordan Valley, large cisterns lined with clay were found inside the Early Bronze Age town walls at Jericho (Kenyon 1960: 93–96) and at Bab edh-Dhraᶜ (Miller 1980: 337). Groundwater was also exploited by protohistoric towns in the southern Levant. Three intramural stepped shafts, one measuring about 100 m long, were carved through bedrock down to the water table at Khirbet Zeira-qoun, a fortified Early Bronze Age town on the northern Jordan plateau (Ibrahim and Mittmann 1987).

Runoff storage systems for protohistoric sedentary communities were developed in currently marginal areas of the southern Levant, as is evident by the location of all of these sites at the edge of the modern rainfall farming zone, near the 200-mm annual rainfall isohyet (fig. 4). These Early Bronze Age fortified towns, with efficient systems for capture and storage of highland runoff and its fertile load of silt, are early examples of an ancient "runoff techno-complex" that extended from Lebanon to Aden in the mountainous Levant and Western Arabia (Roberts 1977). The extramural, but protected, water management features found at Tell el-Handaquq are physical evidence of the technical capabilities of the ancient "irrigation culture" of the Jordan Valley, first hypothesized by Albright (1925). While this runoff conservation system for both agriculture and drinking supply supported a large town at Tell el-Handaquq for a millennium, the cycle of wadi entrenchment that breached the dams made continued flood irriga-tion impossible and prevented diversion of floods into the reservoir. The abandonment of the settlement during the mid-third millennium B.C. was probably due to this failure of the flood diversion and storage system.

Tombs

During March 1988, a group of tombs (NE Tomb Area) 150 m directly north of the eastern hill was brought to our attention by local gold hunters' looting. One recently robbed tomb was an enlarged natural cave (Tomb NE 1) that contained well-preserved skeletal remains and pottery, including red-slipped (Proto-Urban A) ware, and "line-painted" (Proto-Urban B) ware usually dated to late EB I (fig. 5:8–11). At least two other tombs in this area were being opened. A third area of tombs (SE Tomb Area) is visible on the hillside south of the wadi, opposite another group of tombs (E Tomb Area) identified by Muheisen (1988) on the north side of the wadi.

There is a total of at least 100 tombs in these three areas in the hills immediately east of the settlement (fig. 2). Most are enlarged natural caves, though some are carved directly into the limestone conglomerate bedrock. Many tombs have squared and recessed openings, perhaps originally to fit a stone door slab. A large number of the tombs apparently were robbed in antiquity; but because of current looting of pristine tombs a complete survey of the tomb areas and salvage excavation of undisturbed tombs will be top priorities during the next season of fieldwork.

SOUTH BULLDOZER CUT
Jonathan B. Mabry and
Gaetano Palumbo

During his 1985 survey of caves in the eastern Jordan Valley, Muheisen (1988) stopped bulldozers from quarrying the southern end of the western hill for road fill. About 1 m of cultural deposits can now be seen in an upper bulldozer cut. Fifty meters south is a second, lower cut more than 60 m long, showing a maximum depth of about 2.5 m of cultural stratigraphy near the center. This cut (fig. 7) shows in cross-section the massive defensive wall, domestic mudbrick walls with stone foundations, cobble pavements and streets, ceramic vessels lying smashed on house floors, pits, cooking ovens (*tabuns*), hearths, and thick lenses of ash and charcoal.

Between March 11 and 18, 1988, this entire 60-m bulldozer cut was hand-scraped and drawn by Gaetano Palumbo, with the assistance of Wajih Karasneh.

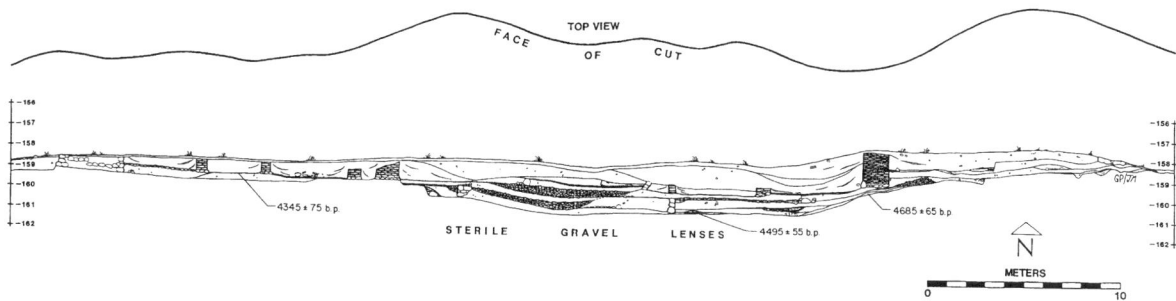

Fig. 7. Stratigraphy of the south bulldozer cut.

Chronologically diagnostic ceramic and lithic artifacts were recovered from each stratum to allow dating of the sequence of deposits. Due to the height of the section (more than 8 m above the present wadi bed), the work was carried out on ladders from below, and in a rope harness tied to a jeep above.

Ceramic Dating of the Stratigraphic Sequence

Seven major phases of architectural construction and cultural deposition were recognized in this cut, dating from the mid-fourth to the mid-third millennia B.C. (EB I–II) on the basis of the artifacts recovered (fig. 8). Three accelerator radiocarbon dates of the carbonized remains of short-lived plants (cereals) were also obtained to anchor the ceramic dating (see below).

The earliest cultural deposits (Stratum VII) exposed at this edge of the site are lenses of silt and ash lying at the deepest level in the center and eastern parts of the cut, directly upon the culturally sterile Pleistocene age gravel. This layer yielded sherds of undecorated everted rim jars (fig. 8:1,2), forms that appear in many Early Bronze I excavated sequences in the Jordan Valley, as well as two radiocarbon dates that support an Early Bronze IA dating of this stratum.

The second phase (Stratum VI) that can be discerned in the cut included escarpment of the underlying gravel and construction of a narrow stone wall, a *tabun*, and earthen floors, one with a sherd from an EB I everted-rim jar (fig. 8:3) lying on it. Wet-wiped body sherds with red trickle paint also characterize this stratum (not illustrated).

The third phase (Stratum V) included further escarpment of the sterile gravel, reuse of the earlier stone wall by raising the floor, and construction of two, more substantial, masonry walls. A stone pile, a cobble pavement, and a thick cobble fill—possibly the foundation for a street—also belong to this phase.

Sherds recovered from Stratum 5 include one from an everted rim jar (fig. 8:4), a body sherd of "Proto-Urban D (or Um Hammad) ware" with raised and indented decoration (fig. 8:5), and another body sherd with raised decoration and a red slip (fig. 8:6). While it is possible that this sherd of Proto-Urban D ware is intrusive from earlier deposits, the context of this distinctive ceramic type supports a late EB I (EB IB) date for this stratum.

During the fourth phase (Stratum IV), the 3-m-wide, boulder-constructed defensive wall was founded upon sterile gravel near the western end of the cut. The underlying gravel in front of the wall was cut into, forming a sloping "fosse." Near the center of the cut a second thick cobble fill was laid above the earlier one during this phase, to raise the level of the street. Several new mudbrick walls with stone foundations also were constructed, probably for houses. Several earthen floors are visible between these mudbrick walls, one of which shows two postholes with carbonized remains of posts. Lying smashed on the floor of another mudbrick structure are several large, holemouth and rolled-rim storage jars with indented ledge handles and "grain-washed" decoration (fig. 8:7,8). A 4-m-wide cobble pavement was laid between the defensive wall and the first wall of this structure, possibly to serve as a foundation for another street behind the town wall. Several pits were also cut into the sterile gravel at the eastern end of the cut during this phase. Sherds from a flat jar base with red slip (fig. 8:9) and a plain rim bowl with red slip inside and outside (fig. 8:10), also point to an EB II date for this stratum, and therefore for the construction of the defensive wall. Again, the ceramic dating of this stratum is supported by a radiocarbon date (below).

The fifth phase (Stratum III) represents reuse of the mudbrick walls of the previous phase by raising the internal floors. Near the center of the cut, one of these earthen floors has a large EB II "pithos" storage jar lying smashed on its side over a length of 1.5 m. The floors of this stratum also yielded sherds of beveled- and thickened-rim holemouth jars (fig. 8:11, 12) and of a high-fired "metallic ware" flared rim jar with red stripes painted over a white slip (fig. 8:13). These forms appear together in the top two strata of the sounding (see below) and suggest a mid-EB II date for this stratum.

The sixth phase (Stratum II) includes thick accumulations of mudbrick debris above the floors of the previous phase and construction of a wide stone wall or foundation at the eastern end of the cut. No chronologically diagnostic artifacts or radiocarbon samples were recovered from this stratum.

The seventh and final phase (Stratum I) visible in the cut represents collapse of Strata VI–IV structures and rapid colluvial deposition from upslope. A trapezoidal "sickle blade" fragment with silica polish along both edges (fig. 9:4) was found in these sediments. The only chronologically diagnostic sherd recovered from this stratum is from an everted-rim amphoriskos with two pierced vertical lugs on the neck (fig. 8:14). This same type of vessel was found at Tel Shalem in the western valley, a late EB I walled town site (Eisenberg 1989: fig. 143). This is

a well-known Early Bronze Age form, but its long use within the period and its context in colluvial sediments does not allow precise dating of the evident abandonment of this part of the site. The latest, datable *in situ* cultural deposits in this sequence belong to Stratum 3, with mid-EB II sherds.

THE SOUNDING

Between March 11 and 18, 1988, a 2.5 × 5 m area on the southeast corner of the western hill (fig. 2) was excavated to a depth of about 2.4 m from the surface (figs. 10, 11; table 1). This location, at the edge of the flat lower mound just inside the southeast gate and corner of the defensive wall, was chosen because the fortifications there have retained the greatest depth of cultural deposits at the site. The underlying, culturally sterile, Late Pleistocene gravels were not reached in the sounding, and the bottom of the sounding trench is still more than 2.5 m above the surface level outside of the defensive wall; a depth of at least 5 m of cultural deposits may be estimated for this part of the site.

This sounding exposed parts of two burials, five strata of trash and mudbrick debris, and five phases of construction or reconstruction of domestic structures.

Fig. 8. Ceramic artifacts from south bulldozer cut, by Stratum.

Location	Description
1. Stratum 7	Everted jar rim, medium-fired, very pale brown 10YR7/4 ware, very coarse grit temper, wet-smoothed exterior.
2. Stratum 7	Everted jar rim, low-fired, light brown 7.5YR6/4 ware, very coarse grit temper, wet-smoothed exterior.
3. Stratum 6	Everted jar rim, low-fired, pink 7.5YR7/4 ware, very coarse grit temper, wet-smoothed exterior.
4. Stratum 5	Everted jar rim, medium-fired, gray 10YR5/1 ware, very coarse grit temper, wet-smoothed exterior.
5. Stratum 5	Medium-fired, red 2.5YR5/6 ware, medium grit temper, raised and indented decoration exterior.
6. Stratum 5	Medium-fired, pink 5YR7/4 ware, medium grit and grog temper, raised decoration, red 10R5/6 wash exterior and part of interior.
7. Stratum 4	Thickened holemouth jar rim, low-fired, pinkish-gray 7.5YR6/2 ware, coarse grit temper, red 10R5/6 "grain wash" exterior.
8. Stratum 4	Rolled jar rim, medium-fired, light brown 7.5YR6/4 ware, coarse grit temper, red 10R5/6 "grain wash" exterior.
9. Stratum 4	Flat jar base, medium-fired, pink 7.5YR7/4 ware, coarse grit temper, red 10R4/6 slip exterior.
10. Stratum 4	Plain bowl rim, medium-fired, pink 5YR8/4 ware, fine grit temper, red 10R5/6 wash interior, dark red 10R3/6 slip exterior.
11. Stratum 3	Beveled rim holemouth jar rim, high-fired, pink 7.5YR7/4 ware, very coarse grit temper.
12. Stratum 3	Thickened holemouth jar rim, medium-fired, reddish-brown 2.5YR5/4 ware, coarse grit temper.
13. Stratum 3	Flared jar rim, high-fired, light red 2.5YR6/6 ware, gray 5YR5/1 core, medium grit temper, white 10YR8/2 slip, dark red 10R3/6 paint exterior and interior.
14. Stratum 1	Everted bottle rim with pierced vertical lug handles on neck, high-fired, very pale brown 10YR8/4 ware, no temper.

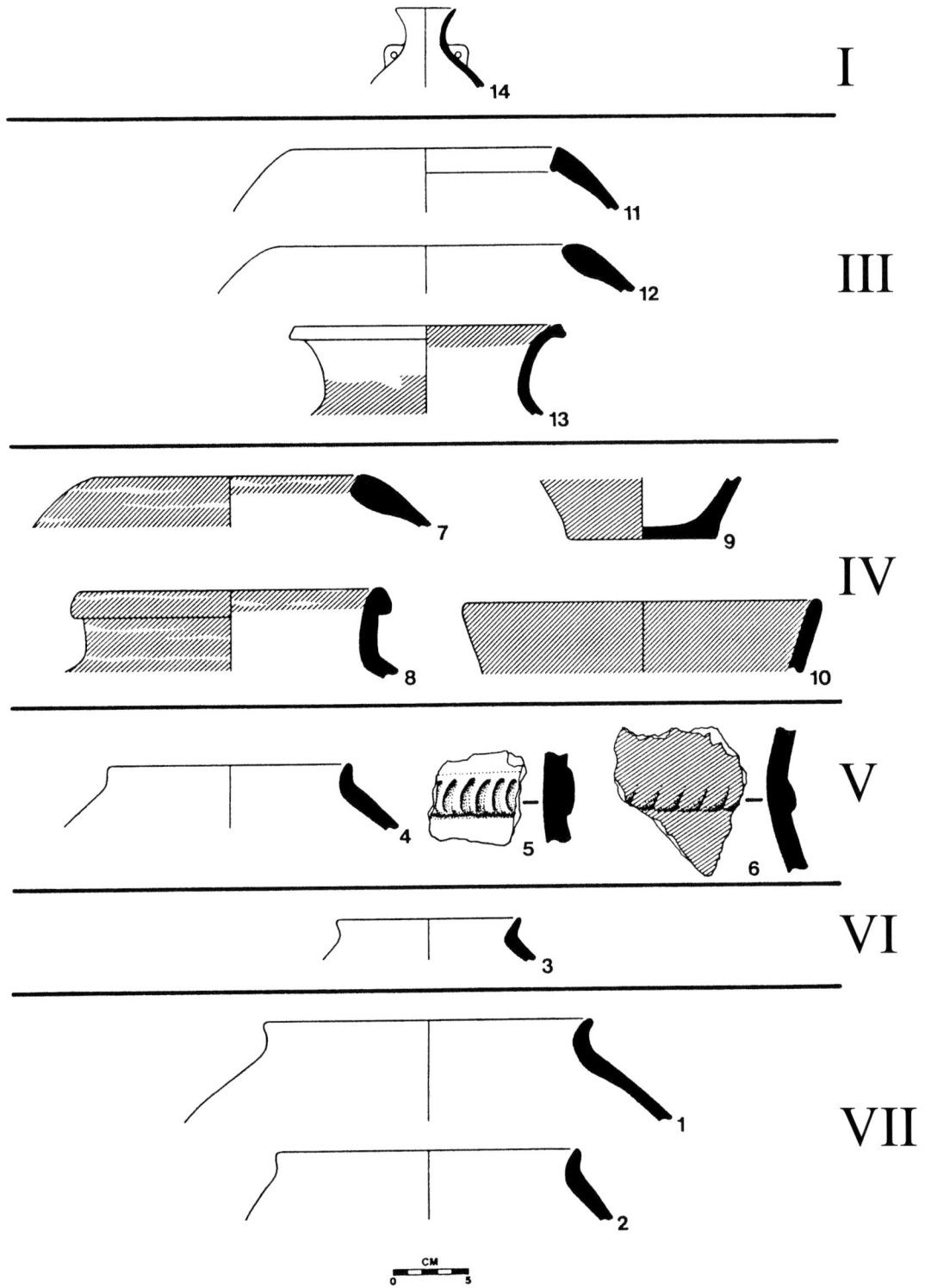

Fig. 8. Ceramic artifacts from south bulldozer cut, by Stratum.

Though only a small area was exposed, the sample of sherds (n=2005) recovered provides a useful ceramic sequence from stratified household deposits dating from near the beginning of the third millennium B.C. (EB I) until the site's abandonment in the mid-third millennium B.C. (EB II). A 25 percent sample of all excavated sediments was sifted through 5-mm mesh screen, while 100 percent from selected loci (all floors and surfaces) was sifted. Well-preserved animal bones were recovered from every stratum, and several sediment samples were taken from areas with large amounts of charcoal for flotation of plant remains. Samples of charcoal also were taken for radiocarbon dating (below).

Stratigraphic Sequence

The earliest cultural deposit (Stratum V) reached in the bottom of the sounding was a 1 × 0.5 m area exposed in the southern part of the trench (fig. 11). In this very limited area exposed, no architecture was found in association with this deposit, which was a gravely silt fill (037) with charcoal fragments, a few animal bones, and pottery sherds. The next phase (Stratum IV) included a surface (036) that covers the earlier fill, a curved stone wall foundation (035) founded on that surface and faced with mud plaster on the interior, and another surface (034) that runs up to the mud plaster (fig. 11).

Above this earlier curved structure were found three phases (Strata III–I) of construction and a rebuild of two parallel walls directly on top of each other, about 2 m apart and oriented from northwest to southeast (fig. 11). Each of these walls had a stone

foundation between one and three courses high and two to three rows (ca. 0.75 m) wide, and a superstructure of unfired mudbricks preserved one or two courses high. In the upper two phases (Strata II, I), smaller subsidiary walls abutted the northeastern face of the longest wall section exposed. Leveling fills, between one and three compacted earthen floors, hearth areas with burned soil, charcoal and ash, animal bones, flint tools and flakes, and flat-lying pottery sherds were found in association with each phase of wall construction/reconstruction (fig. 11). These walls probably formed the sides of a single rectangular house, or of two houses separated by a narrow alley.

Part of the human burial (021), an extended inhumation on its right side and oriented from southwest to northeast, was found beneath a floor (019) between the walls (010, 022) of Stratum II. Fragments of a plain rim lamp with a burnished red slip and soot on the rim, a burnished everted-rim jar, and a ground basalt ring were found in the clayey burial fill (fig. 5:5–7). The cranium of a second skeleton was found in part of another grave (016) that stratigraphically postdates the last building phase on this part of the site (i.e., post-Stratum I).

Ceramic Sequence

The sherds found in each stratum of this sounding, together totalling 2005, form a sequence of typical early- to mid-third millennium B.C. (late EB I–EB II) pottery wares, forms, and decoration, with some types appearing only in lower or upper strata (figs. 5, 12, 13, 14; table 2). Sherds from earlier

---

Fig. 9. Mid-fourth to late third millennium B.C. (Early Bronze Age) chipped stone tools.

Location	Description
1. Sounding, Stratum 2, Locus 026	Bifacially retouched trapezoidal blade fragment, silica polish along both edges.
2. Sounding, Stratum 2, Locus 012	Unifacially retouched blade, silica polish along retouched edge, broken end of longer fragment retouched.
3. Sounding, Stratum 2, Locus 001	Trapezoidal blade fragment, silica polish along both edges.
4. South Cut, Stratum 1	Trapezoidal blade fragment, silica polish along both edges.
5. Surface	Triangular blade fragment, silica polish along one edge.
6. Surface	Trapezoidal blade fragment, silica polish along both edges.
7. Sounding, Stratum 4, Locus 036	Unifacially retouched fan scraper.
8. Sounding, Stratum 1, Locus 002	Unifacially retouched fan scraper.
9. Sounding, Stratum 1, Locus 001	Unifacially retouched scraper fragment.
10. Sounding, Stratum 2, Locus 019	Flint hammerstone with battered edges.

deposits were common in secondary fills; but by excluding these loci from analysis, almost every obviously intrusive sherd can be accounted for. Most of the wares from the earlier strata were low-fired, with gray cores and coarse "grit" (crushed stone) or

"grog" (crushed pottery) temper. Though coarse tempered, low-fired wares continued to occur, high-fired "metallic" wares with fine tempers also appeared in the upper two strata. The majority of the forms were made by hand, though the folded and flared rims

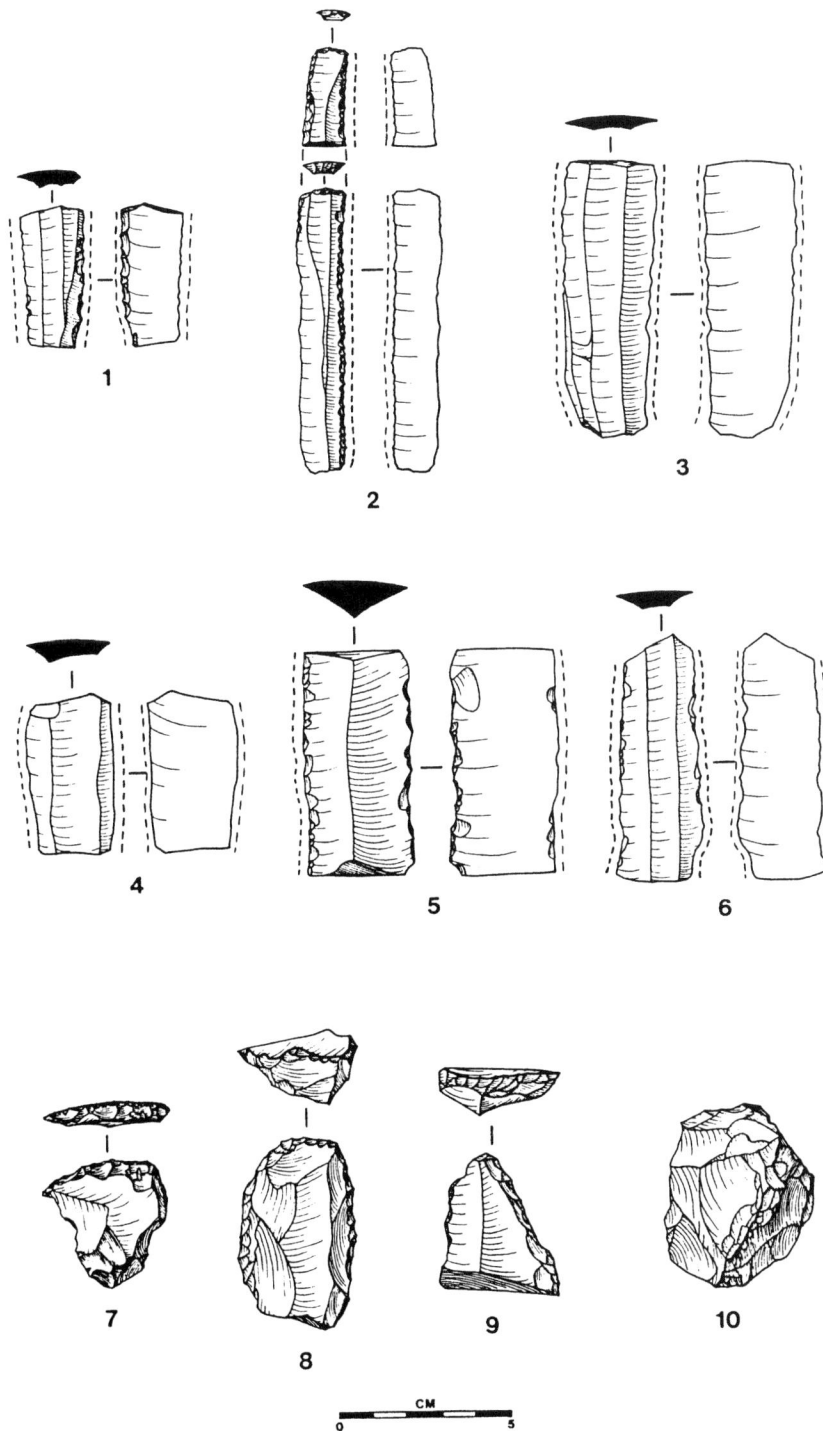

Fig. 9. Mid-fourth to late third millennium B.C. (Early Bronze Age) chipped stone tools.

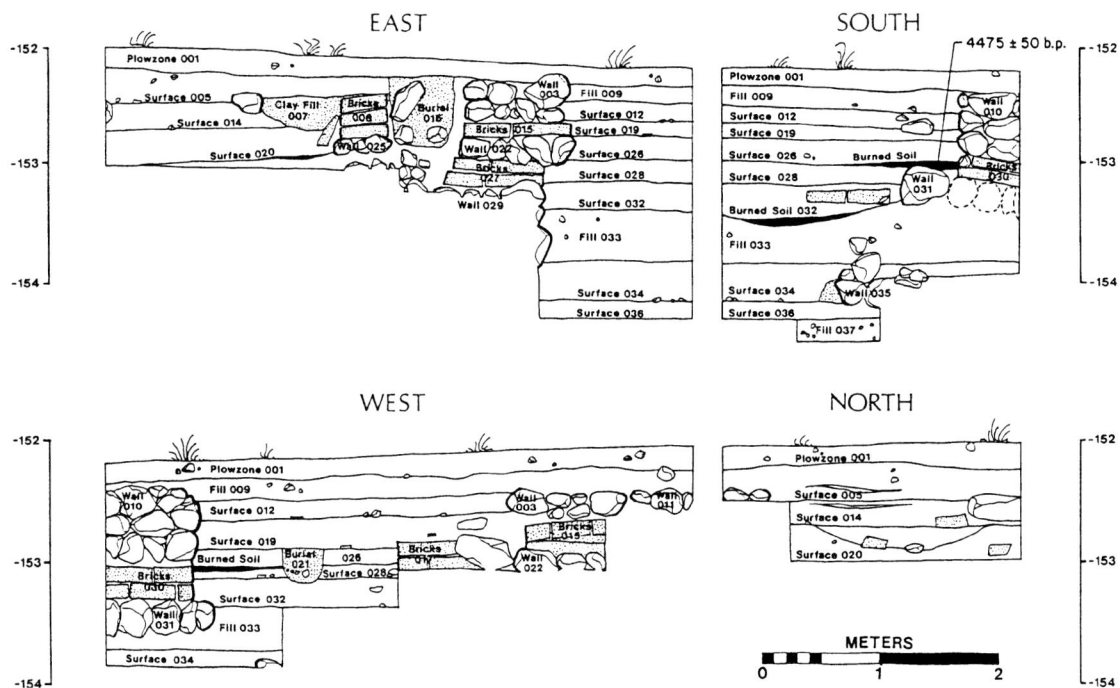

Fig. 10. Sounding sections.

TABLE 1. Description of loci in Tell el-Handaquq sounding, by stratum

Stratum	Locus	Description	Stratum	Locus	Description
V	037	Fill?	II	018	Mud wall?
IV	036	Floor/surface		017	Mudbrick wall
	035	Stone wall foundation		015	Mudbrick superstructure of Wall 022
	034	Floor/surface		010	Stone wall foundation (also used in
III	033	Fill			Stratum I)
	032	Floor/surface		006	Mudbrick superstructure of wall 025
	031	Stone wall foundation	I	014	Floor/surface
	030	Mudbrick superstructure of Wall 031		013	Fill of Wall 003
	029	Stone wall foundation		012	Floor/surface
	028	Floor/surface		011	Stone wall foundation
II	027	Fill of Walls 022, 025		010	Stone wall foundation (also used in
	026	Floor/surface			Stratum II)
	025	Stone wall foundation		009	Fill
	024	Hearth area with burned soil, ashes,		008	Stone line
		and charcoal		007	Clay fill
	023	Stone pile		005	Floor/surface
	022	Stone wall foundation		004	Stone line
	021	Burial fill and skeletal remains		003	Stone wall foundation
	020	Floor/surface	Post-	002	Colluvium
	019	Floor/surface	occupation	001	Plow zone

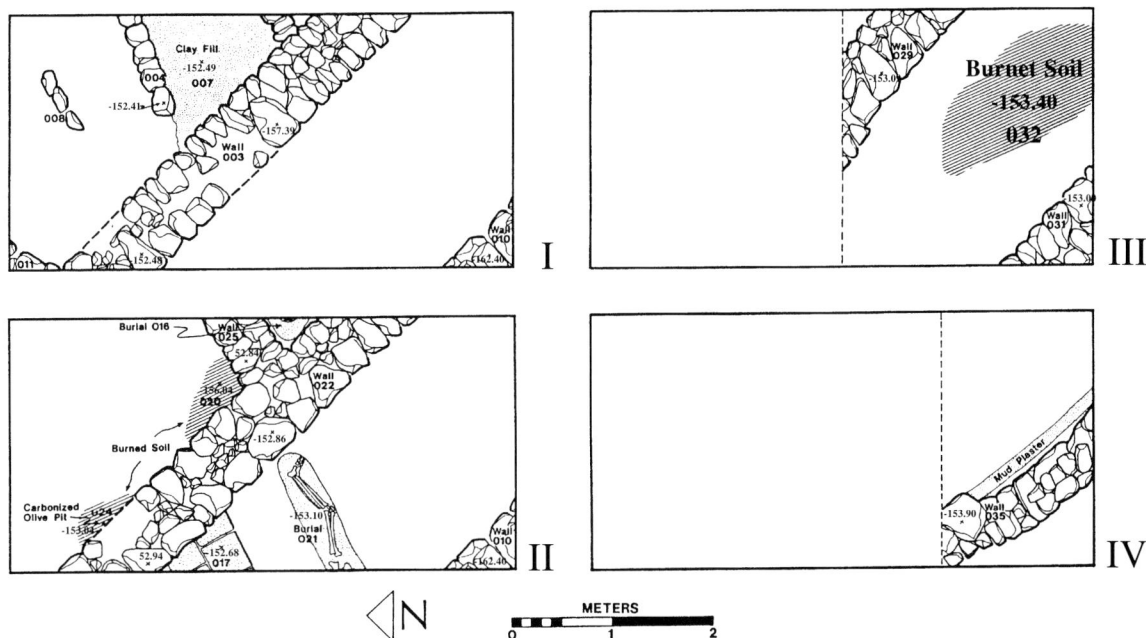

Fig. 11. Sounding Strata.

TABLE 2. Sequence of ceramic types in Tell el-Handaquq North sounding, by stratum

Ceramic types	Site surface	Post-occupation	Sounding Strata				
			1	2	3	4	5
Incised ("Jawa"-type)	X		0.3*				
Red-slipped/incised	X				0.9	0.6	
Um Hammad (PUD)	X						
Line-group painted (PUB)	X		0.3			0.3	
Coarse-tempered/trickle-painted	X	22.9	53.0	43.9	36.7	35.1	40.9
Wiped/trickle-painted	X		1.8	7.4	3.4	11.2	7.6
Grain-washed (band-slipped)	X	30.0	12.5	10.7	19.8	25.2	24.2
Lattice-slipped/burnished	X		0.9	0.7	0.6	0.3	4.5
Red-slipped	X	14.3	10.7	25.0	30.6	20.8	16.7
Red-polished	X	7.1	3.9	3.5	3.4	5.6	6.1
Plain fine-tempered	X	2.9	6.8	3.6	3.8	0.6	
Self-slipped/polished	X	7.1	1.5	0.9	0.8	0.3	
White-slipped/red-painted	X	8.6	6.8	2.3			
Metallic orange	X	1.4	1.5	1.7			
Metallic line-painted	X			0.1			
Metallic reserve-slipped	X	5.7					
Metallic cream-slipped/combed	X						
Stratum total (No. sherds)		70	336	685	526	322	66
Sounding total = 2005							

*Percent of total sherds within stratum.

found in the upper two strata were finished on a slow "tournette" wheel, and the platter-bowls were mass-manufactured quickly on a fast wheel. Table 2 compares the sequence of types of ceramic wares and decorations by stratum.

Sherds of large "coarse ware" jars with thickened and slightly everted rims and occasional red trickle-paint (fig. 12:2–4,10,11) are common in the lower two strata, while this coarse-tempered ware represents between one-third and one-half of the total sherds in every stratum. These fit into the long history of coarse ware forms manufactured locally in the Jordan Valley, extending back to the Pottery Neolithic in the sequence excavated at Tell esh-Shuna North (Gustavson-Gaube 1985; 1986). Body sherds that were "wet-wiped" or finger-streaked and

decorated with parallel lines of trickle-paint appear to be related to the trickle-painted coarse wares; in general, these are more common in the lower strata (Strata V, IV). Finger-streaks and trickle-paint were also common decorations on sherds found in EB IA (Stratum II) deposits at Tell Um Hammad (Helms 1986: fig. 12), Tell Abu el-ᶜAlayiq (Pritchard 1958: pl. 31), and Tell esh-Shuna North (Gustavson-Gaube 1987: fig. 4), indicating a long local history for these decorative techniques as well. The overall impression is that coarse grit temper, surface wiping, and trickle-painting represent a substratum of local pottery traditions that extend back to the Neolithic.

A typical form represented throughout the sequence was the holemouth jar with a flat base, indented ledge handles, and a thickened rim (fig. 12:1,

---

Fig. 12. Ceramic artifacts from sounding Strata V and IV.

Location	Description
1. Stratum 5, Locus 037	Thickened holemouth jar rim, medium-fired, very pale brown 10YR7/3 ware, gray 10YR5/1 core, weak red 10R4/2 "grain wash" exterior.
2. Stratum 5, Locus 037	Thickened and everted jar rim, low-fired, very pale brown 10YR7/3 ware, very coarse grit temper, wet-smoothed exterior.
3. Stratum 5, Locus 037	Thickened and everted jar rim, low-fired, pink 5YR7/4 ware, very coarse grit temper, wet-smoothed exterior.
4. Stratum 5, Locus 037	Flattened holemouth jar rim, low-fired, reddish-yellow 5YR6/6 ware, coarse grit temper, red 10R5/6 slip exterior.
5. Stratum 5, Locus 037	Vertical strap jar handle, low-fired, pink 7.5YR7/4 ware, very coarse grit temper, red 10R5/6 slip exterior.
6. Stratum 5, Locus 037	Everted juglet rim, high-fired, pink 5YR7/4 ware, fine grit temper, light red 10R6/6 slip with vertical burnished stripes exterior.
7. Stratum 4, Locus 036	Thickened holemouth jar rim, low-fired, very pale brown 10YR7/3 ware, gray 10YR5/1 core, coarse grit temper, weak red 10R4/2 "grain wash" exterior.
8. Stratum 4, Locus 034	Thickened holemouth jar rim, low-fired, light gray 10YR7/2 ware, smoothed exterior.
9. Stratum 4, Locus 034	Thickened holemouth jar rim, low-fired, pink 7.5YR8/4 ware, gray 7.5YRN6/ core, smoothed exterior.
10. Stratum 4, Locus 036	Thickened and everted jar rim, low-fired, pink 5YR7/4 ware, gray 5YR5/1 core, wet-smoothed exterior.
11. Stratum 4, Locus 034	Thickened and everted jar rim, low-fired, pink 5YR8/4 ware, very coarse grit temper, wet-smoothed surfaces.
12. Stratum 4, Locus 034	Flared jar rim, medium-fired, very pale brown 10YR7/4 ware, coarse grit temper, dark gray 10YR7/4 ware, coarse grit temper, dark gray 10YR4/1 "grain wash" exterior.
13. Stratum 4, Locus 036	Flat jar base, medium-fired, pink 7.5YR7/4 ware, coarse grit temper.
14. Stratum 4, Locus 034	Flat jar base, low-fired, pink 5YR7/4 ware, reddish-gray 5YR5/2 core, smoothed exterior.
15. Stratum 4, Locus 034	Flat jar base, medium-fired, reddish-yellow 5YR7/6 ware, pinkish-gray 5YR6/2 core, fine grit temper, red 10R5/8 "grain wash" exterior.
16. Stratum 4, Locus 036	Plain bowl rim, medium-fired, very pale brown 10YR7/3 ware, dark gray 10YR4/1 exterior, wet-smoothed interior and exterior, light red 10R6/6 trickle paint interior.
17. Stratum 4, Locus 036	Horn of animal (bull?) figurine, medium-fired, pink 7.5YR8/4 ware, gray 7.5YRN6/ core, very fine grit temper, red 10R6/ polished slip exterior.
18. Stratum 4, Locus 036	Inverted platter-bowl rim with groove below carination, pale red 10R6/4 ware, fine grit temper, weak red 10R4/4 burnished slip exterior.
19. Stratum 4, Locus 036	Inverted platter-bowl rim, medium-fired, reddish-yellow 5YR6/6 ware, very pale brown 10YR7/4 core, fine grit temper.

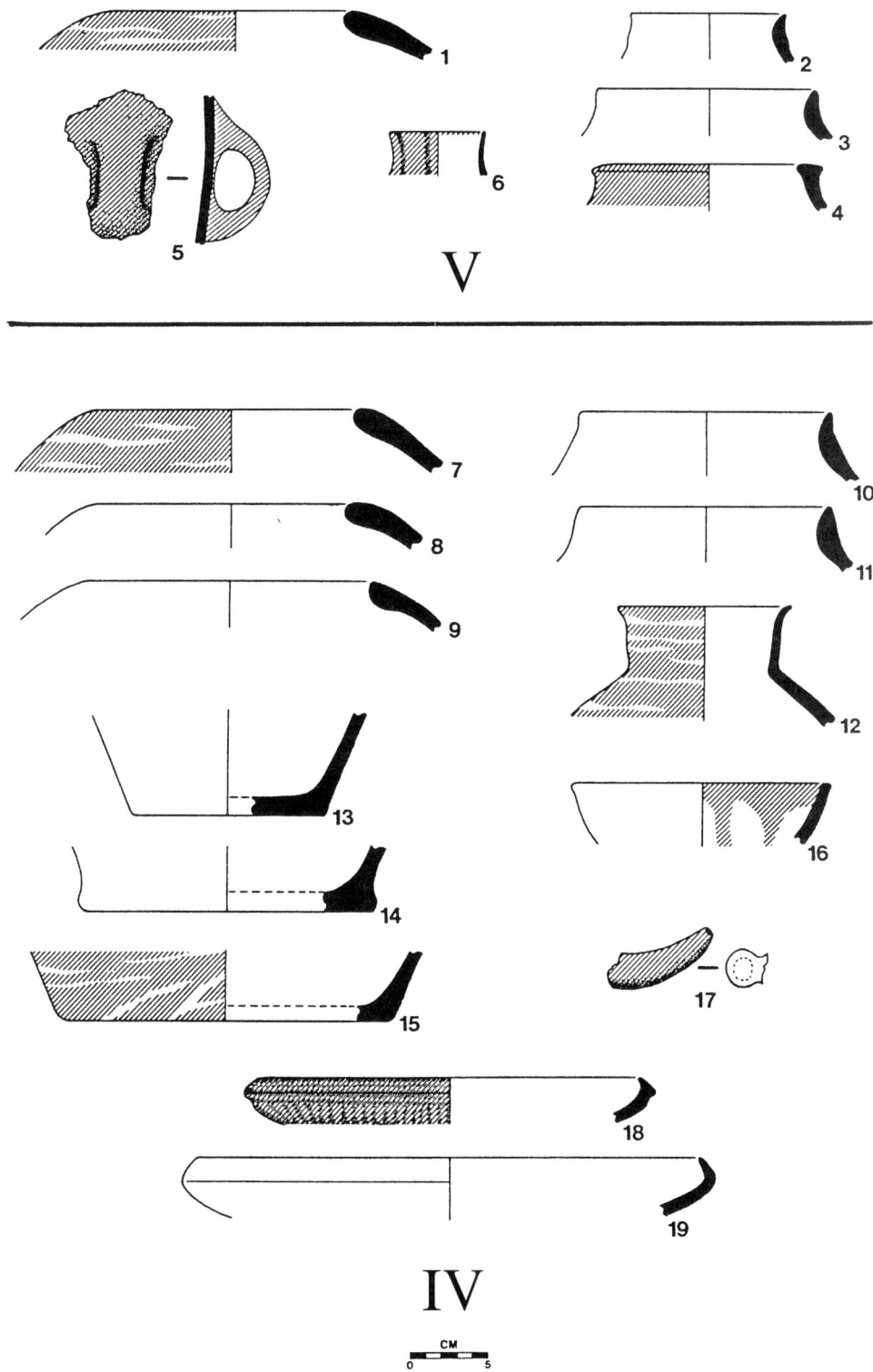

Fig. 12. Ceramic artifacts from sounding Strata V and IV.

7–9; 13:1–2,8,9 14:3;). Beveled, grooved, and "rail" holemouth jar rims (figs. 7:1,2; 13:7) appeared alongside thickened rims in the upper two strata. These variations were not unique to any one phase within the Early Bronze Age, however, as "rail" and beveled holemouth jar rims appeared together even earlier, in EB IB (Stage 3) strata at Tell Um Hammad (Helms 1986: fig. 16). Vertical strap jar handles also occurred throughout the sequence. While a few in each stratum were undecorated, the exteriors of holemouth jars typically were decorated with a red or gray "grain wash" (or "band slip"; figs. 12:1, 7; 13:1, 2, 7, 8). Grain-wash decoration is represented in every stratum but decreases in frequency in the upper two strata. Sherds with lattice-pattern slips and burnishes appear, although sparsely, in the same strata, and these appear to be techniques of decoration re-

lated to grain wash/band slip. Holemouth jars with thick red slips (figs. 13:9; 14:3) also appeared occasionally alongside the grain-washed type throughout the sequence. Jar sherds decorated with stripes of red paint over a thick white slip (figs. 13:14; 14:8) appear only in the upper two strata.

The "grain-washed" (or "band-slip") style was common throughout northern Palestine and Jordan (Glueck 1946) and southern Syria (F. Braemer, personal communication 1988) during the late fourth and early third millennia B.C. Its earliest context in the northern Levant are Phases H and I in the ᶜAmuq sequence (Braidwood and Braidwood 1960), and in the Jordan Valley in stratified EB IB deposits at Tell esh-Shuna North (Gustavson-Gaube 1985; 1986). As well as at Tell el-Handaquq, the grain-washed and red-on-white styles also appear together in "Early

---

Fig. 13. Ceramic artifacts from sounding Strata III and II.

Location	Description
1. Stratum 3, Locus 032	Thickened holemouth jar rim, medium-fired, very pale brown 10YR7/3 ware, gray 10YR6/1 core, weak red 10R5/4 "grain wash" exterior.
2. Stratum 3, Locus 028	Thickened holemouth jar rim, medium-fired, very pale brown 10YR8/3 ware, gray 10YR5/1 core, coarse grit temper, red 10R5/6 "grain wash" exterior.
3. Stratum 3, Locus 028	Indented ledge handle, medium-fired, reddish-yellow 5YR7/6 ware, light gray 10YR7/2 core, coarse grit temper, weak red 10R5/3 "grain wash" exterior.
4. Stratum 3, Locus 032	Flat jar base, medium-fired, pink 7.5YR8/4 ware, gray 10YR6/1 core, coarse grit temper.
5. Stratum 3, Locus 032	Everted jar rim, high-fired light yellowish-brown 10YR6/4 ware, vertically burnished self slip exterior, horizontally burnished red 10R4/6 slip on rim top and interior.
6. Stratum 3, Locus 028	Everted bowl rim, high-fired, pink 5YR8/4 ware, light red 10R6/6 slip exterior and rim interior.
7. Stratum 2, Locus 026	Beveled holemouth jar rim, medium-fired, pink 5YR7/4 ware, light gray 10YR7/1 core, coarse grit temper, gray 5YR5/1 "grain wash" exterior.
8. Stratum 2, Locus 026	Thickened holemouth jar rim, medium-fired, pale brown 10YR7/3 ware, coarse grit temper, light red 10R6/6 "grain wash" exterior.
9. Stratum 2, Locus 026	Thickened holemouth jar rim, medium-fired, very pale brown 10YR8/3 ware, weak red 10R5/3 slip exterior.
10. Stratum 2, Locus 019	Folded jar rim, low-fired, pale brown 10YR6/3 ware, fine grit temper, red 10R4/6 slip exterior.
11. Stratum 2, Locus 026	Folded jar rim, medium-fired, gray 7.5YRN5/ ware, medium grit temper, red 10R4/6 "grainwash" exterior.
12. Stratum 2, Locus 019	Indented ledge handle, high-fired, reddish-gray 10R5/1 ware, medium grit temper, pale yellow 2.5YR8/4 slip exterior.
13. Stratum 2, Locus 019	Flat jar base, medium-fired, pale brown 10YR6/3 ware, gray 10YR6/1 core, coarse grit and grog temper, smoothed exterior.
14. Stratum 2, Locus 019	Flat jar base, medium-fired, pink 7.5YR7/4 ware, very fine grit temper, white 10YR8/2 slip and weak red 10R4/4 painted stripes exterior.
15. Stratum 2, Locus 019	Flat jar base, high-fired, pink 7.5YR7/4 ware, coarse grit temper, red 10R4/6 slip exterior.
16. Stratum 2, Locus 026	Inverted bowl rim, high-fired, brown 10YR5/3 ware, no temper, red 10R5/6 slip exterior.
17. Stratum 2, Locus 026	Inverted platter-bowl rim, medium-fired, weak red 10R5/3 ware, gray 10YR5/1 core, horizontally burnished interior and exterior.

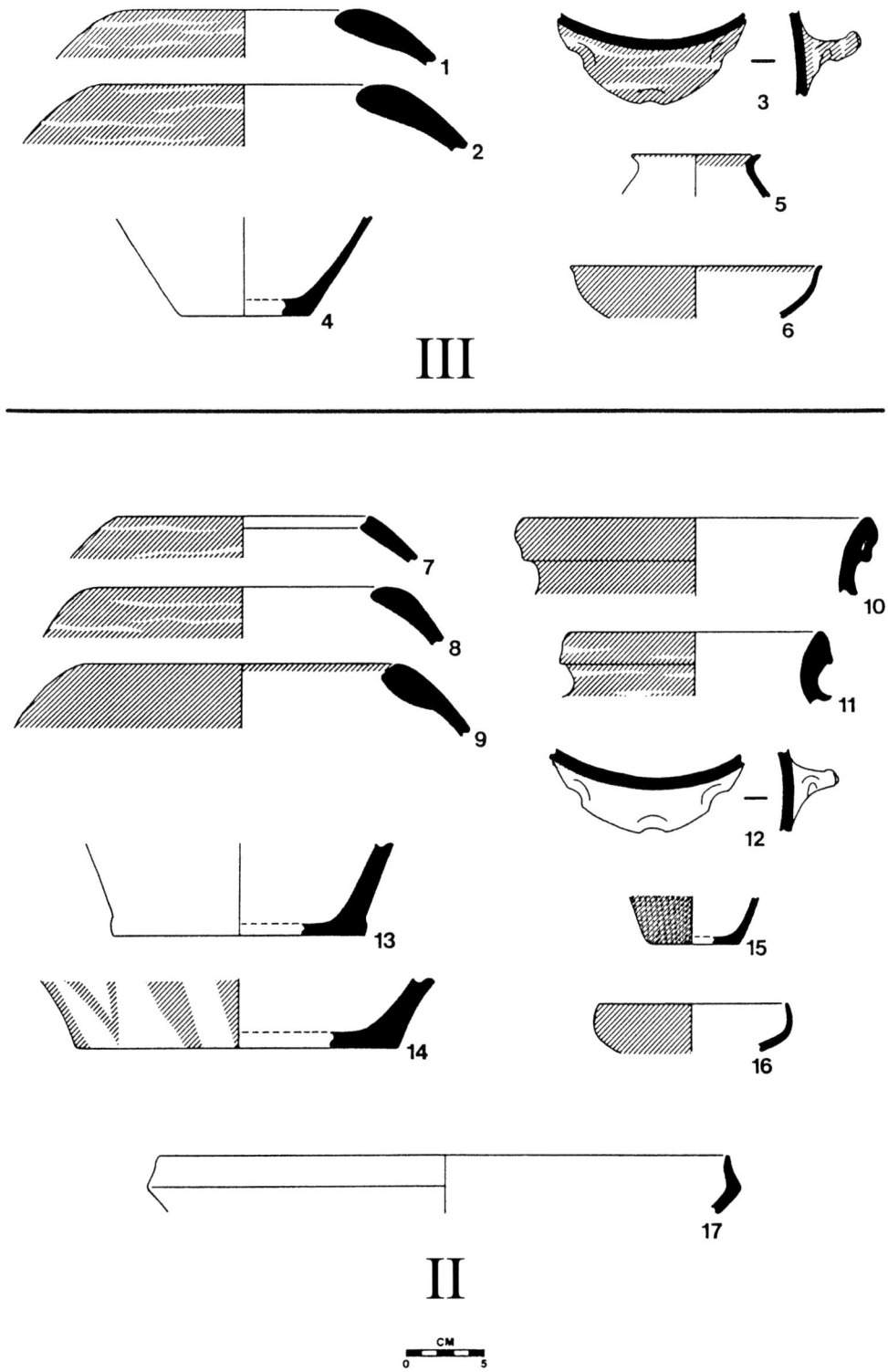

Fig. 13. Ceramic artifacts from sounding Strata III and II.

Bronze I, Phase 1" deposits at Tell el-Far^cah North (Huot 1967), and in Stratum II at Khirbet Kerak (Esse 1982). In the Jordan Valley, red painted stripes over a white slip were found in EB II contexts at Tell el-^cOreimeh (Fritz 1987: 45), and at Tell es-Saidiyeh (J. Tubb, personal communication 1988). In summary, grain-wash and red-on-white decorations were popular in the Jordan Valley and much of the southern Levant from the late EB I through EB II.

In addition to holemouth and everted-rim jars, folded-rim jars decorated with a thick red slip (fig. 13:10) or a grain wash (fig. 13:11) were found on Stratum II floors. Red-slipped sherds are common throughout the sequence, ranging between 10 and 30 percent of the total sherds in each stratum. High-fired, flared-rim jars with straight or everted necks (figs. 12:12; 14:4–6) were represented in all but the lowest stratum. Both forms were decorated with the grain-wash technique, and also with red painted stripes over a thick white slip in the upper two strata (above).

Inverted rim platter-bowls, some with pattern burnished red slips (fig. 12:18), and some with hori-zontal lug handles (fig. 14:12), were common from Stratum IV upwards. Pattern-burnished platter-bowls are common in EB II assemblages, such as at Tell es-Saidiyeh Area DD (Tubb 1988: fig. 32:8). Plain-rim bowls with red trickle paint on the interior (fig. 12:16) were found in Stratum IV, while red-slipped bowls with recessed (fig. 13:6) or inverted rims (fig. 13:16) were found in Strata III and II. These types of bowls were also found in Stage 2 and 3 strata at Tell Um Hammad (Helms 1986: fig. 10). The everted-rim juglet or cup with vertically burnished stripes over a red slip found in the deepest stratum (fig. 12:6) is paralleled in EB IB (Stage 3) deposits at Tell Um Hammad (Helms 1986: fig. 14:12).

High-fired local wares found in the sequence were used for the flared-rim jars described above, for "Abydos ware" juglets with vertical strap handles and vertically burnished or polished red or gray slips and for "metallic orange ware" platter-bowls (fig. 13:17). Red-polished Abydos ware (or, more likely, a local imitation) was found in all strata, while the metallic orange ware was found only in the upper

---

Fig. 14. Ceramic artifacts from sounding Stratum I.

Location	Description
1. Locus 012	Grooved holemouth jar rim, medium-fired, pink 7.5YR5/2 ware, brown 7.5YR5/2 core, coarse grit temper.
2. Locus 012	Beveled holemouth jar rim, medium-fired, light reddish-brown 2.5YR6/4 ware, very coarse grit temper.
3. Locus 012	Thickened holemouth jar rim, medium-fired, pink 7.5YR7/4 ware, coarse grit temper, reddish-brown 2.5YR5/4 slip exterior.
4. Locus 012	Flared jar rim, high-fired, pink 7.5YR7/4 ware, medium grit temper, yellowish-red 5YR5/6 "grain wash" exterior.
5. Locus 012	Flared jar rim, high-fired, light red 2.5YR6/6 ware, pale brown 10YR6/3 core, coarse grit temper, grayish-brown 10YR5/2 "grain wash" exterior.
6. Locus 005	Flared jar rim, high-fired, very pale brown 10YR7/4 ware, medium grit temper, gray 2.5YRN5/ "grain wash" exterior.
7. Locus 012	Indented ledge handle, medium-fired, very pale brown 10YR7/4 ware, coarse grit temper, red 10R5/6 painted stripe exterior.
8. Locus 012	Flat jar base, medium-fired, light red 2.5YR6/6 ware, gray 10YR5/1 core, coarse grit temper, white 5YR8/1 slip and red 10R4/6 paint exterior.
9. Locus 005	Flat jar base, medium-fired, grayish-brown 10YR5/2 ware, coarse grit temper, red 10R5/6 slip exterior.
10. Locus 012	Flat jar base, high-fired, reddish-yellow 5YR6/6 ware, fine grit and grog temper.
11. Locus 012	Inverted platter-bowl rim, high-fired, light reddish-brown 5YR6/4 ware, very fine grit temper, horizontally burnished interior and exterior.
12. Locus 012	Ledge-handled platter-bowl rim, medium-fired, pinkish-gray 7.5YR6/2 ware, coarse grit temper, vertically burnished interior.
13. Locus 002	Flaring rim ovoid jar with two vertical strap handles, very high-fired ("metallic ware"), dark reddish-gray 5YR4/2 ware, fine sand temper, white 10YR8/2 slip and parallel groups of gray 5YR5/1 painted stripes exterior.

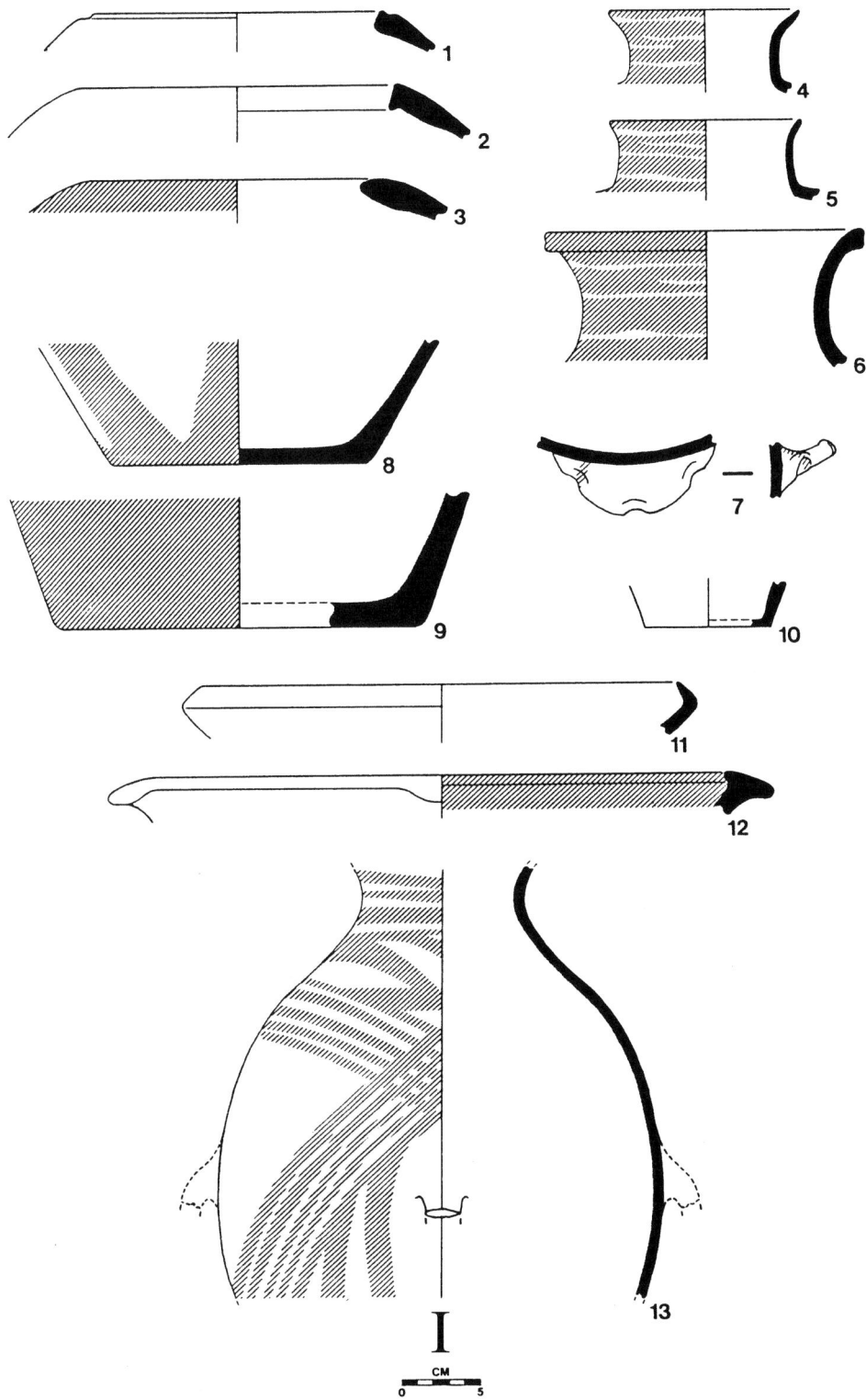

Fig. 14. Ceramic artifacts from sounding Stratum I.

TABLE 3. Stages of occupation and area strata at Tell el-Handaquq North

| Years B.C. | Periods | Area Strata | | | | Stages of occupation |
		Sounding	South cut	Wadi terrace	Tombs	
2000						
	EB IV			1 continued incision	1	5 squatters
2400						
	EB III			2 breach of dams, wadi incision?		4 abandonment
2700						
	EB II	I–III	I–III	3 aggradation	2	3 nucleation, town walls
3000		IV–V	IV	4 dam construction?		
	EB I		V–VII	5 aggradation, burial of houses	3	2 growth
3500						
	Late Chalcolithic			6 house construction		1 establishment
5000						

two strata. Both wares have been found in early- to mid-third millennium B.C. (EB II–III) strata at Khirbet Kerak and Jericho (Hennessy 1967; Esse 1982) in the Jordan Valley.

Reconstructable pieces of a handmade, flared-rim ovoid jar with a sand-tempered, high-fired ("metallic") reddish-gray ware, vertical strap handles, and decorated with parallel groups of gray painted stripes (fig. 14:13) were found in the upper two strata. This unusual, probably nonlocal ware, form, and decoration may be related to the mid- to late Early Bronze Age "scrabbled ware" found in coastal Lebanon (Ehrich 1939: 35) and central Syria (Collon et al. 1975: 38, pl. 19), or the "multiple-brush painted ware" found in northern Syria (Mellaart 1981: 156). Body sherds of a similar nonlocal metallic ware with a white "reserved-slip" decoration were found on the surface of the sounding. This style has been found in ᶜAmuq G strata (Braidwood and Braidwood 1960: 275; figs. 218, 219) and across northern Syria (Mellaart 1981: 154–55; Sanlaville 1985: 105). The presence of these foreign "metallic wares" indicates that the settlement at Tell el-Handaquq had some connections with Syria during the mid-third millennium B.C. (EB II).

Comparisons with other stratified ceramic sequences from the Jordan Valley thus indicate that the five strata of cultural deposits encountered so far in the sounding at Tell el-Handaquq date from the early- to mid-third millennium B.C. (late EB I to mid-

EB II). The lower three strata (Strata III–V) yielded ceramic forms known from stratified EB IB and EB II contexts. Common EB II wares, forms, and decorative styles were found in the Strata II and I, including painted red-on-white decoration on jars, and mass-produced, high-fired, wheel-made forms such as platter-bowls. The sequence so far encountered in the sounding is therefore roughly equivalent to Khirbet Kerak II–III, the middle part of the sequence at Tell esh-Shuna North, Beth Shan XV–XIV, Um Hammad Stage 4, Tell Mahruq 2, Garstang's Jericho IV, and Kenyon's "EB I–II" strata at Jericho. Table 3 shows the possible correlations between strata in the sounding, the South Bulldozer Cut, the Wadi Terrace, and the Tombs.

Lithic Artifacts

Chipped Stone. Analysis of the chipped stone artifact assemblage from Tell el-Handaquq has not been completed. Therefore, only the range of formal tool types represented is discussed here. Of the total of ten formal tools recovered from the sounding, the most common type was the typical third millennium B.C. (Early Bronze Age) "Canaanite sickle-blade" with a triangular or trapezoidal cross section and silica polish along one or both edges (fig. 9:1–6). One very long blade from a Stratum II floor in the sounding (fig. 9:2) was unifacially retouched, with silica polish along the retouched

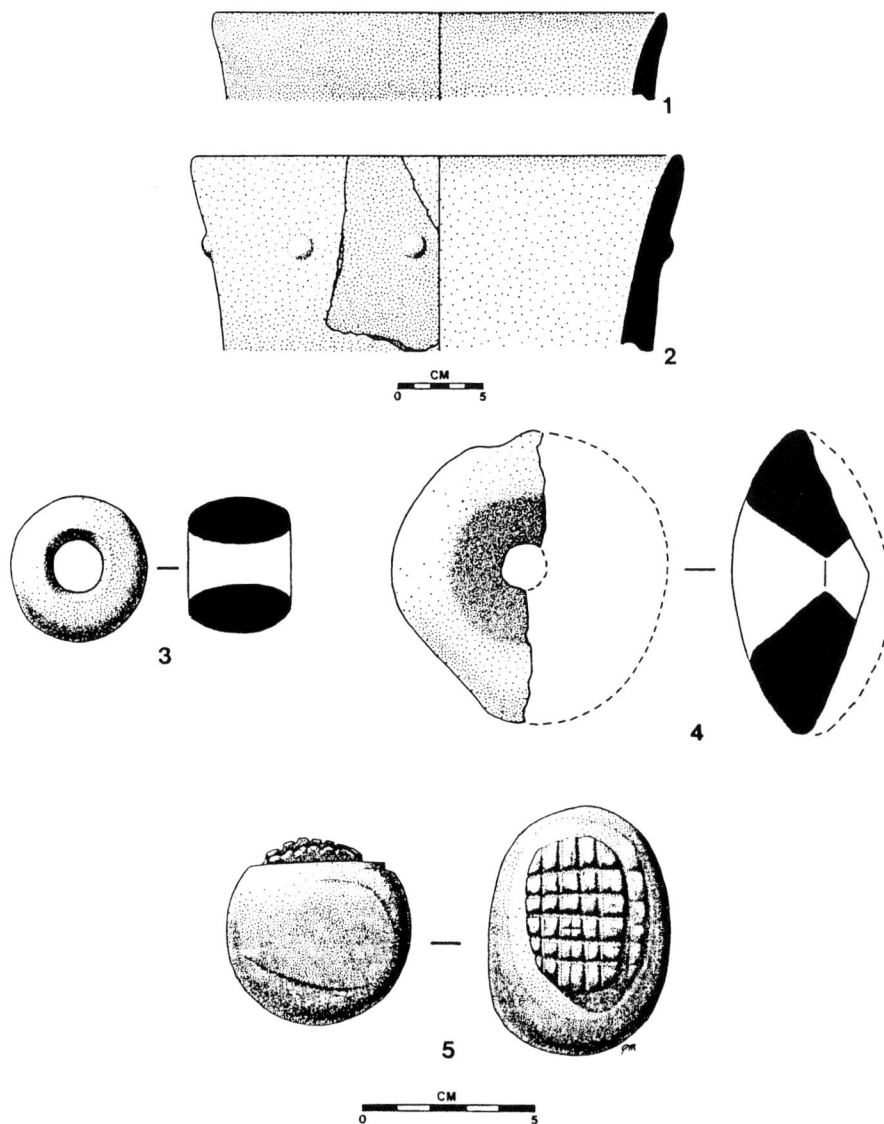

Fig. 15. Ground stone artifacts.

Location	Description
1. Sounding, Stratum 3, Locus 028	Ground basalt bowl rim.
2. Surface	Ground basalt bowl rim with knobs around the exterior.
3. Surface	Ground and drilled basalt ring.
4. Sounding, Stratum 4, Locus 036	Ground and drilled limestone ring (or hoe) fragment.
5. Surface	Ground chalk stamp(?) with carved crossed-line design.

edge. A smaller blade fragment that may have come from the same core was also found on this floor. Unifacially retouched fan scrapers (fig. 9:7–9) and a heavily battered flint hammerstone (fig. 9:10) were also found in the upper two strata of the sounding.

Ground Stone. A rim of a typical EB I ground basalt "V"-shaped bowl was found on a Stratum III floor in the sounding (fig. 15:1). Another example with knobs around the exterior was found on the surface (fig. 15:2). Ground basalt rings were found in the fill of Burial 021 in Stratum II in the sounding

TABLE 4. Identified plant taxa from
Tell el-Handaquq radiocarbon samples

Taxa	Sample 1	Sample 2	Sample 3
Triticum turgidum var. *dicoccum*	7	1	1
Triticum aestivum	1		2
Hordeum sp.	8		6
Spikelet forks	11		2
Unidentified cereal frags.	1		6
Unidentified cereal grain	1		
Ficus carica	2		
Lens esculenta	2		1
Galium sp.	1		
Unknown			3

(fig. 5:7), and on the surface (fig. 15:3). A fragment of a large, ground limestone ring or hoe was also found on the surface (fig. 15:4). Finally, a curious egg-shaped object (possibly an unfinished stamp seal; below), made of ground chalk and carved with a cross-hatched design, was found on the surface (fig. 15:5).

EVIDENCE OF SUBSISTENCE ECONOMY

Plant Remains
Marcia L. Donaldson and Jonathan B. Mabry

During preparation of samples for radiocarbon dating taken from the South Bulldozer Cut, a significant quantity of well-preserved carbonized seeds were recognized in all of the samples. Plant remains separated from charcoal samples representing three stratified contexts in the South Bulldozer Cut were examined. The remains, primarily seeds, include 56 specimens representing six known plant taxa and at least two unknown types (table 4). All of the seeds were charred, and several were quite badly fragmented and weathered. Specimens were identified using a small comparative collection and through comparison with published reports of analyses of plant remains from contemporaneous sites in the Jordan Valley (Hopf 1983). Complete items were measured using a calibrated micrometer with a 10X binocular microscope (table 5).

The great majority of remains represent the cereals wheat and barley. Two types of wheat, emmer (*Triticum turgidum* var. *dicoccum*) and naked bread wheat (*Triticum aestivum*), appear to be represented in these small samples. Unfortunately, there has been

some distortion of the grains due to charring, and erosion of the seed coats is common. Specific identifications, therefore, remain tentative. In these samples, however, it is clear that emmer wheat is more common than naked bread wheat. Domesticated barley (*Hordeum* sp.) is represented by both grains and rachis forks. Those barley grains with intact seed coat surfaces indicate that at least some of the grains were hulled. The presence of quite small specimens of barley grains may indicate the smaller, lateral grains of a six-row hulled barley (*Hordeum vulgare* var. *hexastichum*).

Other domestic taxa recovered include lentils (*Lens esculenta*) and figs (*Ficus carica*), each represented by a few specimens. In addition, one unknown cereal grain was noted in Sample 1, and several fragmented seeds in Sample 3. One of the latter resembled a flax (or linseed) seed (*Linum usitatissimum*) but it appeared too small (length 2.3 mm) to represent even a wild species of flax (*Linum bienne*). Flax seeds from Early Bronze Age strata at Jericho, by comparison, are larger (3.70 × 1.62 mm). However, charring has altered the original dimensions of this specimen, making certain identification impossible. In addition to the carbonized plant remains identified in the radiocarbon samples from the South Bulldozer Cut, sifting recovered one carbonized olive pit (*Olea europaea*) from a Stratum II floor in the sounding.

TABLE 5. Dimensions of Complete Grains in
Tell el-Handaquq Radiocarbon Samples, in mm

	Length	Breadth	Thickness
Triticum turgidum var. *dicoccum*	5.6	2.8	2.6
	5.7	2.6	2.4
	4.8	3.0	2.5
	4.9	2.3	2.2
	5.5	2.1	1.8
Triticum aestivum	6.1	3.2	2.3
	5.8	3.5	2.5
Hordeum sp.	4.2	2.1	1.7
	3.8	1.3	1.0
	4.3	1.5	1.3
	4.4	1.5	1.1
	4.0	1.3	1.3
	6.0	3.0	2.1
	5.8	2.7	2.2
	4.8	2.9	1.9
	4.4	1.6	1.4

TABLE 6. Faunal bone fragments from Tell el-Handaquq sounding,
identified to taxonomic level, by Stratum*

	Class	Order	Family	Genus	Species
Post-occupation	8	4	4	4	4
	(100)	(50)			
Stratum 1	74	19	14	13	6
	(100)	(25.7)	(18.9)	(17.6)	(8.1)
Stratum 2	132	31	25	22	8
	(100)	(23.5)	(18.9)	(16.7)	(6.1)
Stratum 3	137	23	13	10	2
	(100)	(16.8)	(9.5)	(7.3)	(1.5)
Stratum 4	60	17	13	13	2
	(100)	(28.3)	(21.7)	(21.7)	(3.3)
Stratum 5	5	0	0	0	0
	(100)				
All Strata	416	94	69	62	22
	(100)	(22.6)	(16.6)	(14.9)	(5.3)

*Percents are listed in parentheses.

In summary, the plant remains recovered so far from Tell el-Handaquq are indicative of an agricultural economy based on a variety of cereals, pulses, fruits, and possibly fiber and oil plants (flax/linseed). Although two-row hulled barley was the only variety of barley represented in Proto-Urban (EB I) levels at Jericho, six-row hulled barley was the most common variety of barley in EB II and III levels, as it is in these small samples from Tell el-Handaquq. Like barley, lentils are a relatively drought-tolerant crop. But the cultivation of olive and fig trees, as well as bread wheat and (possibly) flax, requires more consistent soil moisture. Their presence at Early Bronze Age Jericho, Bab edh-Dhra[c], and Tell el-Handaquq indicates either higher rainfall than at present in the Jordan Valley, or irrigation (McCreery 1980; Hopf 1983).

A grain of naked bread wheat in Sample 1 yielded an accelerator radiocarbon age (below) that indicates that this hexaploid variety was cultivated in the central Jordan Valley during EB I. Currently, these are the earliest recovered remains of naked bread wheat in the Jordan Valley. Emmer wheat is the most abundant variety represented in the floral samples from Chalcolithic Abu Hamid, 2 km west of Tell el-Handaquq (Neef 1988: 597–98). In the southwestern valley the presence of naked, hexaploid bread wheat in EB II and III strata at Jericho (along with abundant grape seeds) implied artificial irrigation to Hopf (1983: 579, 583); bread wheat is more drought-sensitive and more yield-responsive to

irrigation than are the more drought-tolerant, tetraploid emmer and tetraploid naked hard wheats (*Triticum turgidum* var. *durum*). The relatively large size of the bread wheat grains recovered from Tell el-Handaquq also points to irrigation. The complete bread wheat grains in the Tell el-Handaquq samples (table 5) measured an average of 18 percent larger than those from EB II and III levels at Jericho (Hopf 1983: 583), which averaged 5.3 × 2.90 × 2.55 mm.

Faunal Remains
Katherine Gruspier and Grant Mullen

The sample of faunal bones recovered from the sounding at Tell el-Handaquq is small and therefore not conducive to detailed analysis at this time; future excavations at the site will expand and improve the current database. However, the sample size (n=416 fragments) is comparable to that of ungulate remains recovered from EB II and III strata at Jericho (n=478 fragments; Clutton-Brock 1979). All of the faunal bone fragments from Tell el-Handaquq were identifiable to taxonomic class. Most represented are mammals, followed by mollusks, and a single avian element. No fish remains are represented. The rate of identification to taxonomic species is 5 percent for the entire collection while, inclusive of the above figure, 15 percent are identified to taxonomic genus. The percentages and levels of identification by stratum are summarized in table 6.

TABLE 7. Faunal bone fragments from
Tell el-Handaquq sounding identified to
taxonomic class, by stratum and locus

	Locus	Number	%
Post-occupation	001	6	1.4
	002	2	0.5
Total		8	1.9
Stratum 1	005	4	1.0
	007	2	0.5
	009	16	3.8
	012	32	7.7
	014	20	4.8
Total		74	17.8
Stratum 2	006	1	0.2
	015	3	0.7
	017	2	0.5
	018	3	0.7
	019	36	8.7
	026	83	20.0
	027	4	1.0
Total		132	31.7
Stratum 3	028	23	5.5
	032	25	6.0
	033	89	21.4
Total		137	33.0
Stratum 4	034	47	11.3
	036	13	3.1
Total		60	14.4
Stratum 5	037	5	1.2
Total		5	1.2
Total (All strata)		416	100.0

TABLE 8. Distribution of mammal bone fragments
from Tell el-Handaquq sounding, by body part
and stratum

Stratum	Head	Axial	Limb	Total
Post-occupation	1	1	2	4
1	7	21	42	70
2	26	11	88	125
3	24	17	95	136
4	5	8	46	59
5	—	3	2	5
Total	63	61	275	399
Percent	15.8	15.3	69	100

TABLE 9. Faunal bone from Tell el-Handaquq
sounding, minimum number of individuals,
by stratum

Stratum	MNI*	Identification
Post-occupation	1	Eobania vermiculata
	1	Cerastoderma edule
	1	Unio terminalis
1	1	Capra/Ovis
	1	Ovis aries
	1	Bos taurus
1	2	Capra/Ovis
	1	large Ruminantia
	1	Bos taurus
	1	Canis spp.
	1	Aves
3	1	Capra/Ovis (juv.)
	1	Capra spp.
	1	Ovis spp.
	1	Capreolus capreolus
	1	Gazella gazella
	1	Bovidae
4	2	Capra/Ovis

*Minimum number of individuals.

Table 7 shows the number and percent of fragments identified to taxonomic class, by locus and stratum. The largest samples are available from Strata II and III, with 132 and 137 fragments respectively. Within these, the largest proportion of fragments (41 percent) is derived from two loci. Stratum 2, Locus 026 (a surface/floor), contains 83 fragments, and Stratum III, Locus 033 (a fill layer), yielded 89 fragments. The sample size is too small to suggest implications from this pattern.

In the portion of the sample representing parts of mammalian skeletons (n=399), 69 percent is comprised of limb elements. Strata II and III are the most similar with respect to both numbers and relative proportions of head, axial, and limb fragments. A χ^2 test without an *a priori* hypothesis fails to reject a null hypothesis that the two are the same ($\chi^2=0.722$, df=2, 0.75>p>0.50). The distributions of these elements in both Strata 1 and 4 show much reduced numbers of fragments representing the head (table 8).

Table 9 presents the minimum number of individuals (MNI) represented, by stratum. In all cases

TABLE 10. Minimum numbers (MNI) and percentages of ungulate remains from Tell el-Handaquq sounding compared to other protohistoric sites in the Jordan Valley

Site:	Jelmet esh-Shariyeh (Late Chalcolithic–EB I)		Handaquq (EB I–II)		Jericho (EB II–III)*
Genus	Number	%	Number	%	%
Capra/Ovis	5	45.5	9	64.3	77.8
Bos	2	18.2	2	14.3	12.5
Gazella	1	9.1	1	7.1	5.6
Dama	0	0	0	0	1.5
Capreolus	0	0	1	7.1	0.6
Sus	3	27.3	0	0	1.9

*Percentages of fragments.
(Sources: Clutton-Brock 1979, Gruspier and Mullen 1990)

but one, the animals were relatively mature. In fact, many of the dental remains show the *Capra/Ovis* remains to be of advanced age. When further analysis is undertaken, all ages as derived from dental wear can be calculated and an age profile of the remains can be prepared.

Table 10 presents MNI estimates for selected mammalian genera in comparison to faunal samples from other protohistoric sites in the Jordan Valley. While drawing strong conclusions from this small sample is not merited, the similarities between Tell el-Handaquq and Jericho in the relative proportions of *Capra/Ovis*, *Bos*, and *Gazella* are in marked contrast with the high proportion of *Sus* in the faunal bone sample from Late Chalcolithic–EB I Jelmet esh-Shariyeh (Gruspier and Mullen 1990: 115). However, in Early Bronze Age strata at Jericho, pig (*Sus*) elements represent less than 2 percent of the faunal bone fragments recovered (rather than MNI), and none of these are from domesticated pig (Clutton-Brock 1979). It is possible, then, that wild *Sus* will be represented in a larger sample from Tell el-Handaquq. The presence of roe deer (*Capreolus capreolus*) in the Tell el-Handaquq sample is also paralleled in the Early Bronze Age sample from Jericho, which also contains a small proportion of fallow deer (*Dama mesopotamica*) bone fragments. In addition to these ungulates, domesticated donkey (*Equus asinus*) and fox (*Vulpes*) remains are represented in the sample of mammalian remains at Jericho but are not represented in the Tell el-Handaquq sample. However, dog or jackal (*Canis* sp.) remains are present in the Tell el-Handaquq sample, but not in the Early Bronze Age sample from Jericho; this absence may simply mean that dogs were not commonly eaten at Jericho, however.

TABLE 11. Culturally modified faunal bone from Tell el-Handaquq sounding

Locus	Bone	Description
005	Medium mammal shaft	Calcined
018	Small mammal shaft	Calcined
026	Medium mammal shafts	Calcined
	Medium mammal shaft	Transverse cut marks
	Bos taurus—R. mandibular	
	Coronoid process	Transverse cut marks
032	Large mammal rib	Bone awl
	Medium mammal rib	Possibly worked
	Medium mammal shaft	6 transverse cut marks
033	Large mammal	Many small cut marks,
		Running superior/ inferior
034	Large mammal rib	Evidence of use-wear on edges
	C. capreolus—astragalus	Medial aspect displays Vertical cut marks

A total of twelve bone elements in this sample were culturally modified (table 11). Three mammal limb shafts are completely calcined, the result of extreme heating. One mammal rib was shaped into an awl, while two other showed signs of use-wear or shaping. The remainder showed butchering marks, including both transverse and vertical cut marks. There is no certain explanation for the calcined bone, but a large quantity of calcined caprovine and bovine bones were found on the surface at the EB I sites of Khirbet el-Umbashi and Hebariyeh in southern Syria (Dubretet and Dunand 1954).

In summary, the present sample of faunal bones from the sounding at Tell el-Handaquq indicates that husbandry of sheep, goats, and cattle was an essential part of the settlement's economy, including both meat and secondary products such as milk and hides. The relative importance of secondary products is reflected by the maturity of the sheep and goat remains. The presence of gazelle and roe deer remains also reflects the continued significance of hunted game in the subsistence of the community. The dog or jackal remains in domestic contexts may indicate that, at least occasionally, they also formed part of the diet.

PROTOHISTORIC STAMP
SEAL IMPRESSION

During a collection of artifacts from the surface of Tell el-Handaquq in 1988, a "cross-hatched" design stamp seal impression was found on a sherd from the shoulder of an Early Bronze Age, "grain-washed" holemouth storage jar (fig. 16). Stamp seal impressions with cross-hatched designs have been found at several protohistoric sites in Jordan, stamped on the handles, shoulders, rims, or bases of storage jars dated to the mid- to late fourth millennia B.C., or the EB I period (fig. 17).

In the eastern Jordan Valley, this type of impression has been found at Kataret es-Samra (A. Leonard, personal communication 1989), at Tell Um Hammad esh-Sharqiya (Helms 1984: 47, fig. 11:15–17; 1987: 55, fig. 4; Leonard 1992: pl. 35:4), at Tell Mafluq (Leonard 1992: pl. 35:3), and now at Tell el-Handaquq. Sherds from EB I with the same type of stamped impression also have been found at Sbeiheh in the lower Wadi Zerqa (Hanbury-Tenison 1987: fig. 5:48) and at Jawa in the eastern desert (Helms 1981: 227; fig. B4:6). Use of cross-hatched stamp seals thus linked a string of mid- to late fourth millennium B.C. settlements from the Jebel Druze, through the Wadi Zerqa, to the Jordan Valley. This cross-hatched design may have been standardized, as among the set of known impressions there are only three minor variations (fig. 17; Helms 1991 presents a more thorough discussion of the variations of southern Levantine stamp seal designs). No stamp impressions with this design have been found west of the Jordan River to date, although the impressions of spiral and animal design stamps have been found.

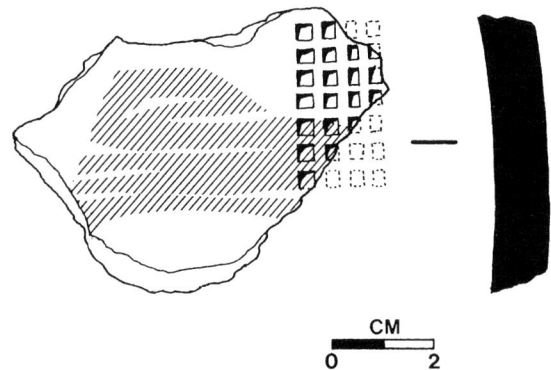

Fig. 16. Stamp seal impression from Tell el-Handaquq North.

Stamp seals, and this particular motif, have parallels from Syria dating back to at least the sixth millennium B.C., while the earliest stamp seals and impressions found in the southern Levant date to the early fifth millennium B.C.—the late Pottery Neolithic or Early Chalcolithic. In the Jordan Valley, Chalcolithic stamp seals with a circular design of drilled holes have been found at Teleilat Ghassul (Mallon, Koeppel, and Neuville 1934: 75, fig. 28:1) and at Tell esh-Shemdin (Tzori 1958: 47, pl. 5A). The stamp seal impression of irregular crossed lines found on a piece of partially baked clay in an Early Chalcolithic stratum at Tel Tsaf (Gophna and Sadeh 1989: 32, fig. 12:16) may represent the predecessor of the cross-hatched design.

Both the chronology and the pattern of distribution of these finds suggests that stamp seals spread from the northern to the southern Levant, where they became widely used by the nonurban, preliterate society of the southern Levant during the fifth and fourth millennia B.C. The "Protohistoric" period in the southern Levant, from the Early Chalcolithic period to the end of the Early Bronze Age, can thus be defined both by contemporaneity with neighboring literate societies and by widespread use of standardized glyptic symbols before the use of the Canaanite alphabet in the Middle Bronze Age.

Systematic use of seals to mark only large storage vessels in the late fourth millennium B.C. is an intriguing pattern that suggests developed concepts of property, the passing of goods out of the owner's hands, and differential access to whatever valuable commodity the vessels contained (probably agricultural surpluses in this case). Helms (1987a: 41–43; 1987b; 1991) has argued that these EB I stamp seals functioned as "economic control devices" by signifying ownership, a specific commodity, or a place of origin.

TYPES

<u>1</u>   <u>2</u>   <u>3</u>

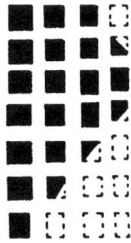      

HANDAQUQ   JAWA

UM HAMMAD

SBEIHEH   KATARET ES-SAMRA   MAFLUQ

3 cm

Fig. 17. Stamp seal impressions from protohistoric sites in Jordan.

TABLE 12. AMS-Method Radiocarbon Dates from Tell el-Handaquq

Sample No.	Material	Uncalibrated Date b.p.*	Calibrated Date B.C.**	Lab No.
Wadi 1	Charcoal	4710 ± 65	3631–3369	AA-10269
South Cut 1	Charred grain	4685 ± 65	3626–3361	AA-5284
South Cut 3	Charred grain	4495 ± 55	3344–3046	AA-5286
Sounding 1	Charcoal	4475 ± 50	3334–2944	AA-5287
South Cut 2	Charred grain	4345 ± 75	3078–2889	AA-5285
Surface 1	Sherd residue	3780 ± 65	2396–2041	AA-7814

*Calculated according to 5568-year "Libby" half-life, in years before A.D. 1950 datum.
**1-σ range (68%) of probability, based on Stuiver and Becker 1993.

Logically, stamp seal impressions could have been used for a variety of purposes, including potters' trademarks, marks of ownership, labels of contents, seals of quality, place-of-production tags, or addresses of destination. It is likely that they conveyed some combination of those meanings.

The spread of stamp seal use in the southern Levant during the late fourth and early third millennia B.C. coincided with—and may have been related to—the development of highland rain-fed horticultural production, intensification of lowland irrigated cereal and flax production, increase in long-distance trade with Egypt, and a trend toward nucleation of population into fortified towns. Although a number of reconstructions can be considered, it seems likely that emerging elite classes in the developing towns of the southern Levant borrowed the use of seals from the more socially and economically advanced Syrians, first to organize local agricultural production and later to facilitate long-distance trade in these surpluses with the Egyptians.

Cylinder seal impressions found in the Jezreel Valley at EB I ᶜEn Shadud (Braun and Gibson 1984: 38) and contemporaneous Stage V deposits at Megiddo (Engberg and Shipton 1934: fig. 11:B) represent elaboration of stamp seals in the late fourth millennium B.C. At Bab edh-Dhraᶜ, southeast of the Dead Sea, cylinder seal impressions also have been found on late EB I sherds (Lapp 1989). But a widespread shift from the use of simple stamp seals to cylinder seals with more complicated designs did not occur in the southern Levant until the early third millennium B.C. (Ben-Tor 1978), perhaps due to a necessity to transmit additional information to manage increased long-distance trade. At the very least, the use of such administrative technology at Tell

el-Handaquq, along with runoff conservation technology, linked this settlement to other protohistoric towns in the southern Levant. It may also imply some organized trade in agricultural surpluses, and some degree of socioeconomic stratification.

RADIOCARBON DATES

Six samples of organic material were radiocarbon dated by the accelerator mass spectrometry (AMS) method at the National Science Foundation—University of Arizona Accelerator Facility for Radioisotope Analysis (table 12). These included one sample of wood charcoal from the wadi, three samples of charred cereal grains from the South Bulldozer Cut, one sample of wood charcoal from the sounding, and an organic residue chemically extracted from a surface pottery sherd. The dates are reported here in uncalibrated radiocarbon years b.p. (before present, A.D. 1950 datum); i.e., based on the short, 5568-year "Libby" half-life. Date ranges expressed in years B.C. represent 1 σ range of probability (68%) in dendrocalibrated years, based on the calibration curve of Stuiver and Becker (1993).

A sample of wood charcoal from a depth of about 1.2 m below the surface in the south bank of Wadi es-Sarar, within a relatively well-sorted silt deposit accumulated behind a masonry dam and containing Late Chalcolithic sherds and chipped stone tools (above), yielded a radiocarbon age of 4710 ± 65 b.p. (AA-10269). Dendrocalibration indicates a 1 σ range of 3631–3369 B.C., which falls near the juncture of the Late Chalcolithic and EB I periods; it supports the artifact-based dating of the underlying structures to the former period, and of the masonry dams to (at least) the latter period.

A radiocarbon age of 4685 ± 65 b.p. (AA-5284) was provided by a single charred grain of naked bread wheat from a basal cultural deposit (Stratum VII), an ashy lense or hearth, exposed in the eastern part of South Bulldozer Cut about 2.5 m below the surface. A second date of 4495 ± 55 b.p. (AA-5286) was obtained from a single charred grain of barley (*Hordeum* sp.) in another ashy lense near the base of the center part of the cultural deposits exposed in the Cut (Stratum 7) about 2.5 m below the surface. A single charred grain of emmer wheat in a sample from a house floor about 0.75 m below the surface in the western part of the South Bulldozer Cut (Stratum IV) provided a third date of 4345 ± 75 b.p. (AA-5285). In dendrocalibrated years, the age of these samples from the South Cut fall between 3626 and 3361 B.C., 3344 and 3046 B.C., and 3078 and 2889 B.C. respectively. Because of the short annual life cycle of cereals, these samples are ideal for accelerator radiocarbon dating. The first two dates indicate occupation of this part of the site by the mid-fourth millennium B.C. In the Jordan Valley, these fall closest to dates obtained from Proto-Urban (EB I) contexts at Jericho (Burleigh 1983). The last date, from an EB II context postdating construction of the town wall, indicates that the settlement was already fortified before the beginning of the third millennium B.C.

Currently, the latter is the oldest radiocarbon age associated with a walled settlement in the Jordan Valley, falling earlier than radiocarbon dates from EB II strata at Jericho (Burleigh 1983). When calibrated, however, it compares closely with the four reliable radiocarbon dates obtained from a carbonized olive stone and charred wheat grains from the early EB II (post-town wall) Stratum IV at Tell Areini, which average 3015 B.C. (Barker, Burleigh, and Meeks 1971: 182–83); the stratigraphy of that site is not well understood, however. This new radiocarbon date from Handaquq supports the association of "late Early Bronze I" ceramic types with a double-wall fortification with a sloped glaçis at Tel Shalem in the west-central Jordan Valley (Eisenberg 1986). Likewise, the 2.5-m wide mudbrick wall on stone foundations enclosing the Proto-Urban occupation at Jericho (Kenyon 1981) and the 2.8-m wide mudbrick wall in the EB I stratum at Tell el-Farah (de Vaux 1962) do not seem so precocious now. It is now clear that the first town walls in the southern Levant were constructed near the end of the fourth millennium B.C., close to the beginning of the First Dynasty in Egypt, and thus supporting a "high" chro-

nology for the Early Bronze Age in Palestine and Jordan (Callaway and Weinstein 1977).

A sample of wood charcoal from a house floor about 0.75 m below the surface in the sounding (Stratum II, Locus 026) yielded a radiocarbon age of 4475 ± 50 b.p. (AA-5287). Dendrocalibration indicates a 1-σ age range between 3334 and 2944 B.C. for this sample. In the Jordan Valley, this date falls closest to those from EB I contexts at Jericho and from the South Bulldozer Cut; but this unidentified wood charcoal is associated with an EB II ceramic assemblage. Representing a longer-lived perennial species, the early date obtained from this sample may be due to the "old wood" problem (i.e., heartwood dates older than the outer rings, and dead wood may lie on the desert surface without decomposing for centuries before being collected and burned).

Finally, fatty acid (lipid) residue chemically extracted and isolated from a sherd of a high-fired, cream-slipped "combed ware" jar on the site surface (fig. 5:2) yielded an accelerator date of 3780 ± 65 b.p. (AA-7814), or 2396–2041 B.C. in dendrocalibrated years. Although this date is the preliminary result of an experimental technique still under development by a group at the University of Arizona, it falls within the expected age range of this EB III–IV ceramic ware in the Jordan Valley. This date also supports the ceramic evidence that the ruins of Tell el-Handaquq were at least occasionally occupied during the EB IV.

SUMMARY

Tell el-Handaquq is an important example of early town development and community water management in Jordan. Surface finds indicate uninterrupted occupation of the site from the early fourth to the mid-third millennium B.C., followed by occasional encampments during the late third millennium B.C. The fortifications, large "public" buildings, intramural precincts, large-scale water management features, and the use of mass-produced pottery and stamp seals all indicate that this settlement was an organized community capable of labor cooperation and sophisticated engineering. Perhaps the best ethnohistoric analogy for organization of this protohistoric agricultural community is the "irrigation community," in which kinship units are linked by the necessity to pool labor, share productive resources, exchange surpluses, and defend territory.

Where foundations are still visible on the surface, a relatively high density of housing is indicated.

If a density of 200 people per hectare is assumed (a conservative estimate based on ethnographic measurements of up to 300/ha in contemporary tell settlements, e.g., Van Beek 1982), the population reached a peak of at least 5,000 by the time the 25–30 ha settlement was fortified during the late fourth millennium B.C. This figure seems high, but a peak population of more than 1,000 does not seem unrealistic. Tell el-Handaquq is comparable in size to several other EB I walled towns in Jordan and southern Syria, including Jebel Mutawwaq (28 ha) and Khirbet el-Umbashi (20 ha). It is significantly larger, however, than contemporaneous Jawa (12 ha), Leboueh (11 ha), and Um Hammad esh-Sharqiyeh (16 ha). As Schaub (1982), Falconer (1987), and Hanbury-Tenison (1989) have pointed out, however, these walled fourth-millennium B.C. towns are not truly urban-scale settlements. They are similar in size to the open settlements of the Chalcolithic period, and—in terms of material culture—were directly developed from them. Enclosure of protohistoric settlements in the southern Levant was more likely due to indigenous development (de Miroschedji 1971; Schaub 1982; Joffe 1991) than to an invasion of an already urbanized population from the north (Lapp 1970; de Vaux 1971; Kenyon 1979).

Calculations indicate that the reservoir easily could have supported this population by storage of only part of the present amount of the flood flow of Wadi es-Sarar. The use of channel-bottom check dams indicates an aggradational regime during occupation. The cycle of wadi incision that breached the dams and prevented further flood diversion was probably the cause of the town's abandonment during the mid-third millennium B.C. This was the mid-Holocene cycle of downcutting that occurred throughout the Jordan Valley, and may have been the primary factor in the abandonment of almost every protohistoric town in the region (Mabry 1992).

The material culture found on the surface, in the South Cut, and in the sounding also links this settlement with other early fortified towns in the southern Levant that relied on runoff conservation and used standardized stamp seals. The ceramic wares represented include both local and Syrian types, and range in date from Late Chalcolithic to Early Bronze IV. Handmade pottery was found in all strata, while wheelmade pottery appeared only in upper ones. The samples of floral and faunal remains reflect a mixed farming and herding economy, including irrigation of drought-sensitive crop varieties and careful livestock management. The charred grains of naked bread wheat, which predominated in the samples, are currently the earliest evidence of cultivation of this variety in the southern Levant. In this region, the accelerator radiocarbon dates obtained from the remains of short-lived plants found in stratified contexts are also the earliest associated with an EB I material culture, and with a town wall.

The discoveries at Tell el-Handaquq were not unexpected, given the physiographic and hydrological conditions in the Jordan Valley. Even before any major archaeological fieldwork had been conducted in this region, Albright (1925) suggested that fortified towns, based on water management, developed in the Jordan Valley earlier than anywhere else in the southern Levant. At least he was right when he predicted, "It would be extremely interesting to learn more about the civilization of the Jordan Valley in the third millennium. . . . Without a doubt we have some great surprises in store for us" (Albright 1925: 73).

ACKNOWLEDGMENTS

The primary author directed the fieldwork with the assistance of Gaetano Palumbo from the University of Rome, and Wajih Karasneh from the Jordan Department of Antiquities. The topographical-architectural survey team included Michael Rawlings and Marcus Woodburn from the British Institute for Archaeology in Amman. The work at Tell el-Handaquq would not have been possible without the permission of Adnan Hadidi, former director of the Department of Antiquities of Jordan, and the logistical help of David McCreery, former director of the American Center for Oriental Research in Amman. Svend Helms generously gave access to the sherd collection from Tell Um Hammad esh-Sharqiya for comparison and provided helpful comments on earlier drafts of this manuscript. The fieldwork was funded by a grant from the Shell Oil Corporation through the ASOR Shell Fellowship for archaeological research in Jordan. Douglas Donahue, director of the National Science Foundation—University of Arizona Accelerator Facility for Radioisotope Analysis, donated six accelerator radiocarbon dates. This report was part of a dissertation research project completed under the supervision of John Olsen, William Dever, and Vance Haynes of the University of Arizona Department of Anthropology.

REFERENCES

Abel, F. M.
1991   Exploration de la Vallee du Jourdain. *Revue Biblique* 8: 408–36.

Albright, W. F.
1925   The Jordan Valley in the Bronze Age. *Annual of the American Schools of Oriental Research* 6: 13–74. New Haven: American Schools of Oriental Research.

Amiran, R.
1978   *Early Arad I.* Jerusalem: Israel Exploration Society.

Barker, H.; Burleigh, R.; and Meeks, N.
1971   British Museum Natural Radiocarbon Measurements VII. *Radiocarbon* 13: 157–88.

Ben-Tor, A.
1978   *Cylinder Seals of Third-Millennium Palestine.* American Schools of Oriental Research, Supplement Series 22. Cambridge, MA: American Schools of Oriental Research.

Braemer, F.
1988   Prospections archéologiques dans le Hawran II. Les reseaux de l'eau. *Syria* 65 (1–2): 99–137.

Braidwood, R. J., and Braidwood, L. S.
1960   *Excavations in the Plain of Antioch I.* Oriental Institute Publications 61. Chicago: The Oriental Institute of the University of Chicago.

Braun, E., and Gibson, S.
1984   ᶜEn-shadud: An Early Bronze I Farming Community in the Jezreel Valley. *Bulletin of the American Schools of Oriental Research* 253: 29–40.

Burleigh, R.
1983   Additional Radiocarbon Dates for Jericho. Pp. 760–65 in *Excavations at Jericho V*, eds. K. M. Kenyon and T. A. Holland. London: British School of Archaeology in Jerusalem.

Callaway, J. A.
1978   New Perspectives on Early Bronze Age III Canaan. Pp. 46–58 in *Archaeology in the Levant*, eds. R. Moorey and P. Parr. Warminster: Aris and Phillips.

Callaway, J. A., and Weinstein, J. M.
1977   Radiocarbon Dating of Palestine in the Early Bronze Age. *Bulletin of the American Schools of Oriental Research* 225: 1–16.

Clutton-Brock, J.
1979   The Mammalian Remains from the Jericho Tell. *Proceedings of the Prehistoric Society* 45: 135–57.

Collon, D.; Otte, C. M.; and Zaqzouq, A.
1975   *Sondages au Flanc Sud du Tell de Qalᶜat el-Mudiq.* Fouilles d'Apamee de Syrie, Miscel-

lanea. Fasc. 11. Brussels: Centre Belge de Recherches Archeologiques a Apamee de Syrie.

de Contenson, H.
1960a   Three Soundings in the Jordan Valley. *Annual of the Department of Antiquities of Jordan* 4/5: 12–98.
1960b   La chronologie relative du niveau le plus ancien de Tell esh-Shuna. *Melanges de l'Universite Saint-Joseph de Beyrouth* 37: 57–77.

Dollfus, G., and Kafafi, Z.
1986a   Preliminary Results of the First Season of the Joint Jordan-French Project at Abu Hamid, *Annual of the Department of Antiquities of Jordan* 30: 353–79.
1986b   Abu Hamid, Jordanie: Premiers Resultats, *Paléorient* 12(1): 91–100.
1987   Tell Abu Hamid. Pp. 231–35 in *Studies in the History and Archaeology of Jordan III*, ed. A. Hadidi. Amman: Department of Antiquities of Jordan.

Dubretet, L., and Dunand, M.
1954   Les gisements ossiferes de Khirbet el-Umbashi et de Hebariye (Safa) et les installations correspondantes. *Les Annales Archeologiques Arabes Syriennes* IV: 59–76.

Ehrich, A.
1939   *Early Pottery of the Jebeleh Region.* Memoirs of the American Philosophical Society 13. Philadelphia: American Philosophical Society.

Eisenberg, E.
1986   Tel Shalem. Pp. 96–97 in *Excavations and Surveys in Israel 1986*, Vol. 5. Jerusalem: Israel Department of Antiquities.
1989   Tel Shalem—1988. Pp. 165–66 in *Excavations and Surveys in Israel 1988/1989*, Vols. 7–8. Jerusalem: Israel Department of Antiquities.

Engberg, R. M., and Shipton, G. M.
1934   *Notes on Chalcolithic and Early Bronze Age Pottery of Megiddo.* Studies in Ancient Oriental Civilization 10. Chicago: The Oriental Institute of the University of Chicago.

Esse, D. L.
1991   *Subsistence, Trade and Social Change in Early Bronze Age Palestine.* Chicago: University of Chicago.

Falconer, S. E.
1987   *Heartland of Villages: Reconsidering Early Urbanism in the Southern Levant.* Unpublished doctoral dissertation, University of Arizona.

Fitzgerald, G. M.
1935   The Earliest Pottery of Beth Shan. *University of Pennsylvania Museum Journal* 24, no. 1: 5–22.

Fritz, V.
1987   Kinneret: A Biblical City on the Sea of Galilee. *Archaeology* 40, no. 40: 42–49.
Glueck, N.
1945   A Chalcolithic Settlement in the Jordan Valley. *Bulletin of the American Schools of Oriental Research* 97: 10–22.
1946   Band-Slip Ware in the Jordan Valley and Northern Gilead. *Bulletin of the American Schools of Oriental Research* 101: 3–20.
1951   *Explorations in Eastern Palestine IV.* Annual of the American Schools of Oriental Research 25–28. New Haven: American Schools of Oriental Research.
Gophna, R., and Sadeh, S.
1989   Excavations at Tel Tsaf: An Early Chalcolithic Site in the Jordan Valley. *Tel Aviv* 15–16: 3–36.
Gordon, R., and Villiers, L.
1983   Telul edh-Dhahab and its Environs: Survey of 1980 and 1982: Preliminary Report. *Annual of the Department of Antiquities of Jordan* 27: 275–89.
Gruspier, K. L., and Mullen, G. J.
1990   Preliminary Analysis of Faunal Remains from Jelmet esh-Shariyeh, WY120. *Annual of the Department of Antiquities of Jordan* 34: 115.
Gustavson-Gaube, C.
1985   Tell esh-Shuna North 1984: A Preliminary Report. *Annual of the Department of Antiquities of Jordan* 29: 43–87.
1986   Tell esh-Shuna North 1985: A Preliminary Report. *Annual of the Department of Antiquities of Jordan* 30: 69–98.
1987   Tell esh-Shuna North: 1984 and 1985. Pp. 237–40 in *Studies in the History and Archaeology of Jordan III*, ed. A. Hadidi. Amman: Department of Antiquities of Jordan.
Hanbury-Tenison, J. W.
1986   *The Late Chalcolithic to Early Bronze I Transition in Palestine and Transjordan.* B.A.R. International Series 311. London: British Archaeological Reports.
1987   Jerash Region Survey, 1984. *Annual of the Department of Antiquities of Jordan* 31: 129–57.
1989   Desert Urbanism in the Fourth Millennium? *Palestine Exploration Quarterly*: 55–63.
Helms, S. W.
1975   Jawa 1973: A Preliminary Report. *Levant* 7: 20–38.
1976a   Jawa Excavations 1974: A Preliminary Report. *Levant* 8: 1–35.
1976b   *Urban Fortifications of Palestine during the Third Millennium B.C.* Unpublished doctoral dissertation, University of London Institute of Archaeology.

1977   Jawa Excavations 1975: Third Preliminary Report. *Levant* 9: 21–35.
1981   *Jawa: Lost City of the Black Desert.* Ithaca: Cornell University.
1982   Paleo-Beduin and Transmigrant Urbanism. Pp. 97–113 in *Studies in the History and Archaeology of Jordan I*, ed. Adnan Hadidi. Amman: Department of Antiquities of Jordan.
1984   Excavations at Tell Um Hammad esh-Sharqiya in the Jordan Valley. *Levant* 16: 35–54.
1986   Excavations at Tell Um Hammad, 1984. *Levant* 18: 25–50.
1987a   A Question of Economic Control during the Proto-Historical Era of Palestine/Transjordan (c. 3500–2000 B.C.). Pp. 41–51 in *Studies in the History and Archaeology of Jordan III*, ed. A. Hadidi. Amman: Department of Antiquities of Jordan.
1987b   A Note on Some 4th Millennium Stamp Seal Impressions from Jordan. *Akkadica* 52: 29–31.
1991   Stamped, Incised, and Painted Designs on Pottery. Pp. 110–39 in *Excavations at Jawa 1972–1986: Stratigraphy, Pottery and Other Finds*, ed. A. V. G. Betts. Edinburgh: Edinburgh University.
1992   The 'Zarqa Triangle': A Preliminary Appraisal of Protohistoric Settlement Patterns and Demographic Episodes. Pp. 129–35 in *Studies in the History and Archaeology of Jordan IV*. Amman: Department of Antiquities of Jordan.
Hennessy, J. B.
1967   *The Foreign Relations of Palestine during the Early Bronze Age.* London: Colt.
Hopf, M.
1983   Jericho Plant Remains. Pp. 576–621 in *Excavations at Jericho V*, eds. K. M. Kenyon and T. A. Holland. London: British School of Archaeology in Jerusalem.
Huot, J.
1967   Typologie et chronologie relative de la ceramique du Bronze Ancien a Tell el-Far^cah. *Revue Biblique* 74: 517–54.
Ibrahim, M., and Mittmann, S.
1987   Khirbet Zeiraqoun. *Newsletter of the Institute of Archaeology and Anthropology, Yarmouk University 4*, no. 2: 3–6.
Ibrahim, M.; Sauer, J.; and Yassine, K.
1976   The East Jordan Valley Survey. *Bulletin of the American Schools of Oriental Research* 222: 41–66.
Joffe, A.
1991   Early Bronze I and the Evolution of Social Complexity in the Southern Levant. *Journal of Mediterranean Archaeology* 4, no. 1: 3–58.

Kenyon, K. M.
1952   Excavations at Jericho, 1952. *Palestine Exploration Quarterly* 1952: 62–82.
1960   Excavations at Jericho, 1957–58. *Palestine Exploration Quarterly* 1962: 88–108.
1979   *Archaeology in the Holy Land.* 4th ed. New York: Horton.
1981   *Excavations at Jericho III.* London: British School of Archaeology in Jerusalem.

Lapp, N. L.
1989   Cylinder Seals and Impressions of the Third Millennium B.C. from the Dead Sea Plain. *Bulletin of the American Schools of Oriental Research* 273: 1–15.

Lapp, P. W.
1970   Palestine in the Early Bronze Age. Pp. 101–31 in *Near Eastern Archaeology in the Twentieth Century: Essays in Honor of Nelson Glueck*, ed. J. A. Canders. Garden City, NY: Doubleday.

Leonard, A., Jr.
1983   The Proto-Urban/Early Bronze I Utilization of the Kataret es-Samra Plateau. *Bulletin of the American Schools of Oriental Research* 251: 37–60.
1992   *The Jordan Valley Survey, 1953: Some Unpublished Soundings Conducted by James Mellaart.* Annual of the American Schools of Oriental Research, 50. Winona Lake, IN: Eisenbrauns.

Mabry, J. B.
1989   Investigations at Tell el-Handaquq, Jordan (1987–88). *Annual of the Department of Antiquities of Jordan* 33: 59–95.
1992   *Alluvial Cycles and Early Agricultural Settlement Phases in the Jordan Valley.* Unpublished doctoral dissertation, Department of Anthropology, University of Arizona, Tucson.

Mabry, J. B., and Palumbo, G.
1988   The 1987 Wadi el-Yabis Survey. *Annual of the Department of Antiquities of Jordan* 32: 275–305.

al-Maqdissi, M.
1984   Compte Rendu des Travaux Archeologiques dans le Ledja en 1984. *Berytus* 32: 7–17.

Mallon, A.; Koeppel, R.; and Neuville, R.
1934   *Teleilat Ghassul I.* Rome: Pontifical Biblical Institute.

McCreery, D.
1980   Flotation of the Bab edh-Dhra[c] and Numeira Plant Remains. *Annual of the American Schools of Oriental Research* 46: 165–69.

McNicoll, A. W.; Smith, R. H.; and Hennessy, J. B.
1982   *Pella in Jordan 1.* Canberra: Australian National Gallery.

Mellaart, J.
1981   The Prehistoric Pottery from the Neolithic to the Beginning of E.B. IV (c. 7000–2500 B.C.). Pp. 131–321 in *The River Quoeiq, Northern Syria, and its Catchment: Studies Arising from the Tell Rifa'at Survey 1977–79*, ed. J. Matthers. Oxford: British Archaeological Reports S98.

de Miroschedji, P. R.
1971   *L'Epoque Pre-urbaine en Palestine.* Paris: Cahiers de la Revue Biblique.

Miller, R.
1980   Water Use in Syria and Palestine from the Neolithic to the Bronze Age. *World Archaeology* 11: 331–41.

Muheisen, M. Sh.
1988   A Survey of Prehistoric Cave Sites in the Northern Jordan Valley. Pp. 503–23 in *The Prehistory of Jordan: The State of Research in 1986*, eds. A. Garrard and H. Gebel. B.A.R. International Series 396. London: British Archaeological Reports.

National Water Master Plan of Jordan
1977   *Potential Surface Water Resources*, Map SW-8 N.

Neef, R.
1988   Les activites agricoles et horticoles. Pp. 29–30 in *Abu Hamid: Village du 4e millenaire del vallee du Jourdain.* Amman: French Cultural Center.

North, R.
1961   *Ghassul 1960, Excavation Report.* Analecta Biblica 14. Rome: Pontifical Biblical Institute.

Palumbo, G.; Mabry, J.; and Kuijt, I.
1990   The Wadi el-Yabis Survey: Report on the 1989 Field Season. *Annual of the Department of Antiquities of Jordan* 34: 95–118.

Pritchard, J. B.
1958   *The Excavations at Herodian Jericho, 1951.* Annual of the American Schools of Oriental Research 32–33. New Haven: American Schools of Oriental Research.

Roberts, N.
1977   Water Conservation in Ancient Arabia. *Proceedings of the Seminar for Arabian Studies* 7: 134–46.

Sanlaville, P., ed.
1985   *Holocene Settlement in North Syria.* B.A.R. International Series 238. London: British Archaeological Reports.

Schaub, R. T.
1982   The Origins of the Early Bronze Age Walled Town Culture of Jordan. Pp. 67–75 in *Studies in the History and Archaeology of Jordan I*, ed. A. Hadidi. Amman: Department of Antiquities of Jordan.

Smith, R. H.
  1973   *Pella of the Decapolis I.* Wooster, OH: College
          of Wooster.
Steuernagel, D. C.
  1925   Der Adschlun. *Zeitschrift des deutschen Palas-
          tina-Vereins* 48: 1–144, 201–392.
Stuiver, M., and Becker, B.
  1993   High-Precision Decadal Calibration of the
          Radiocarbon Timescale, A.D. 1950–600 B.C.
          Radiocarbon 35, no. 1: 35–65.
Tubb, J. N.
  1988   Tell es-Sa^cidiyeh: Preliminary Report on the
          First Three Seasons of Renewed Excavations.
          Levant 20: 23–87.
Tzori, N.
  1958   Neolithic and Chalcolithic Sites in the Valley
          of Beth-Shan. *Palestine Exploration Quarterly*
          90: 44–51.
Van Beek, G. W.
  1982   A Population Estimate from Marib: A Contem-
          porary Tell Village in North Yemen. *Bulletin of
          the American Schools of Oriental Research*
          248: 61–67.
de Vaux, R.
  1962   Les fouilles de Tell el-Far^cah: rapport prelim-
          inaire sur les 7^e, 8^e, 9^e campagnes, 1958–1960
          (Suite). *Revue Biblique* 69: 212–53.
  1971   Palestine in the Early Bronze Age. Pp. 208–37
          in *The Cambridge Ancient History of the Mid-
          dle East*, Vol. I, Pt. 2, ed. I. Cambridge: Cam-
          bridge University.

DATE DUE

DEMCO 38-297